T0305570

The New Multinationals

A new breed of multinational companies is reshaping competition in global industries. For most of the nineteenth and twentieth centuries, multinational firms came from the most technologically advanced countries in the world. Over the last two decades, however, new multinational firms from upper-middle-income economies (e.g. Spain, Ireland, Portugal, South Korea, and Taiwan), developing countries (e.g. Egypt, Indonesia, and Thailand), and oil-rich countries (e.g. United Arab Emirates, Nigeria, Russia, and Venezuela) have become formidable global competitors. These firms do not necessarily possess technological or marketing skills. In contrast to the classic multinationals, they found strength in their ability to organize, manage, execute, and network. They pursued a variety of strategies including vertical integration, product diversification, learning by doing, exploration of new capabilities, and collaboration with other firms. This book documents this phenomenon, identifies key capabilities of the new multinationals, and provides a new conceptual framework for understanding its causes and implications.

MAURO F. GUILLÉN is the Director of the Joseph H. Lauder Institute at the University of Pennsylvania and holder of the Dr. Felix Zandman Endowed Professorship in International Management at the Wharton School. Trained as a sociologist and political economist, he has studied multinational firms and the process of globalization for more than two decades. He is a recipient of best paper awards from both the Academy of Management and the American Sociological Association, and book awards from the Gustavus Myers Center and the Social Science History Association. In 2005 he won the IV Fundación Banco Herrero Prize, awarded annually to the best Spanish social scientist under the age of forty. He is a former holder of the Rafael del Pino Chair.

ESTEBAN GARCÍA-CANAL is Professor of Management at the University of Oviedo and a member of the Institute of Business and Humanism at the University of Navarra. His research interests lie at the intersection of interorganizational relations, organizational economics, and international management. He is the author of more than sixty articles published in scientific journals. He is, or has been, a member of the editorial boards of international journals such as the *Journal of International Business Studies*, *Management International Review*, and *M@n@gement*.

The New Multinationals
Spanish Firms in a Global Context

MAURO F. GUILLÉN
The Wharton School

ESTEBAN GARCÍA-CANAL
University of Oviedo

CAMBRIDGE
UNIVERSITY PRESS

CAMBRIDGE
UNIVERSITY PRESS

University Printing House, Cambridge CB2 8BS, United Kingdom

One Liberty Plaza, 20th Floor, New York, NY 10006, USA

477 Williamstown Road, Port Melbourne, VIC 3207, Australia

314-321, 3rd Floor, Plot 3, Splendor Forum, Jasola District Centre, New Delhi - 110025, India

79 Anson Road, #06-04/06, Singapore 079906

Cambridge University Press is part of the University of Cambridge.

It furthers the University's mission by disseminating knowledge in the pursuit of education, learning and research at the highest international levels of excellence.

www.cambridge.org
Information on this title: www.cambridge.org/9780521516143

© Mauro F. Guillén and Esteban García-Canal 2010

First published 2010

A catalogue record for this publication is available from the British Library

Library of Congress Cataloging in Publication data
Guillén, Mauro F.
  The new multinationals : Spanish firms in a global context /
Mauro F. Guillén, Esteban García-Canal.
    p. cm.
  Includes bibliographical references and index.
  ISBN 978-0-521-51614-3
  1. International business enterprises–Spain. 2. Spain–Foreign economic
relations. I. García-Canal, Esteban. II. Title.
  HD2887.G837 2010
  338.8'8946–dc22
                                                          2010023746

ISBN 978-0-521-51614-3 Hardback

Contents

Figures

Tables

Preface

Over the last two decades, the world has witnessed the fall of the Soviet bloc, an increase in the number of failed states, the rise of international terrorism, trade liberalization coupled with the formation of new trade blocs, a series of devastating financial crises, the expansion of the Internet, the beginnings of a green revolution, a spike in migration, and a drastic geographical reconfiguration of production. While these changes represent major shifts and discontinuities in the global political and economic landscape, looking towards the future the one that is likely to bring about the deepest consequences is the rise of the new multinationals from upper-middle-income, emerging, and developing countries. The international growth of these new multinationals marks the coming of age of a tier of countries that have hitherto being passive players in global economic, financial, and political affairs. It is hard to underestimate the importance of this phenomenon as one industry after another feels the impact of the increasing size, sophistication, and geographical reach of the new multinationals, challenging our assumptions regarding the division of labor between developed and emerging countries.

While research on the new multinationals has blossomed in parallel with the phenomenon itself, little has been said or documented about the capabilities that the new multinationals bring to the table. Often dismissed as creatures of protected home markets, beneficiaries of subsidized lending, and technology laggards, the new multinationals have been the subject of multiple jokes, condescending comments, and dire predictions of ultimate failure. And yet, here they are, investing not only in other countries at a similar level of development but also making daring acquisitions and conquering market shares in the most advanced economies. The rise of the new multinationals clearly shows that their countries of origin have more to offer than domestic markets to be exploited and cheap labor force. In expanding around the world on the basis of know-how, project-execution, networking, and political skills, the new multinationals represent not only a challenge to their established counterparts in developed economies but also to our traditional ways of understanding the multinational firm. We argue that the new multinationals do not require a wholesale revision of the theory of foreign direct investment and the multinational firm, but they do make it necessary to revisit some of the assumptions about the role of the home country, the process of capability building, and the pace and sequence of international growth.

This book is the result of a long-standing collaboration between two scholars located on different sides of the Atlantic Ocean. While most of the evidence presented in these pages focuses on the new multinationals from Spain, as they compare to those from the United States and the more advanced parts of Western Europe, we also used our research on Asian, Latin American, and Middle Eastern multinationals to elucidate the drivers and the consequences of the rise of this new type of firm.

We would like to thank the Fundación Rafael del Pino for offering not only financial support but also, and most importantly, the intellectual guidance that helped us focus on an important topic that is likely to reshape the global economy for decades to come. Over the years, Amadeo Petitbò and his team have encouraged us to re-examine our assumptions, revisit traditional arguments, and develop a new theory to tackle the rapid ways in which the business world is changing.

We would have been utterly unable to complete the book without the diligent assistance of several teams of research assistants. At Wharton, Wifredo Fernández, Arun Hendi, Jason Chien Jee, Chelsea Lew, and Maya Perl-Kot compiled numerous datasets and case studies used in the various chapters of the book. At Oviedo, Laura Fernández Méndez and Francisco Javier García Canal worked on the detailed case histories of Spanish multinational firms. Andrea Martínez-

Noya, Pablo Sánchez-Lorda and Ana Valdés provided valuable insights. Purificación Flórez provided research on a variety of topics related to the project and undertook several of the editorial tasks. Jue Pu coordinated a team of assistants in Beijing who provided further insights on Chinese multinationals. We have also used evidence collected under the auspices of the Centro de Estudios Comerciales of the Ministry of Trade and Industry, and the Instituto Español de Comercio Exterior, and of the Centre d'Economia Industrial of the Universitat Autònoma de Barcelona. José Manuel Campa, Julio García Cobos, Alvaro Cuervo, Andrea Goldstein, and Emilio Ontiveros provided us with innumerable ideas to improve the book.

We would like to dedicate this book to our respective families. They allowed us to focus the attention on the task at hand during the late hours of the evening, many weekends, and a few field trips. We cannot return the time to them, but we hope that they will see in the final product that it was worth all the effort.

1   The new multinationals

> The new multinationals have some distinct advantages in their sprint
> to the fore of global business. They are often family-owned or family-
> controlled (even when they are public companies), which helps them
> to make decisions quickly. They often enjoy cheap finance from state
> banks. But they also face particular problems, because they are trying
> to break into a world economy in which globalization is already well
> advanced.
>
> *The Economist* (January 10, 2008)
>
> Emerging-market multinationals might be relative newcomers to
> globalization, but they are quickly making up for lost time.
>
> Mark Foster (Accenture 2008: 6)

The global competitive landscape is becoming increasingly populated by multinational enterprises (MNEs) originating from countries that are not among the most advanced in the world in terms of
technology or brand reputation. These "new" multinationals come
from:

(1) upper-middle-income economies such as Spain, Ireland, Portugal,
    South Korea, or Taiwan;
(2) emerging economies like Brazil, Chile, Mexico, China, India, or
    Turkey;
(3) developing countries such as Egypt, Indonesia, or Thailand; or
(4) oil-rich countries like the United Arab Emirates, Nigeria, Russia, or
    Venezuela.

The new multinationals operate internationally using multiple
modes ranging from alliances and joint ventures to wholly owned
subsidiaries. Some of them are small and product focused, while
others are large and even diversified across many industries. The literature has referred to them in a variety of ways, including "third-
world multinationals" (Wells 1983), "latecomer firms" (Mathews
2002), "unconventional multinationals" (Li 2003), "challengers"

(BCG 2009), or "emerging multinationals" (Accenture 2008; *The Economist* 2008; Goldstein 2007; Ramamurti and Singh 2009). In some cases, these firms are labeled according to their region of origin, using terms such as "dragon multinationals" (Mathews 2002), or "multilatinas" (Cuervo-Cazurra 2008). The new multinationals have become key actors in foreign direct investment and cross-border acquisitions (UNCTAD 2008). While they may not possess the most sophisticated technological or marketing skills in their respective industries, they have expanded around the world in innovative ways. The purpose of this book is to identify and analyze their competitive capabilities, which have to do with organizational, managerial, project-execution, political, and network skills.

The proliferation of the new multinationals has taken observers, policymakers, and scholars by surprise. Many of these firms were marginal competitors just a decade ago; today they are challenging some of the world's most accomplished and established multinationals in a wide variety of industries and markets. In this book, we chart and analyze the rise of the new multinationals from Spain, a country that one generation ago lacked firms of international stature but is presently home to some of the world's largest. Like South Korea, Taiwan, or Singapore, Spain was a developing country until the early 1970s. Within thirty years, these countries transformed themselves into industrial economies with rapidly rising incomes. They have also seen a globally competitive service sector grow in areas such as infrastructure and financial services. Studying the ways in which Spanish firms managed to develop the capabilities needed to make a dent in global competition offers a view of things to come as companies from Asia, Latin America, and the Middle East increasingly build a global presence in key industries.

One of the most intriguing features of the rise of the new multinationals is that it has happened very swiftly. Since 1990 a number of countries and their firms have come to play an important role in the global economy not just as exporters but also as foreign direct investors. Foreign direct investment (FDI) includes acquisitions and greenfield transactions in which the investor holds at least 10 percent of the equity of the invested foreign subsidiary. While the motivations for direct investment may be diverse, the goal always is to exercise managerial control over the invested company. Table 1.1 presents data on the world's most important sources of FDI. Leaving aside Hong Kong and the Netherlands, which serve as hubs for trade and investment, the United States, the United Kingdom, France and Germany continue to be the largest foreign direct investors. In recent years, Spain has raced ahead of Italy, with a total stock of cumulative outward FDI of nearly $602 billion as of the end of 2008, an amount equivalent to 37.5 percent of the country's gross domestic product (GDP). Other important new foreign direct investing countries include Russia ($203 billion), Taiwan (175), Brazil (162), China (148), South Korea (96), Malaysia (68), South Africa (62), India (62), the United Arab Emirates (51), Mexico (45), Chile (32), and Argentina (29). As in the cases of Hong Kong and the Netherlands, the figures for Singapore (189) and Ireland (159) reflect not only the investments of their own companies but also those of others that use the two countries as a platform for trade and investment. Taken together, the developing countries' share of total FDI stock has increased from 8.1 percent in 1990 to 14.5 in 2008.

One important characteristic of the countries that are home to the new MNEs is that they are not technology leaders, as measured by patents, with the exceptions of South Korea and Taiwan (Furman *et al.* 2002). By contrast, some of these countries stand out for the large numbers of quality management certificates, relative to the size of their economies, especially China, Taiwan, Malaysia, and Spain (Table 1.2). These data suggest that companies in these countries are efficient, world-class implementers whose innovations have to do with managerial and organizational skills. The sustainability of the competitive advantages that have enabled them to become major investors depends, to a large extent, on their ability to upgrade capabilities, as discussed at length in Chapter 2.

The largest non-financial new multinationals in terms of foreign assets appear in Table 1.3. They operate in a variety of industries

Table 1.1. *Outward foreign direct investment stocks, 1990 and 2008*

	Outward FDI stock				Number of multi-national firms[a]
	$ billion		% of GDP		
Country	1990	2008	1990	2008	
Brazil	41.0	162.2	9.4	10.3	226
Russia	–	202.8	–	12.0	–
India	0.1	61.8	–	5.0	815
China	4.5	147.9	1.1	3.4	3,429
Singapore	7.8	189.1	21.2	103.9	–
Hong Kong	11.9	775.9	15.5	360.3	1,167
Taiwan	30.4	175.1	18.4	44.6	606
South Korea	2.3	95.5	0.9	10.3	7,460
Malaysia	0.8	67.6	1.7	30.4	–
Argentina	6.1	28.7	4.3	8.7	106
Chile	0.6	31.7	0.5	18.7	99
Mexico	2.7	45.4	1.0	4.2	–
Turkey	1.2	13.9	0.6	1.9	2,871
United Arab Emirates	0.1	50.8	–	19.5	77
Egypt	0.2	3.7	0.4	2.3	10
South Africa	15.0	62.3	13.4	22.5	261
Ireland	14.9	159.4	31.2	58.6	39
Spain	15.7	601.8	3.0	37.5	1,598
United States	430.5	3,162.0	7.4	22.2	2,418
France	112.4	1,397.0	9.1	48.9	1,267
Germany	151.6	1,450.9	8.8	39.8	6,115
Italy	60.2	517.1	5.3	22.5	5,750
Netherlands	106.9	843.7	35.9	96.9	4,788
United Kingdom	229.3	1,510.6	23.1	56.7	2,360
Japan	201.4	680.3	6.7	13.9	4,663
Developing countries	144.9	2,356.6	4.0	14.0	21,425
World total	1,785.3	16,205.7	8.5	26.9	82,053

Note: [a] Most recent available year.

Source: UNCTAD (2009).

Table 1.2. *Technology and quality management indicators*

Country	GDP[a] $ billion	Patents[b] Number	Patents[b] Per billion GDP	Quality management certificates[c] Number	Quality management certificates[c] Per billion GDP
Brazil	1,976.6	2,210	1.1	15,384	8.4
Russia	2,288.4	2,456	1.1	11,527	5.5
India	3,388.5	4,082	1.2	46,091	14.9
China	7,903.2	7,222	0.9	210,773	29.9
Singapore	238.5	4,466	18.7	4,150	18.0
Hong Kong	306.5	9,275	30.3	3,251	11.1
Taiwan[d]	402.6	86,798	226.4	10,402	27.1
South Korea	1,358.0	62,767	46.2	15,794	13.2
Malaysia	383.7	1,117	2.9	7,838	22.1
Argentina	571.5	1,052	1.8	8,808	16.6
Chile	242.4	272	1.1	4,013	17.4
Mexico	1,541.6	1,912	1.2	3,946	2.9
Turkey	1,028.9	238	0.2	12,802	13.9
United Arab Emirates[e]	226.1	–	–	2,422	12.4
Egypt	441.6	94	0.2	1,535	3.8
South Africa	492.2	3,456	7.0	3,283	7.1
Ireland	197.1	2,558	13.0	1,999	10.6
Spain	1,456.1	6,301	4.3	65,112	46.3
United States	14,204.3	2,096,055	147.6	36,192	2.6
France	2,112.4	99,397	47.1	22,981	11.1
Germany	2,925.2	261,683	89.5	45,195	16.6
Italy	1,840.9	44,125	24.0	115,359	64.9
Netherlands	671.7	34,423	51.2	18,922	30.4
United Kingdom	2,176.3	99,760	45.8	35,517	17.4
Japan	4,354.6	718,729	165.1	73,176	17.1
World total	69,697.6	3,854,057	55.3	951,486	14.5

Notes:

[a] In current US dollars at purchasing power parities, 2008.

[b] Granted by the US Patent and Trademark Office between 1977 and 2008 to residents of the country who are listed as the first-name inventor.

6 THE NEW MULTINATIONALS

Notes to Table 1.2 *(cont.)*

c ISO 9001:2000 quality management certificates issued by national quality organizations to processes that comply with a set of guidelines, as of the end of 2007.

d Source: National Statistics, Republic of China (Taiwan) http://eng.stat.gov.tw/mp.asp?mp=5.

e GDP data for 2005.

Sources: US Patent and Trademark Office; International Organization for Standardization.

ranging from oil and mining to cement and chemicals, automobiles and electronics, and various infrastructure sectors like electricity, transportation, and telecommunications. Similarly, the Boston Consulting Group publishes an annual list of the Global Challengers, most of which are important foreign investors. Chinese, Indian, and Brazilian companies top the list, which excludes Spanish, Irish, South Korean, and Taiwanese firms (Table 1.4). Yet another way to show the national distribution of the new multinationals is to examine the Fortune Global 500 ranking of the world's largest corporations in terms of revenue. China, South Korea, and Spain lead the ranking (Table 1.5). Although they define and measure the population of new MNEs in different ways, these rankings indicate unambiguously that the global economy is increasingly inhabited by companies based in countries that few people would identify as being at the leading edge of technological or brand development.

The first "new" MNEs emerged from the so-called Asian tiger economies – those that industrialized during the 1960s (Haggard 1990). Taiwan, a country that excels both at technological and process innovation, has proved to be the most fertile ground for outward foreign investors, including such powerhouses as Formosa Plastics, Taiwan Semiconductor, and Acer. Following a path to development much more oriented towards large-scale industry, South Korea is home to some of the best-known names in the electronics and appliances industries (Samsung and LG), and automobiles (Hyundai and Kia).

Table 1.3. *The largest new non-financial multinationals ranked by foreign assets, 2006*

Company	Country	Industry	Foreign assets ($ bn)	Total sales ($ bn)	Number of foreign affiliates
Telefónica	Spain	Telecom	101.9	66.4	165
Hutchison Whampoa	Hong Kong	Diversified[a]	70.7	34.4	115
Grupo Ferrovial	Spain	Infrastructure	60.2	9.1	–
Repsol YPF	Spain	Oil	38.3	64.4	71
Endesa	Spain	Electricity	31.4	25.8	65
Petronas	Malaysia	Oil	30.7	51.0	4
Samsung Electronics	South Korea	Electronics	27.0	91.9	78
Cemex	Mexico	Cement	24.4	18.1	493
CRH	Ireland	Building materials	22.9	23.5	514
Hyundai Motor	South Korea	Automobiles	19.6	68.5	19
SingTel	Singapore	Telecom	18.7	8.6	103
CITIC Group	China	Diversified[b]	17.6	10.1	12
Formosa Plastic Group	Taiwan	Chemicals	16.8	50.4	11

Table 1.3 (cont.)

Company	Country	Industry	Foreign assets ($ bn)	Total sales ($ bn)	Number of foreign affiliates
Jardine Matheson	Hong Kong	Diversified[c]	16.7	16.3	108
LG Corporation	South Korea	Electronics	15.0	70.6	3
CVRD	Brazil	Mining	15.0	46.7	17

Notes:

[a] Ports, telecommunications, property, hotels, retail, energy, and infrastructure services, among others.

[b] Telecommunications, construction, media, and financial services, among others.

[c] Transportation, construction, retail, IT services, and financial services, among others.

Source: UNCTAD (2008).

Table 1.4. *The new multinationals on the 2009 Boston Consulting Group 100 Global Challengers list, by country*

Country	Number of firms	Country	Number of firms
China	36	Malaysia	2
India	20	Indonesia	2
Brazil	14	Thailand	2
Mexico	7	Turkey	2
Russia	6	Argentina	1
United Arab Emirates	4	Hungary	1
Chile	2	Kuwait	1

Note: BCG does not include firms from Spain, South Korea, and Taiwan.

Source: BCG (2009).

The city-state of Singapore has bred multinationals in food and beverages (Fraser and Neave, Want Want), electronics (Olam), telecommunications (SingTel), real estate (CapitaLand), transportation (Neptune Orient Lines), and hotels (City Developments). For its part, Hong Kong is home to a large number of multinationals in a similar set of industries, led by Hutchison Whampoa, the world's largest port operator.

More recently, the new multinationals from Brazil, Russia, India, and China (BRIC) have made great inroads into the global economy. Among Brazilian firms, Companhia Vale do Rio Doce (CVRD) and Metalúrgica Gerdau are among the largest firms in mining and steel, Embraer holds with Bombardier of Canada a duopoly in the global regional jet market, and Natura Cosméticos has a presence in both Latin America and Europe. Lukoil, Gazprom and Severstal are among the top Russian multinationals, while India boasts an army of firms not only in IT and outsourcing services, in which companies like Infosys, Tata Consultancy Services (TCS), and Wipro are among the largest in the world, but also in steel, automobiles, and

Table 1.5. *The new multinationals on the Fortune Global 500 ranking by country, 2008*

Country	Number of companies
China	37
South Korea	14
Spain	12
India	7
Taiwan	6
Brazil	6
Mexico	4
Russia	8
Ireland	1
Malaysia	1
Poland	1
Portugal	2
Saudi Arabia	1
Singapore	2
Thailand	1
Turkey	1

Note: Ranking is based on total revenue during 2008.
Source: Fortune magazine.

pharmaceuticals. Chinese firms have erupted with force in global markets not only as exporters but also foreign investors, and in every industry from mining and oil to chemicals and steel. In electrical appliances and electronics, China boasts three increasingly well-known firms, Haier, Lenovo, and Huawei.

In Spanish-speaking Latin America some firms from Mexico and Argentina have become formidable global competitors. In food-processing, Bimbo and Gruma are among the largest firms in the world in their respective market niches, namely, packaged bread and tortillas. In cement, Cemex is the second- or third-largest, depending on the specific product. Grupo Modelo is the third-largest brewery in the world. These companies have made acquisitions or greenfield investments in North America, Asia, and Europe. Argentina's Tenaris is the global leader in seamless steel tubes, and Industrias Metalúrgicas Pescarmona a major firm in the crane business.

The Middle East is also becoming the home base of major multinational corporations, including DP World of Dubai (the world's second-largest port operator), Orascom (the Egyptian construction and telecommunications group with major operations throughout Africa and the Middle East), Mobile Telecommunications Company (the Kuwaiti giant), and Enka Insaat ve Sanayi (the Turkish infrastructure group). These firms are making inroads around the world and hitting the headlines, especially because of their rapid growth via mergers and acquisitions.

Table 1.6 provides information on the new multinationals with the largest global market positions as of the end of 2008. It is important to note that the new multinationals have become global leaders not only in traditional industries like food processing or beverages, but also in high-technology fields like aircraft and information services. Another important pattern is country specialization. Argentine and Mexican multinationals stand out in both consumer and producer goods, while Brazilian multinationals stand out in mining and aircraft. Taiwanese, South Korean, and Chinese firms tend to excel in electronics, while Indian firms are world leaders in information and outsourcing services.

THE SPANISH EXPERIENCE

Together with South Korea and Taiwan, Spain has produced the largest number of truly global multinationals among the countries that back in the 1960s were still attempting to develop a solid industrial base. Table 1.7 lists the most prominent examples of Spanish firms with a leading presence abroad. It includes companies in major industries, except chemicals, electronics, and automobiles, in which there are only a few remaining Spanish-owned companies. In foodprocessing, Spanish companies have made important acquisitions in

Table 1.6. *New multinationals with the largest global market positions, end of 2008*

Company	Home country	Industry	Global market position
Arcor	Argentina	Confectionery	No. 1 in candy
Bimbo	Mexico	Food processing	No. 2 in bread
Modelo	Mexico	Beverages	No. 3 in beer
CVRD	Brazil	Mining	No. 3 in mining
Tenaris	Argentina	Steel	No. 1 in seamless tubes
POSCO	South Korea	Steel	No. 4 in steel
Bharat Forge	India	Metals	No. 2 in forging
Cemex	Mexico	Cement	No. 2 in cement
Acer	Taiwan	Personal computers	No. 3 personal computer brand
Lenovo	China	Personal computers	No. 4 personal computer brand
BYD	China	Electronics	No. 1 in nickel-cadmium batteries
Samsung Electronics	South Korea	Consumer electronics	No. 2 in consumer electronics
Embraer	Brazil	Aircraft	No. 1 in regional jets
Gazprom	Russia	Utility	No. 1 utility
DP World	Dubai	Port operator	No. 4 port operator
Infosys	India	Information services	Top 5 in information services
TCS	India	Information services	Top 5 in information services

Table 1.6 *(cont.)*

Company	Home country	Industry	Global market position
Wipro	India	Outsourcing services	Top 5 in outsourcing services

Note: Table excludes multinationals from Spain. See Table 1.7.
Source: Compiled by Mauro F. Guillén from company reports.

Europe, Asia, and the Americas, turning themselves into the world's largest producers of rice and olive oil, and the second-largest producer of pasta. For its part, Viscofán is the largest producer of artificial casings for the meat industry. In wines, Freixenet has been the world's largest sparkling wine producer for over two decades. These companies will be analyzed in depth in Chapter 3. In the textiles and clothing sector, Spain has also produced companies of international stature, such as global denim leader Tavex (now merged with Brazil's Santista), Inditex, which owns the world's second most valuable clothing brand (Zara), and Pronovias, the largest bridal wear designer and manufacturer. The growth path and capabilities of Spanish clothing manufacturers will be analyzed in Chapter 4, and compared to companies from emerging economies.

While Spanish companies are not global leaders in capital-intensive industries such as chemicals, metals, electronics, and automobiles, a handful stand out as formidable global competitors in certain market niches. For instance, Acerinox is the third-largest producer of stainless steel, with factories in Spain, the United States, South Africa, and Malaysia. Spanish automobile component manufacturers have traditionally been efficient and highly-regarded by assemblers (Andersen Consulting 1994). Grupo Antolín is the largest maker of interior linings, and has established factories on four continents. Zanini is the largest producer of wheel trims, a company that we will analyze in Chapter 5 together with some firms that have made great strides in the

Table 1.7. *The Spanish multinationals with the largest global market positions, end of 2008, compared with their main rivals from Spain, and oldest position found in international rankings*

Company	Industry	Global market position and main Spanish rivals (including global position in the same ranking when available)	Oldest global market position found
Ebro Puleva	Food processing	No. 1 producer of rice, and 2nd of pasta Main rival: SOS Cuétara	No. 1 producer of rice in 2001
Grupo SOS	Food processing	No. 1 producer of olive oil	No. 1 producer of olive oil
Chupa Chups	Food processing	No. 1 producer of lollipops and no. 2 of candy	
Viscofán	Food processing	No. 1 producer of artificial casings for the meat industry	No. 1 producer of artificial casings for the meat industry in 2005
Freixenet	Sparkling wine	No. 1 producer of sparkling wine Main rival: Codorniu (not on the ranking)	No. 1 producer of sparkling wine in 2002
Tavex	Textiles	No. 1 producer of denim	No. 1 producer of denim in 2005
Zara (Inditex)	Clothing	No. 2 most valuable clothing brand	No. 2 most valuable clothing brand in 2005
Pronovias	Clothing	No. 1 maker of bridal wear	

Acerinox	Steel	No. 3 producer of stainless steel Main rival: Sidenor	No. 3 producer of stainless steel in 2003
Repsol-Gas Natural[a]	Gas	No. 3 distributor of natural gas Main rival: Enagas (no. 13)	No. 2 distributor of natural gas in 2006
Roca	Sanitary equipment	No. 1 maker of sanitary equipment	No. 1 maker of sanitary equipment in 2000
Grupo Antolín	Automobile components	No. 1 producer of interior linings	
Zanini	Automobile components	No. 1 producer of wheel trims	
Gamesa	Machinery	No. 3 manufacturer of wind turbines Main rivals: Acciona (no. 8)/Ecotècnia (now a subsidiary of Alstom) (no. 14)	No. 2 manufacturer of wind turbines in 2000
Indo	Optical equipment	No. 3 manufacturer of lenses	
Mondragón	Diversified	No. 1 worker-owned cooperative group	No. 9 worker-owned cooperative group in 2005
Grupo Ferrovial	Infrastructure	No. 3 developer and manager of transportation infrastructure (Public Works Financing 2009)	No. 2 developer and manager of transportation infrastructure in 2000

Table 1.7 (cont.)

Company	Industry	Global market position and main Spanish rivals (including global position in the same ranking when available)	Oldest global market position found
ACS	Infrastructure	No. 2 construction company (Forbes Ranking) Main rivals: ACS (no. 1), FCC (no. 2)	No. 1 Dragados (now a subsidiary of ACS) in 2000 (Public Works Financing Ranking
Acciona	Infrastructure	No. 1 developer of wind farms Main rivals: ACCIONA (no. 9)/FCC (no. 16) Main rivals: Iberdrola, Endesa	
Iberdrola	Electricity	No. 1 Iberdrola Renovables (Wind Farm Operator) Main rivals: Acciona Energy (no. 4), Endesa (no. 8)	
Telefónica	Telecom	No. 3 telecom operator by total customers	No. 3 telecom operator by total customers in 2006

Santander	Banking	No. 4 bank by market capitalization; no. 1 retail banking Main rivals: BBVA: no. 10 bank by market capitalization; no. 6 in retail banking	No. 4 bank by market capitalization in 2001 in Eurozone
Prosegur	Security	No. 3 company by sales	
Sol Meliá	Hotels	No. 17 Sol Meliá hotels by number of beds Main rivals: NH Hoteles (no. 23), Barceló (no. 24)	No. 10 resort hotel chain by number of beds in 2000
Real Madrid	Sports	No. 1 football club by revenue Main rival: FC Barcelona (no. 3)	No. 2 football club by revenue in 2000

Note: [a] Joint venture between Repsol-YPF and Gas Natural.

Source: Compiled by William Chislett, Esteban García-Canal, and Mauro F. Guillén from company reports.

machinery industry, like Gamesa, the world's third-largest maker of wind turbines, and Ficosa and Corporación Gestamp, among the world leaders in rearview systems and metal components, respectively.

The areas in which Spanish multinationals have become best known internationally are infrastructure, leisure, and financial services, a reflection no doubt of the fact that the country has not developed a sound technology base. Spanish companies in electricity, transportation, telecommunications, banking, and hospitality are among the largest in the world in their respective areas of activity. For example, through acquisitions and privatization contracts, Grupo Ferrovial has become the largest transportation infrastructure developer and manager, Acciona the largest developer of wind farms, Telefónica the third-largest telecommunications operator by total customers, and Sol Meliá the biggest resort hotel chain. Although the situation changes by the day, Santander is one of the eighth largest banks in the world in terms of market capitalization and revenue.

The increasing presence of Spanish multinationals in the global economy can be charted over time with the help of aggregate data on foreign direct investment (FDI). Figure 1.1 shows the evolution of Spain's foreign direct investment position as a percentage of GDP. Back in the early 1980s, both inward and outward stocks were low, no more than 5 percent of GDP. In 1986 Spain became a full member of the European Union, at the time called the European Economic Community. The treaty of accession called for the sudden removal of trade barriers for manufactured goods, but a seven-year transition period was negotiated for services, including the infrastructure and financial sectors. European firms engaged in a number of high-profile acquisitions of Spanish manufacturing firms, frequently in oligopolistic industries. As a result, the stock of inward FDI grew to over 15 percent of GDP by the mid 1990s.

Outward FDI by Spanish firms did not gather speed until the mid 1990s, and it was mostly focused on infrastructure and financial services. The trigger was the end of the transition period negotiated back in 1986 and the coming into effect of the Single European Act

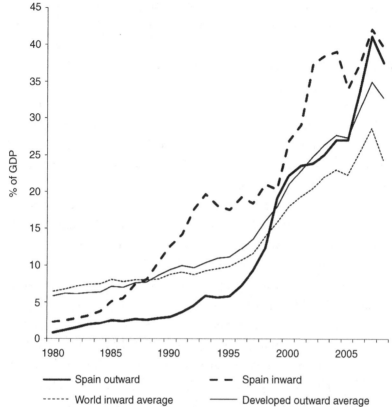

FIGURE I.I Spain's foreign direct investment position, 1980–2008
Note: Excluding transit capital.
Source: UNCTAD, *World Investment Report* (several years).

in 1993, which meant the removal of barriers to trade and competition in services. The largest Spanish companies in electricity, water, oil, gas, transportation, telecommunications, and banking started to make big acquisitions. By the end of the 1990s, the stock of outward FDI had grown to more than 20 percent of GDP. In 1999 the stock of outward FDI almost reached the level of inward FDI, the same year that Spain overtook the average developed country in the world in terms of its cumulative investments abroad (see Figure 1.1).

With the adoption of the euro as the currency in 1998 Spanish companies maintained their rates of foreign investment into the early years of the twenty-first century, given the ease with which they could raise funds at rates unimaginable just a few years back. The example of Repsol's 1999 acquisition of YPF in a deal worth nearly €5 billion illustrates the beneficial effect of monetary union. The Argentine company's by-laws stipulated that any acquisition had to be in cash only. As a eurozone company, Repsol could appeal to European equity and debt markets. "It's practically impossible to think of a Spanish company launching such a big issue and placing it with success without the euro," observed Repsol chief executive Alfonso Cortina at the time.[1]

One important characteristic of Spanish outward FDI is its geographical and industry concentration. Nearly 90 percent has Latin America or Europe as its destination, and over 80 percent has involved firms in infrastructure and financial services. Companies undergoing privatization in Spain were especially prone to invest abroad during this period, including Endesa (whose privatization process started in 1988), Repsol (1989), Argentaria (1993), Gas Natural (1996) and Telefónica (1996). As shown in Figure 1.2, Spanish companies invested primarily in Latin America during the 1990s. This was due in part to the obvious cultural and linguistic affinities, but most importantly because Spanish companies in infrastructure and financial services were looking for emerging markets in which to invest so as to enjoy bigger profit margins and grow bigger (Guillén 2005). As Casanova (2002) has put it, they eventually came to the realization that "the best defense is an attack." Their strategic response to the threat of acquisition by their more powerful European rivals was to grow bigger. Size can be an effective anti-takeover measure, especially if the expansion takes place in riskier, more volatile markets. The fact that several Latin American governments decided to privatize their state-owned firms in those industries at about the same time presented a unique opportunity (García-Canal and Guillén 2008). Once firmly

---

[1] *Business Week*, May 22, 2000.

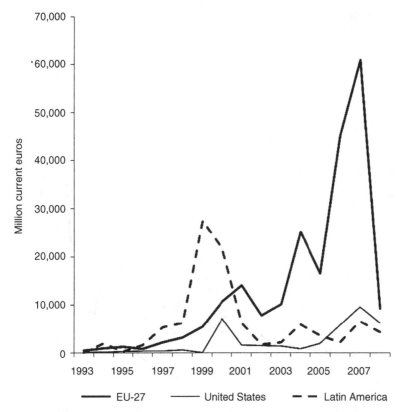

FIGURE I.2 Spain's net outward foreign direct investment flows by destination, 1993–2008
Note: Excluding transit capital.
Source: State Secretariat for Foreign Trade.

positioned in Latin America, Spanish multinationals turned their attention toward Europe, which became the most important destination since 2001.

When broken down by industry, the annual flows of Spanish outward FDI exhibit very sharp ups and downs, driven by the timing of large acquisitions. Chief among them are the multi-billion dollar acquisitions of Argentina's YPF by Repsol in 1999, several banks in Mexico and Brazil by BBVA and Santander in 2000, telecommunications operators in Europe and the United States by Telefónica also in 2000, Abbey National of the United Kingdom

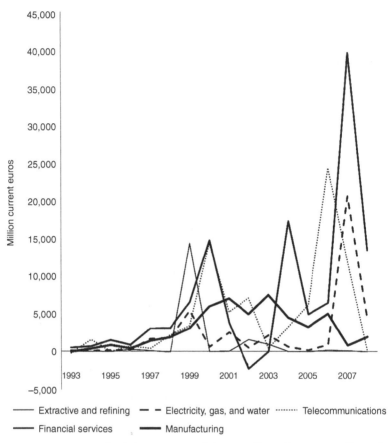

FIGURE 1.3 Spain's net outward foreign direct investment flows by industry, 1993–2008
Note: Excluding transit capital.
Source: State Secretariat for Foreign Trade.

by Santander in 2004, O2 by Telefónica in 2006, Scottish Power by Iberdrola in 2007, and Compass in the United States by BBVA and parts of ABN AMRO by Santander also in 2007. Due to the global economic and financial crisis, outward foreign investments during 2008 declined sharply.

In total, as of the end of 2008 there were 2,064 Spanish multinational companies, or 1,835 if companies belonging to the same group (e.g. Telefónica or Ferrovial) are counted as one. These companies undertook one or more cross-border acquisitions, green-field investments, or joint ventures. If one also includes alliances with a foreign firm as an act of international expansion, there were 2,495 firms (2,241 taking groups into account) with a stable presence abroad. These firms concluded some 9,000 acquisitions, investments, alliances, or bidding processes for public contracts in a foreign country between 1986 and 2008. About 60 percent of those actions were accounted for by service-sector firms, with infrastructure and financial services representing half of that figure or 30 percent of the total. Within manufacturing, i.e. the remaining 40 percent, relatively small firms in food-processing, transportation equipment, electronics, metals, chemicals, and machinery were the most active.[2]

The recent evolution of Spanish outward FDI illustrates many of the peculiarities associated with the activities of the new multinationals. First, the international expansion of Spanish firms was largely based not on the possession of intangible technological assets, but rather on other types of know-how such as organizational, managerial, project-execution, political, and network skills. Second, foreign expansion is clustered geographically in that most firms have invested in one, or at most two, regions of the world. And third, acquisitions and alliances have been the most important ways of attaining geographical reach and upgrading competitive capabilities. At the beginning of their process of internationalization, most Spanish multinationals used shared-control entry modes such as joint ventures or alliances. Over time, they started to use full acquisitions and wholly owned greenfield investments more assiduously. While in the late 1980s only about 40 percent of all foreign investments were majority owned by the Spanish firm, by 2008 some 80 percent were (Guillén and García-Canal 2009).

[2] Guillén and García-Canal (2009). Citing official Spanish sources, the World Investment Report indicates that as of the end of 2006 Spain was home to 1,598 multinationals (see Table 1.1). Our data show that as of the end of 2006 there were 1,870 Spanish multinationals (Guillén and García-Canal 2009).

PLAN AND METHOD

Our theoretical and empirical analysis is organized following a logic of systematic comparison across countries, industries, and firms. Chapter 2 presents a conceptual framework for understanding the peculiarities of the new multinationals, their distinctive capabilities, and their pattern of growth. We propose that the traditional way of looking at multinational corporations and foreign direct investment is becoming obsolete, although its basic postulates are still valid. Thus, we propose a series of arguments that qualify, redirect, and enrich existing theories of the multinational enterprise.

Chapters 3–7 each focus on the process of internationalization of firms in different kinds of industries. Chapter 3 deals with the traditional sectors, including food-processing and wines. The interplay between comparative advantage and firm capabilities lies at the core of competitive dynamics in this industry, which has been revolutionized by mergers and acquisitions and the incorporation of new technology. Chapter 4 addresses the internationalization of firms making durable consumer goods such as clothing, simple assembled devices, and electrical appliances, in which different levels of access to proprietary product technology and distribution channels shape competition and entry modes into foreign markets. Chapter 5 analyzes the foreign expansion of firms in the producer goods sector, including construction materials, wind turbines, and automobile components. Chapter 6 focuses on the regulated infrastructure industries, in which large firms from emerging economies as well as Spain have reached prominence around the world. Chapter 7 examines the internationalization of firms in service activities such as multimedia, education, transportation, and turnkey projects. Finally, Chapter 8 draws conclusions regarding the ways in which the new multinationals have managed to develop capabilities and access foreign markets, and proposes a framework to integrate the new multinationals within existing theories of the multinational enterprise.

Our approach to the study of the new multinationals follows the comparative case-study method. Case studies are used in scholarly research for the purposes of empirical description and classification, theory building and testing, clinical diagnosis, professional preparation, and program evaluation (Flyvbjerg 2006; Hamel 1993; Yin 2003). They have become increasingly popular in the field of management research. In a widely cited article, Eisenhardt (1989) proposed them as an ideal methodology for exploring an empirical phenomenon and building theory based on the evidence collected. In this book, we systematically compare cases of companies within a given industry in order to test specific arguments about the motivations, drivers, and performance consequences of the international growth patterns of the new multinationals.

In order to ensure that our analysis has internal validity and can be generalized within a certain set of parameters, we study firms in specific industries following the matched-case comparative design (Gerring 2007; Gupta and Guillén 2009). The key idea behind this methodology is to strategically choose cases for systematic comparative study so that some variables are controlled for while others enable the researcher to build and test theory. In particular, we use the 2 × 2 research design within each industry, systematically analyzing how the internationalization pattern of the firm is affected by pairs of variables such as vertical integration and product diversification, the importance of proprietary product technology and the difficulty of access to foreign markets, and the firm's strategic independence and its reliance on alliances for the exploration of new capabilities. In each industry, we provide in-depth analyses of each company's pattern of international growth and compare it to its peers in Spain and other countries, both at higher and lower levels of development. In so doing, we are in a better position to propose some calibrated generalizations about the extent to which the domestic and global competitive contexts, the firm's strategic decisions, and the reaction of its competitors shape the process of internationalization in the case of the new multinationals. In the concluding chapter we develop an integrative framework to analyze the process through which the new multinationals accumulated and developed the resources and capabilities that sustained their international expansion, and discuss the implications of the rise of the new multinationals for the theory of the multinational firm.

2 Traditional and new multinationals

Control of the foreign enterprise ... is desired in order to appropriate fully the returns on certain skills and abilities.

Stephen Hymer (1960: 25)

Few challengers have mastered the use of innovation as a means of obtaining competitive advantage. But those that succeed at innovation will be well positioned to become global leaders in their fast-changing industries.

Boston Consulting Group (BCG 2009: 28)

The traditional model of multinational enterprise (MNE), characterized by foreign direct investment (FDI) aimed at exploiting firm-specific capabilities developed in the home country and a gradual, country-by-country, approach to internationalization dominated the global economy during much of the twentieth century. This model has its origins in the second industrial revolution of the late nineteenth century. British, North American, and continental European firms expanded around the world on the basis of intangible assets such as technology, brands, and managerial expertise. The climax of their worldwide expansion was reached during the 1960s and early 1970s, as trade and investment barriers gradually fell around the world (Chandler 1990; Kindleberger 1969; Vernon 1979; Wilkins 1974).

While significant variations in the strategy and structure of North American and European multinationals were documented at the time (e.g. Stopford and Wells 1972), and the rise of Japanese multinationals during the 1970s and 1980s added yet more diversity to the global population of multinational corporations (Kenney and Florida 1993), firms expanding from relatively rich and technologically advanced countries tended to share a core set of features. Chief among them were their technological, marketing, and managerial strengths, which enabled them to overcome the so-called "liability of foreignness" in a variety of markets, investing for the most part in wholly or majority owned subsidiaries, transferring technology, products, and knowledge from headquarters to far-flung operations around the globe, and relying on elaborate bureaucratic and financial controls.

In the last two decades, however, new MNEs from emerging, upper-middle-income, or oil-rich countries have followed completely different patterns of international expansion. The unexpected rise to prominence of firms such as Cemex of Mexico, Embraer of Brazil, Haier of China, Tata Consultancy Services of India, or Banco Santander of Spain begs three fundamental types of questions. First, do these firms share some common distinctive features that distinguish them from the traditional MNEs? Second, what advantages have made it possible for them to operate and compete not only in host countries at the same or lower levels of economic development but also in the richest economies? Third, how come they have been able to expand abroad at dizzying speed, in defiance of the conventional wisdom about the virtues of a staged, incremental approach to international expansion? Before being in a position to answer these questions, one must begin by outlining the established theory of the MNE and explore the extent to which its basic postulates need to be re-examined.

THE THEORY OF THE MULTINATIONAL FIRM

Although MNEs have existed for a very long time, scholars first attempted to understand the nature and drivers of their cross-border activities during the 1950s. The credit for providing the first comprehensive analysis of the MNE and of foreign direct investment goes to an economist, Stephen Hymer, who in his doctoral dissertation observed that the "control of the foreign enterprise is desired in order to remove competition between that foreign enterprise and enterprises in other countries ... or the control is desired in order to appropriate fully the returns on certain skills and abilities" (Hymer 1960: 25). His key insight was that the multinational firm possesses certain kinds of proprietary advantages that set it apart from purely domestic firms, thus helping it overcome the "liability of foreignness."

Multinational firms exist because certain economic conditions and proprietary advantages make it advisable and possible for them to profitably undertake production of a good or service in a foreign location. It is important to distinguish between vertical and horizontal foreign expansion in order to fully understand the basic economic principles that underlie the activities of MNEs in general and the novelty of the "new" MNEs in particular. Vertical expansion occurs when the firm locates assets or employees in a foreign country with the purpose of securing the production of a raw material, component, or input (backward vertical expansion) or the distribution and sale of a good or service (forward vertical expansion). The necessary condition for a firm to engage in vertical expansion is the presence of a comparative advantage in the foreign location. The advantage typically has to do with the prices or productivities of production factors such as capital, labor, or land. For instance, a clothing firm may consider production in a foreign location due to lower labor costs.

It is important, though, to realize that the mere existence of a comparative advantage in a foreign location does not mean that the firm ought to vertically expand. The necessary condition of lower factor costs or higher factor productivity, or both, is not sufficient. After all, the firm may benefit from the comparative advantage in the foreign location simply by asking a local producer to become its supplier. The sufficient condition justifying a vertical foreign investment refers to the possible reasons encouraging the firm to undertake foreign production by itself rather than rely on others to do the job. The main two reasons are uncertainty about the supply or asset specificity. If uncertainty is high, the firm would prefer to integrate backward into the foreign location so as to make sure that the supply chain functions smoothly, and that delivery timetables are met. Asset specificity is high when the firm and the foreign supplier need to develop joint assets in order for the supply operation to take place. In that situation the firm would prefer to expand backward in order to avoid the "hold-up" problem, i.e. opportunistic behavior on the part of the foreign supplier trying to extract rents from the firm. These necessary and sufficient conditions also apply in the case of forward vertical expansion into a foreign location. Uncertainty and asset specificity with, say, a foreign distributor, would compel the firm to take things in its own hands and invest in the foreign location in order to make sure that the goods or services reach the buyer in the appropriate way and at a reasonable cost.

Horizontal expansion occurs when the firm sets up a plant or service delivery facility in a foreign location with the goal of selling in that market, and without abandoning production of the good or service in the home country. The decision to engage in horizontal expansion is driven by forces different than those for vertical expansion. Production of a good or service in a foreign market is desirable in the presence of protectionist barriers, high transportation costs, unfavorable currency exchange rate shifts, or requirements for local adaptation to the peculiarities of local demand that make exporting from the home country unfeasible or unprofitable. Like in the case of vertical expansion, these obstacles are merely a necessary condition for horizontal expansion, but not a sufficient one. The firm should ponder the relative merits of licensing a local producer in the foreign market or establishing an alliance against those of committing to a foreign investment. The sufficient condition for setting up a proprietary plant or service facility has to do with the possession of intangible assets – brands, technology, know-how, and other firm-specific skills – that make licensing a risky option because the licensee might appropriate, damage, or otherwise misuse the firm's assets.[1]

---

[1] For a summary of the basic economic model of the multinational firm, see Caves (1996). Stephen Hymer (1960) was the first to observe that firms expand horizontally to protect (and monopolize) their intangible assets. Other important contributions are Buckley and Casson (1976), Teece (1977), and Hennart (1982).

Scholars in the field of international management have also acknowledged that firms in possession of the requisite competitive advantages do not become MNEs overnight, but in a gradual way, following different stages. According to the framework originally proposed by researchers at the University of Uppsala in Sweden (Johanson and Vahlne 1977; Johanson and Wiedersheim-Paul 1975), firms expand abroad on a country-by-country basis, starting with those more similar in terms of socio-cultural distance. They also argued that in each foreign country firms typically followed a sequence of steps: on-and-off exports, exporting through local agents, sales subsidiary, and production and marketing subsidiary. A similar set of explanations and predictions were proposed by Vernon ([1966] 1979) in his application of the product life cycle to the location of production. According to these perspectives, the firm commits resources to foreign markets as it accumulates knowledge and experience, managing the risks of expansion and coping with the liability of foreignness. An important corollary is that the firm expands abroad only as fast as its experience and knowledge allows.

ENTER THE "NEW" MULTINATIONALS

The early students of the phenomenon of MNEs from developing, newly industrialized, emerging, or upper-middle-income countries focused their attention on both the vertical and the horizontal investments undertaken by these firms, but they were especially struck by the latter. Vertical investments, after all, are easily understood in terms of the desire to reduce uncertainty and minimize opportunism when assets are dedicated or specific to the supply or the downstream activity, whether the MNE comes from a developed country or not (Caves 1996: 238–41; Lall 1983; Lecraw 1977; Wells 1983). The horizontal investments of the new MNEs, however, are harder to explain because they are supposed to be driven by the possession of intangible assets, and firms from developing countries were simply assumed not to possess them, or at least not to possess the same kinds of intangible assets as the classic MNEs from the rich countries (Lall

1983: 4). This paradox becomes more evident with the second wave of FDI from the developing world, the one starting in the late 1980s. In contrast with the first wave FDI from developing countries that took place in the 1960s and 1970s (Lall 1983; Wells 1983), the new MNEs of the 1980s and 1990s aimed at becoming world leaders in their respective industries, not just marginal players (Mathews 2006). In addition, the new MNEs do not come only from emerging countries. Some firms labeled as born-global or born-again born-globals (Bell *et al.* 2001; Rialp *et al.* 2005) have emerged from developed countries following accelerated paths of internationalization that challenge the conventional view of international expansion.

The main features of the new MNEs, as compared to the traditional ones, appear in Table 2.1. The dimensions in the table highlight the key differences between new and conventional MNEs. Perhaps the most startling one has to do with the accelerated pace of internationalization of the new MNEs, as firms from emerging economies have attempted to close the gap between their market reach and the global presence of the MNEs from developed countries (Mathews 2006).

A second feature of the new MNEs is that, regardless of the home country, they have been forced to deal not only with the liability of foreignness, but also with the liability and competitive disadvantage that stems from being latecomers lacking the resources and capabilities of the established MNEs from the most advanced countries. For this reason, the international expansion of the new MNEs runs in parallel with a capability upgrading process through which newcomers seek to gain access to external resources and capabilities in order to catch up with their more advanced competitors, i.e. to reduce their competitiveness gap with established MNEs (Aulakh 2007; Li 2007; Mathews 2006). However, despite lacking the same resource endowment of MNEs from developed countries, the new MNEs usually have an advantage over them, as they tend to possess stronger political capabilities. As the new MNEs are more used to deal with discretionary and/or unstable governments in their home country, they are better prepared than

Table 2.1. *The new multinational enterprises compared to traditional multinationals*

Dimension	New MNEs	Traditional MNEs
Speed of internationalization	Accelerated	Gradual
Competitive advantages	Weak: upgrading of resources required	Strong: required resources available in-house
Political capabilities	Strong: firms used to unstable political environments	Weak: firms used to stable political environments
Expansion path	Dual path: entry into developing countries for market access and developed countries for resource upgrading	Single path: from less to more distant countries
Preferred entry modes	External growth: alliances, joint ventures, and acquisitions	Internal growth: wholly owned subsidiaries
Organizational adaptability	High, because of their recent and relatively limited international presence	Low, because of their ingrained structure and culture

the traditional MNEs to succeed in foreign countries character-ized by a weak institutional environment (Cuervo-Cazurra and Genc 2008; García-Canal and Guillén 2008). Taking into account the high growth rates of emerging countries and their peculiar

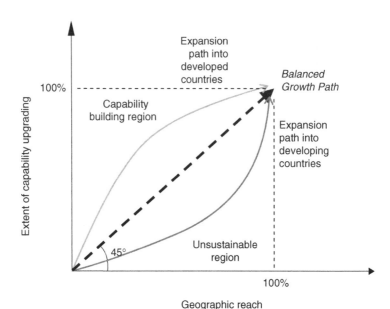

FIGURE 2.1 Expansion paths of new MNEs in developed and developing countries

institutional environment, political capabilities have been especially valuable for the new MNEs.

The first three features taken together point to another key characteristic of the new MNEs, they face a significant dilemma when it comes to international expansion because they need to balance the desire for global reach with the need to upgrade their capabilities. They can readily use their home-grown competitive advantages in other emerging or developing countries, but they must also enter more advanced countries in order to expose themselves to cutting-edge demand and develop their capabilities. This tension is reflected in Figure 2.1. Firms may evolve in a way that helps them to upgrade their capabilities or gain geographic reach, or both. Although some emerging market multinationals can focus only on emerging markets for their international expansion, becoming what Ramamurti and Singh (2009) call local optimizers, the corporate expansion of the new multinationals typically entails moving simultaneously in both directions: capability upgrading and geographic reach. Along the diagonal, the firm pursues a balanced growth path, which is the typical expansion pattern of the established multinationals. Above the diagonal it enters the region of capability building, in which the firm sacrifices the number of countries entered (i.e. its geographic reach) so as to close the gap with other competitors, especially in the advanced economies. Below the diagonal the firm enters the unsustainable region because prioritizing global reach without improving firm competences jeopardizes the capability upgrading process. The tension between capability upgrading and gaining global reach forces the new MNEs to enter developed and developing countries simultaneously since the beginning of their international expansion. Entering developing countries helps them gain size, operational experience, and generate profits, while venturing into developed ones contributes primarily to the capability upgrading process. The new MNEs have certainly tended to expand into developing countries at the beginning of their international expansion and limit their presence in developed countries to only a few locations where they can build capabilities, either because they have a partner there or because they have acquired a local firm. As they catch up with established MNEs, they begin to invest more in developed countries in search of markets, though they also make acquisitions in developed markets in order to secure strategic assets such as technology or brands.

A fifth feature of the new MNEs is their preference for entry modes based on external growth (see Table 2.1). Global alliances (García-Canal *et al.* 2002) and acquisitions (Rui and Yip 2008) are used by these firms to simultaneously overcome the liability of foreignness in the country of the partner/target and to gain access to their competitive advantages with the aim of upgrading their own resources and capabilities. When entering into global alliances, the new MNEs have used their home market position to facilitate the entry of their partners in exchange for reciprocal access to the partners' home markets and/or technology. Besides the size of the domestic market, the stronger the position of new MNEs in it, the greater the bargaining power of the new MNEs to enter into these alliances.

This fact is illustrated by the case of some new MNEs competing in the domestic appliances industry like China's Haier, Mexico's Mabe or Turkey's Arçelik, whose international expansion was boosted by alliances with world leaders that allowed them to upgrade their technological competences (Bonaglia *et al.* 2007). Capability upgrading processes based on acquisitions have been possible in some cases due to the new MNEs' privileged access to financial resources, because of government subsidies or capital market imperfections, as illustrated by the Chinese MNEs (Buckley *et al.* 2007).

A final feature of the new MNEs is that they enjoy more freedom to implement organizational innovations to adapt to the requirements of globalization because they do not face the constraints typical of established MNEs. As major global players with long histories, many MNEs from the developed economies suffer from inertia and path dependence due to their deeply ingrained values, culture, and organizational structure. Mathews (2006) shows how the new MNEs from Asia have adopted a number of innovative organizational forms that suited their needs, including networked and decentralized structures.

When analyzing the foreign investments of the new MNEs of the 1960s and 1970s, scholars focused their attention on two important questions, namely, their motivations and their proprietary, firm-specific advantages, if any. Table 2.2 summarizes the main motivations identified in the literature. As noted above, scholars documented and readily explained the desire of some of the new MNEs to create backward linkages into sources of raw materials or forward linkages into foreign markets in order to reduce uncertainty and opportunism in the relationship between the firm and the supplier of the raw material, or between the firm and the distributor or agent in the foreign market. Research documented, especially in the cases of South Korean and Taiwanese firms, their drive to internalize backward and forward linkages through the creation of trading companies, in some cases with government encouragement and financial support (Fields 1995: 183–237). For example, while during

Table 2.2. *Motivations for foreign direct investment by the new multinational enterprises*

Motivation	Description	References
Backward linkage into raw materials	Firm seeks to secure supplies of crucial inputs in the face of uncertainty or asset specificity.	Fields 1995; Lall 1983; UNCTAD 2006; Wells 1983
Forward linkage into foreign markets	Firm seeks to secure access to the market in the presence of asset specificity.	Fields 1995; UNCTAD 2006; Wells 1983;
Home-country government curbs	Firm attempts to overcome growth restrictions imposed by the government in its home market.	Lall 1983; UNCTAD 2006; Wells 1983
Spreading of risk	Firm locates assets in different countries to manage risk.	Lecraw 1977
Move personal capital abroad	Firm invests abroad so that owner(s) diversify their exposure to any one country.	Wells 1983
Follow a home-country customer to foreign markets	Firm follows home-country customers as they expand	UNCTAD 2006; Wells 1983

Table 2.2 *(cont.)*

Motivation	Description	References
	horizontally to other countries.	
Invest in new markets in response to economic reforms in the home country	Firm enjoying monopolistic or oligopolistic position in the home market is threatened by liberalization, deregulation, and/ or privatization policies.	Goldstein 2007; Guillén 2005
Acquire firm-specific intangible assets	Firm invests or acquires assets in more developed countries.	Lall 1983; UNCTAD 2006
Exploit firm-specific intangible assets	See Table 2.3	

the 1960s a tiny proportion of South Korea's exports reached foreign markets through the distribution and sale channels established by South Korean firms, by the 1980s roughly 50 percent of them were fully internalized, that is, handled by the exporters themselves (Cho 1987). As would be expected, the new MNEs felt the pressures of uncertainty and asset specificity more strongly if they had developed intangible assets. For instance, using evidence on a representative cross-sectional sample of 837 Spanish exporting firms as of 1992, Campa and Guillén (1999) found that those with greater expenditures on R&D were more likely to internalize export operations. A recent survey of the empirical evidence concluded that many of the new MNEs, especially in the extractive and manufacturing sectors, became multinationals when they internalized backward or forward linkages (UNCTAD 2006).

Scholars also documented that developing-country MNEs wished to expand abroad in order to overcome limitations imposed by the home-country government in the domestic market. In many developing and newly industrialized countries, limitations such as licensing systems, quota allocations, and export restrictions deprived firms from having enough growth opportunities at their disposal; hence the desire to expand abroad (Lall 1983; Wells 1983). In part related to the previous motive, firms felt the need to spread risks by locating assets in different countries (Lecraw 1977). This motivation was driven by the macroeconomic and political volatility characteristic of so many developing and newly industrialized countries. The home country tended to be characterized by macroeconomic and political volatility. A variation on this effect has to do with the case of family-owned MNEs from developing countries under the threat of government scrutiny or confiscation (Wells 1983).

The early literature on the new MNEs also identified buyer–supplier relationships as motives for a supplier establishing production facilities in a foreign country in which the buyer already had a presence (UNCTAD 2006; Wells 1983). In some cases, both the buyer and the supplier are home-country firms that followed each other abroad, while in others the buyer is a multinational from a developed country that asks its supplier in a developing or newly industrialized country to co-locate either in its home country or in other countries (Guillén 2005).

Scholars also devoted attention to the proprietary, firm-specific intangible assets of the new MNEs, noting that they engaged in foreign direct investment with the purpose of not only acquiring such assets but also exploiting existing ones. Foreign expansion with a view to acquiring intangible assets, especially technology and brands, was not very important during the 1970s and 1980s, but has become widespread in the last two decades (UNCTAD 2006). With the advent of current account and currency exchange liberalization in many developing and newly industrialized countries, the new MNEs have enjoyed more of a free hand in terms of making acquisitions, including multi-billion dollar deals. Many of these have targeted troubled companies or divisions located in the United States and Europe that possess some brands and product technology that the new MNE is in a better position to exploit because of its superior or more efficient manufacturing abilities.[2]

Acquisitions have not been the only way to gain access to intangible assets. The evidence suggests that the acceleration in the international expansion of the new MNEs has been backed by a number of international alliances aimed at gaining access to critical resources and skills that allow these firms to catch up to MNEs from developed countries. As argued above, these alliances and acquisitions have been critical for these firms to match the competitiveness of MNEs from developed countries. For this reason the international expansion of new MNEs runs in parallel with the process of upgrading their capabilities. Sometimes, however, capability upgrading precedes international expansion. This is the case, for instance, for some state-owned enterprises that undergo a restructuring process before their internationalization and privatization (Cuervo and Villalonga 2000). In other cases the capability upgrading process can follow international expansion. This can happen in regulated industries, where firms face strong incentives to commit large amounts of resources and to establish operations quickly, whenever and wherever opportunities arise, and frequently via acquisition as opposed to greenfield investment (García-Canal and Guillén 2008; Sarkar et al. 1999). As opportunities for international expansion in these industries depend on privatization and deregulation, some firms lacking competitive advantages expand abroad on the basis of free cash-

---

[2] Hennart (2009) argues that the greater efficiency in markets for assets and asset services in developed countries makes firms less diversified and, for this reason, more modular, i.e. easier to be took over and integrated by an emerging market multinational willing to acquire external technology and know-how.

flows as opportunities arise. As noted above, horizontal investments seemed to pose a challenge to established theories of the MNE. The literature had emphasized since the late 1950s that MNEs in general undertake horizontal investments on the basis of intangible assets such as proprietary technology, brands, or know-how. The early literature on the new multinationals simply assumed that firms from developing or newly industrialized countries lacked the kind of intangible assets characteristic of US, Japanese, or European multinationals (Lall 1983: 4). In fact, study after study found that the new multinationals scored lower on technology, marketing skill, organizational overhead, scale, capital intensity, and control over foreign subsidiaries than their rich-country counterparts (e.g. Lall 1983; Lecraw 1977; Wells 1983).

Still, horizontal investments cannot be explained without the presence of intangible assets of some sort. Table 2.3 summarizes the main types of intangible assets possessed by the new MNEs, as reflected in the existing literature. During the 1970s and 1980s, scholarly attention focused on capabilities such as the adaptation of technology to the typically smaller-scale markets of developing and newly industrialized countries, their cheaper labor, or imperfect input markets (Ferrantino 1992; Heenan and Keegan 1979; Lall 1983; Lecraw 1977; Tolentino 1993). Consumer-goods MNEs from these countries were also found to possess a different kind of intangible asset, namely, "ethnic brands" that appealed to customers not only in the home market but also to the ethnic diaspora in foreign countries, especially in Europe and the United States (Ferrantino 1992; Goldstein 2007: 117–22; Lecraw 1977; Wells 1983). Other scholars noted that the new MNEs possessed an uncanny ability to incrementally improve available products and to develop specialized variations for certain market niches (Lall 1983; UNCTAD 2006).

During the 1980s, students of the so-called East Asian miracle highlighted yet another intangible asset, one having to do with the ability to organize production and to execute large-scale projects efficiently with the help of technology borrowed from abroad in

Table 2.3. *Intangible assets of the new multinational enterprises*

Intangible asset	Description	References
Technology adaptation	Adaptation of available technology to small-scale product markets, cheap labor and/or imperfect input markets.	Heenan and Keegan 1979; Ferrantino 1992; Lall 1983; Lecraw 1977; Tolentino 1993
Early adoption of new technology	Implementation of new technology developed by someone else, especially in infrastructure industries such as construction, electricity, or telecommunications.	Guillén 2005; UNCTAD 2006
Ethnic branding	Consumer brands with appeal to immigrant home-country communities abroad.	Ferrantino 1992; Heenan and Keegan 1979; Lall 1983; Lecraw 1977; Wells 1983
Efficient production and project execution	Ability to absorb technology, combine resources and innovate from an organizational point of view in ways that reduce costs and enhance learning.	Amsden and Hikino 1994; Goldstein 2007; Guillén 2000; Kock and Guillén 2001; Mathews 2006; Ramamurti 2009; Ramamurti and Singh 2009; UNCTAD 2006

Table 2.3 *(cont.)*

Intangible asset	Description	References
Product innovation	Incremental product improvements; specialized products for market niches.	Lall 1983; UNCTAD 2006
Institutional entrepreneurial ability	Skills or know-how needed to operate in the peculiar institutional conditions of less developed countries.	Caves 1996; Lall 1983; Lecraw 1993; Ramamurti 2009
Expertise in the management of acquisitions	Experience gained in the home country in the management of M&As and corporate restructuring that help to extract value from cross-border acquisitions.	García-Canal and Guillén 2008; Guillén 2005
Networking skills	Ability to develop networks of cooperative relationships.	Buckley *et al.* 2007; Dunning 2002; Mathews 2006
Political know-how	Advantage in dealing with host governments and with political risk in less developed countries.	García-Canal and Guillén 2008; Goldstein and Pritchard 2009; Lall 1983; Lecraw 1977

industries as diverse as steel, electronics, automobiles, shipbuilding, infrastructure development, and turnkey plant construction (Amsden and Hikino 1994). Scholars also proposed that these capabilities facilitated the growth of diversified business groups (Guillén 2000; Kock and Guillén 2001; Ramamurti 2009; Ramamurti and Singh 2009), which in turn made it easier for firms within the same group to expand and invest abroad by drawing on shared financial, managerial and organizational resources (Goldstein 2007: 87–93; Guillén 2002; Lall 1983: 6; Mathews 2006; UNCTAD 2006). A specific type of managerial skill that becomes critical in accelerated internationalization is the ability to manage effectively mergers and acquisitions or strategic alliances. These abilities become critical when extracting value from such organizational combinations, that are necessary to learn and gain access to critical resources to increase the international competitiveness of the firm (Kale *et al.* 2000; Zollo and Singh 2004). The accrued skills in the management of M&As and corporate restructuring by Spanish large firms competing in regulated industries were critical for their international expansion in Latin America (García-Canal and Guillén 2008; Guillén 2005). Buckley *et al.* (2007), analyzing the success of Chinese firms capitalizing on the Chinese diaspora, argued that some firms have the ability to engage in beneficial relationships with other firms having valuable resources needed to succeed in global markets. The adoption of network based structures has also helped the development of the new MNEs by making easier the coordination of the international activities (Mathews 2006). However, home-country networks in several cases have also allowed these firms to take advantage of the experience of the firms with whom they have a tie (Elango and Pattnaik 2007; Yiu *et al.* 2007).

In more recent years, students of the new MNEs have drawn the attention to other types of intangible assets. On the technology side, research has documented that firms in developing, newly industrialized and upper-middle-income countries face lower hurdles when it comes to adopting new technology than their more established counterparts in rich countries. This is especially the case in industries such as construction, electricity, port operators, or telecommunications, in which companies from Brazil, Chile, Mexico, South Korea, Spain, and Dubai, among other countries, have demonstrated a superior ability to borrow technology and organize efficient operations across many markets (Guillén 2005; UNCTAD 2006). Another area of recent theoretical and empirical research has to do with the political know-how that the new MNEs seem to possess by virtue of having been forced to operate in heavily regulated environments at first, and then rapidly deregulating ones, as illustrated by the expansion of Spanish banking, electricity, water, and telecommunications firms throughout Latin America and, more recently, Europe (García-Canal and Guillén 2008). This "political" capability was not lost on the early students of the new MNEs; they duly pointed out that these firms possessed an "institutional entrepreneurial ability" that enabled them to operate effectively in the peculiar political, regulatory, and cultural conditions characteristic of developing countries (Caves 1996; Goldstein 2007: 99–102; Lall 1983; Lecraw 1993; Ramamurti 2009). Political and regulatory risk management was identified in some early studies as a key competitive capability (Lall 1983; Lecraw 1977). In the last twenty years, a new twist has been added to this theoretical insight after observing that the new MNEs are making acquisitions and increasing their presence in the infrastructure industries of the rich countries of Europe and North America, including electricity generation and distribution, telecommunications, water, and airport, ports, and toll-highway operation, among others (Guillén 2005; see also Goldstein and Pritchard 2009). The recent corporate expansion into Latin America of Spanish firms from regulated industries illustrates how firms tend to invest in those countries where their political capabilities are more valuable, i.e. those with high political instability. Over time, Spanish firms from regulated industries reduced their propensity to invest in politically unstable countries, showing that it is easier to move from politically unstable countries to stable ones than the other way around (García-Canal and Guillén 2008).

It is cardinal to note that, while the managerial, organizational, and political skills of the new multinationals may not be "patentable," they are rare, difficult to imitate, and valuable, the three conditions identified in the resource-based view of the firm as characterizing a true "capability" (Barney 1986; Markides and Williamson 1996; Peteraf 1993). The international expansion of the new multinationals cannot be understood without taking into account these non-technological proprietary intangible assets, which have enabled them to obtain scarcity rents in addition to the extraordinary profits arising from imperfect competition. Thus, intangible assets have played a key role in the rise of the new multinationals, but the assets themselves tend not to be technology and brands, as in the case of traditional multinationals (Caves 1996), but managerial, organizational, and political in nature.

An important point that early students of the new MNEs underplayed was that, depending on the home country, these foreign-investing firms tended to emerge from certain industries and not others (UNCTAD 2006). Thus, the South Korean MNEs have excelled in automobiles and electronics, the Taiwanese in component manufacturing, the Brazilian in automotive and aerospace products, the Mexican in ethnic brands and in producer goods such as cement, the Spanish in regulated and infrastructure industries, the Indian in information services, and the Chinese (so far) in simple assembled goods. In so doing, firms originating from developing, newly industrialized, and upper-middle-income countries have accumulated proprietary intangible assets that have enabled them to successfully compete through internalized exports and horizontal investments even in the most advanced countries in the world.

This process of "reverse" foreign direct investment from home countries at a lower level of development than the host countries to which it is directed is only anomalous in a superficial way. The overall level of development of a country, as measured by such aggregate indicators as GDP per capita, more likely than not conceals a heterogeneous mix of backward and world-class industries and firms.

Many countries around the world include pockets or enclaves of excellence surrounded by relatively mediocre or even inefficient producers. The literature on geographical clusters and agglomeration economies has shown that firms build capabilities as they interact with others located in close proximity (Cortright 2006; Porter 1998). This literature emphasizes that the country level of analysis is not the appropriate one for understanding the impact of location and geography. Ironically, one of the facilitating factors in the development of these clusters and enclaves of excellence could be incoming FDI and outsourcing agreements from firms located in developed countries that contributed to the formation of industrial clusters in less developed ones (McKendrik *et al.* 2001; Meyer 2004). One of the main purposes of this book is precisely to uncloak these patterns of industrial specialization at the local level with a view to documenting the sources of competitive advantage that have enabled the new MNEs to expand throughout the world.

The new MNEs have tended to follow some of the patterns of expansion consistent with product life cycle and staged theories of internationalization, as they have tended to expand first into countries located within the same region (Goldstein 2007; Lall 1983; Wells 1983). In addition, when stepping outside their home region, they have tended to emphasize areas culturally, politically, or economically similar, as in the case of the Spanish firms' expansion into Latin America (Guillén 2005). However, notable exceptions to this pattern have to do with investments in search of strategic assets (Goldstein 2007: 85–7) and the rapid pace at which they have expanded their global reach (Mathews 2006). This book also seeks to provide an understanding of the choices that the new MNEs have made in terms of foreign markets for expansion.

In sum, our analytical approach involves comparing the ways in which the new MNEs develop capabilities and obtain global reach. As reflected in Table 2.4, we focus the attention on three ways of developing capabilities, namely, internally, through alliances or via acquisitions. Similarly, the new MNEs have sought to increase

Table 2.4. *Capability development, global reach, and the new multinationals*

Ways of developing capabilities:	Ways of gaining global reach:		
	Greenfield	Alliances	Acquisitions
Internally	The firm develops technological, marketing, or organizational capabilities internally, and exploits them in a variety of markets through greenfield investment.	The firm possesses technological, marketing, or organizational capabilities, and uses alliances to overcome competitive or regulatory barriers to entry into foreign markets.	The firm possesses technological, marketing, or organizational capabilities, and uses acquisitions to overcome competitive or regulatory barriers to entry into foreign markets.
Alliances	The firm uses alliances to develop technological, marketing, or organizational capabilities, reserving for itself the right to enter certain foreign markets.	The firm uses alliances both to develop capabilities and	The firm uses alliances to develop technological, marketing, or organizational

Acquisitions	Lacking capabilities, the firm makes acquisitions in certain markets which then enable it to enter new markets by itself.	Lacking capabilities, the firm makes acquisitions to develop them, and then uses alliances to expand into other markets characterized by barriers to entry.	to gain access to foreign markets.	capabilities, but resorts to acquisitions in order to overcome competitive or regulatory barriers to entry into foreign markets.
				Lacking capabilities and market access, the firm makes acquisitions to address both problems simultaneously.

their global reach by means of the three most common foreign-entry modes, i.e. greenfield, alliances, and acquisitions. In the chapters that follow we systematically analyze the circumstances under which Spanish firms have developed capabilities and pursued global reach in a variety of manufacturing and service industries, comparing their strategies to their European and emerging-market competitors.

CONCLUSION

The new MNEs are the result of both imitation of established MNEs from the rich countries – which they have tried to emulate strategically and organizationally – and innovation in response to the peculiar characteristics of emerging and developing countries. The context in which their international expansion has taken place is also relevant. The new MNEs have emerged from countries with weak institutional environments and they are used to operate in countries with weak property-rights regimes, legal systems and so on. Experience in the home country became especially valuable for the new MNEs because many countries with weak institutions are growing fast and they had developed the capabilities to compete in such challenging environments.

In addition, the new MNEs have flourished at a time of market globalization in which, despite the local differences that still remain, global reach and global scale are crucial. The new MNEs have responded to this challenge by embarking into an accelerated international strategy based on external growth aimed at upgrading their capabilities and increasing their global market reach. When implementing this strategy, the new MNEs took advantage of their market position in the home country and, ironically, their meager international presence allowed them to adopt a strategy and organizational structure that happens to be most appropriate to the current international environment in which emerging economies are growing very fast.

It is also important to note that the established MNEs from the rich countries have adopted some of the patterns of behavior of the new multinationals. Increased competitive pressure from the latter in industries such as cement, steel, electrical appliances, construction, banking, and infrastructure has prompted many US and European firms to become much less reliant on traditional product-differentiation strategies and vertically integrated structures. To a certain extent, the rise of networked organizations (e.g. Bartlett and Ghoshal 1989) and the extensive shift towards outsourcing represent competitive responses to the challenges faced by established MNEs. Finally, a special type of new MNE is the so-called born-global firm, which resembles the new MNE in many ways but has emerged from developed countries.

Taking all of these developments into account, it is clear that the traditional model of the MNE is fading. In effect, globalization, technical change, and the coming of age of the emerging countries have facilitated the rise of a new type of MNE in which foreign direct investment is driven not only by the exploitation of firm-specific competences but also by the exploration of new patterns of innovation and ways of accessing markets. In addition, the new MNEs have expanded very rapidly, without following the gradual, staged model of internationalization.

It is important to note, however, that the decline of the traditional model of the MNE does not necessarily imply the demise of existing theories of the MNE. In fact, the core explanation for the existence of MNEs remains, namely, that in order to pursue international expansion, the firm needs to possess capabilities allowing it to overcome the liability of foreignness; no firm-specific capabilities, no multinationals. Our analysis of the new MNEs has shown that their international expansion was possible due to some valuable capabilities developed in the home country, including project-execution, political and networking skills, among other non-conventional ones. Thus, the lack of the classic technological or marketing capabilities does not imply the absence of other valuable capabilities that may provide the foundations for international expansion. It is precisely for this reason that the new MNEs are here to stay. In the following chapters we provide a more fine-grained analysis of the process by which the new multinationals leverage and upgrade their competitive advantages by studying selected cases of new multinationals from different industries.

A NOTE ON OLIGOPOLISTIC RIVALRY

In summarizing the theory of the multinational enterprise, Richard Caves observed that "multinational enterprises are large firms that typically operate in concentrated industries and earn both monopoly profits and rents to their proprietary assets" (Caves 1996: 97). Indeed, most foreign direct investment takes place in moderately concentrated industries such as oil, chemicals, automobiles, electronics, or banking. As fragmented industries become more concentrated or as monopolies are deregulated and liberalized, one observes a spike in foreign direct investment (Goldstein 2007: 99–102; Guillén 2005; UNCTAD 2006). There is evidence indicating that this phenomenon occurs in developing, newly industrialized, and upper-middle-income as well as in developed countries. For instance, South Korean manufacturing firms in moderately concentrated industries were more likely to invest in China during the late 1980s and 1990s than those in other industries (Guillén 2002). Moreover, research has shown that firms in moderately concentrated industries follow each other to foreign markets, a pattern of behavior known as "oligopolistic reaction" (Knickerbocker 1973). Same-industry competitors in South Korea and Spain, for instance, have tended to follow each other to foreign markets (Guillén 2001). In addition to documenting and explaining patterns of firm-specific competitive advantage by industry and of foreign market choice, this book aims at elucidating the process of oligopolistic rivalry that has led many of the new MNEs to pursue foreign expansion. In the next chapters we analyze each of these three dynamics, showing how the interplay among comparative location advantages, proprietary capabilities, and market structures have generated distinct types of new MNEs in various countries around the world.

3 Diversification and vertical integration in traditional industries

We know best practices in baking. We travel around the globe looking closely at all practices in baking plants. We can compare everywhere, and we can detect a good number of opportunities to raise productivity.

Daniel Servitje, CEO, Grupo Bimbo (quoted by Siegel 2008: 13)

Only renowned brands enable you to play in the global economy. This does not mean that if you lack such a brand you cannot grow, but it is a requirement for playing in the big leagues.

Josep Lluis Bonet Ferrer, Chairman and CEO, Freixenet[1]

The agro-food and beverages industries belong to the set of "traditional" industries in which natural endowments and comparative advantage have historically shaped the structure of competition. However, fundamental technological and competitive changes over the last three decades have enabled the rise of numerous new multinational firms in these industries. In addition to the incorporation of new technologies, foreign direct investment involving firms in the industry has increased sharply. Whereas in 1990 the cumulative stock of outward FDI from the agriculture, fishing, food, beverages, and tobacco industries amounted to just $77 billion, by 2007 it had grown to $472 billion, a rate of change slightly faster than for the manufacturing sector as a whole. While only about 1 percent of the stock is attributable to firms from developing countries, activity by the new multinationals has increased ten-fold, from $0.6 to $6.0 billion (UNCTAD 2009: 219).

The value of mergers and acquisitions (M&A) in agriculture, fishing, agro-food, and beverages has also increased. In 2008

---

[1] *Fomento de la Producción*, no. 1240, December 1, 2004.

it amounted to $115.1 billion or 17.1 percent of total M&A activity in the world in terms of sales, and $82.7 billion or 12 percent in terms of purchases, indicating that the industry attracts acquirers primarily based in other industries. These figures represent a 53 percent increase over 2007 sales, and a 69 percent increase over 2007 purchases, primarily driven by rising agricultural commodity prices and consolidation in the beverage and beer industries (UNCTAD 2009: 274). Much M&A activity in agro-food has to do with multibillion dollar deals by the two largest companies, Nestlé ($104.1 billion in sales) and Unilever (57.1). Increasingly, new multinationals from developing and emerging economies are making a dent in the industry on a global scale, including Bimbo and Gruma of Mexico, and Arcor of Argentina in food products, and San Miguel of the Philippines or Modelo of Mexico in beverages.

As in the case of other Southern European, Latin American, and Asian countries, Spanish firms in the agro-food and beverages industries have traditionally remained small and primarily oriented towards the domestic market. However, technological, branding, and scale improvements over the last two decades have enabled them to play an increasingly important role globally. After undertaking a series of foreign investments and acquisitions in Europe, North America, and Asia, Ebro Puleva has become the world's largest producer and marketer of rice and the second-largest of pasta, Grupo SOS the biggest company in olive oil, Chupa-Chups the second-largest candy company, Viscofán the largest maker of artificial casings for the meat industry, and Freixenet the largest sparkling wine maker. While these firms are dwarfed by the large food and beverages multinationals from the most developed countries in the world, they have managed to carve out a profitable niche, albeit with different degrees of vertical integration and product diversification (see Table 3.1).

Due to its climatic and geographic diversity, Spain is home to one of the world's largest and most sophisticated agricultural sectors. The country is the tenth-largest food producer in value terms. In 2008 the primary food sector (agriculture, cattle-rearing, hunting,

Table 3.1. *Growth strategies in the agro-food and beverage sector*

Product diversification:	Vertical integration	
	Low	High
High	Bimbo, Arcor*	Ebro Puleva, SOS, Viscofán
Low	Gruma	Freixenet*

Note: *Arcor and Freixenet started their internationalization process prior to 1985.

and fishing) employed 879,000 workers, and the food processing and beverage industries 509,000, and exported 27.1 billion euros worth of meat, fruit, vegetables, oil, and beverages, 81 percent to the rest of the European Union (MMAMRM 2009: 88, 1014, 1017–19). Spain is both a large exporter and a large importer of food, with exports exceeding imports by a mere 2.5 percent. While there is some specialization in trade depending on natural endowments, Spain exemplifies the importance of paying attention to economies of scale and product differentiation in explaining complex patterns of international trade and investment (Krugman 1979, 1980). The strategies and success of Spanish agro-food and beverages companies cannot be understood without paying attention to technology, scale, and differentiation, as the cases of Ebro Puleva, Grupo SOS, Viscofán, and Freixenet illustrate.

EBRO PULEVA
Ebro Puleva is the world's largest producer and marketer of rice, and the second-largest of pasta. In Spain it leads the market in sugar and dairy products as well. It has a strong market presence throughout Europe and the North American Free Trade Agreement countries. It is the largest rice and pasta company in the United States and Canada. In 2008 annual sales amounted to €2.4 billion and it employed 6,650 people worldwide. Twenty-eight percent of sales were in Spain, 44

percent in Europe, and 28 percent in North America. Pasta is the largest division (41 percent of sales), followed by rice (38) and dairy (21). In late 2008 it sold its sugar producing and refining division to Associated British Foods for €385 million, a business mired by low margins, overcapacity, and stringent EU regulations. The company is also present in biotechnology and bio-fuels. The company is the result of the 2001 merger of a fifty-year-old sugar company and a dairy producer.

Ebro Puleva is a publicly listed firm with a market capitalization of €2.2 billion as of the end of 2009. Its equity ownership, however, is rather concentrated. As of the end of 2008, about 15 percent of the equity was controlled by the Instituto Hispánico del Arroz, Spain's leading rice seed producer, owned by the family of Antonio Hernández Callejas, the President and CEO of Ebro Puleva. The state holding company SEPI held 8.4 percent, regional savings banks a combined 11 percent, and other beverage and food companies another 11 percent. The Hernández Callejas family has played a key role in corporate governance since 1988, when Ebro Agrícolas and Sociedad General Azucarera merged, in a deal orchestrated by the Spanish Ministry of Agriculture as a way to provide the company with a stable shareholding structure after the scandals associated with the presence of the Kuwait Investment Office in the chemicals and sugar industries. The Hernández family had been active in the rice business through Arrocerías Herba, a company that Ebro acquired in a series of all-equity deals, allowing the family to gradually gain control of Ebro Puleva. Antonio Hernández Callejas became Vice-President of Ebro Puleva in 2002, and President and CEO in 2005.

Prior to their merger, neither Ebro nor Puleva had developed strong capabilities that set them apart from other firms in the industry. In fact, they were prime targets for foreign acquirers given their meager competitive capabilities by international standards but large domestic market shares. The Spanish food sector has traditionally been populated by small and medium-sized enterprises. The large European and US food multinationals arrived in the 1960s and 1970s, mainly through greenfield investments. During the 1980s, however, foreign firms turned to acquisitions of local family-controlled firms experiencing difficulties. As part of its global portfolio diversification program, the Kuwait Investment Office built up its initial stake in Ebro Agrícolas to 34 percent. The government was keenly aware that Spanish firms lacked the competitive capabilities to succeed in a single European market. In the oligopolistic sugar market, which provided badly needed jobs in Spain's interior, the government felt that firms were too small to compete, and was eager to encourage mergers. The main idea was that economies of scale and a revamping of ownership and managerial structures might give Spanish companies a fighting chance. With the domestic market growing quickly during the 1990s, the strategy seemed to work. Ebro Agrícolas continued to be a dominant local player. The next step was to orchestrate a merger with Puleva, a dairy producer, inspired by the idea that there were important synergies in branding and distribution channels that could be exploited across a wider set of food products.

Armed with a stable ownership structure, greater scale, new management, and a commanding share of the domestic market, Ebro Puleva started to think about foreign expansion. Rather than pursuing entry into the crowded and highly regulated European markets, the company saw opportunities in the United States. Cheap financing thanks to the euro and a favorable exchange rate with the dollar facilitated the 2004 acquisition of Houston-based rice producer and marketer Riviana Foods for $380 million, and the 2006 acquisition of New World Pasta, also in the United States, for $362 million, which added Ronzoni and American Beauty to its already strong portfolio of pasta brands (Riviana and Panzani). In 2006 Ebro Puleva reached an agreement with Kraft Foods to purchase Minute Rice's US and Canadian operations for $280 million. In 2008 Ebro Puleva was the largest pasta company in the US market with a 29 percent share, and the largest in Canada with a 41 percent share.

The company is keen on focusing on branded, high value-added, and high-technology areas. Rice and pasta are its core strategic products for international growth, and they deliver most of the profits. It has factories throughout Western and Eastern Europe, the United States, Puerto Rico, Algeria, Libya, Morocco, Tunisia, Egypt, Israel, India, and Thailand. The rice division was set up as a separate entity in 2001. International acquisitions started in 1986. Its best-known brands include Brillante, La Cigala, Oryza, Reis Fit, Ris Fix, Bosto, Riceland, Mahatma, Success, and Carolina. Biotechnology activities are focused on organic and medicinal foods. In 2001 it established Puleva Biotech, which is a publicly listed company with a market capitalization of €58 million. Bio-fuels research and production are presently undergoing a strategic review given changing energy prices and the sale of the sugar division.

Ebro Puleva's transformation into a major new multinational firm took place via acquisitions in developed markets like France and the United States, which gave it both market share and brands. Greenfield investments and alliances have not played as important a role in acquiring capabilities and extending market reach.

GRUPO SOS

Grupo SOS is a vertically integrated Spanish company dedicated to the production and sale of branded oil, rice, olives, vinegars, and other foodstuffs. It is the world's largest olive oil producer and marketer, and Spain's second-largest agro-food firm. In 2008 sales amounted to €1.4 billion, of which 52 percent are in the European Union (Spain representing about half), 25 percent in the United States and Canada, 12 percent in Latin America, and 6 percent in the Middle East. The largest division, oil, accounted for 69 percent of sales, and rice for 26 percent. Although some of its brands – Sasso, Louit, SOS, and Carbonell – are more than 100 years old, the beginning of Grupo SOS as we know it only goes back to 1990. It was then when Jesús and Jaime Salazar joined forces with both private and institutional investors to acquire Arana Maderas, a food company listed on the Bilbao stock exchange. The Salazar brothers transformed the firm into what became known as Grupo Industrial Arana. Within two years, majority stakes were acquired in Interván and Pictolin. In 1992 they acquired Hijos J. Sos Borrás, a firm in the rice production business. A restructuring process in 1994 brought together all of these companies, giving birth to Sos Arana Alimentación.

The firm undertook its first international acquisitions in 1994 with the purchase of Bernabé Biosca Tunisie, a rice producer in Tunisia, and in 1997, when it came to control Arrocera del Trópico, a Mexican rice producer. Two years later, in 1999, Arroz Sos Sevilla was established from the industrial assets acquired from Arrocerías Dársena. This served as a buyer for the farmers and cooperatives of Andalucía, given that it is located in Los Palacios, province of Seville, the heart of the main rice-producing area in Spain. During the following year, 2000, the company purchased Grupo SIPA (Saludães Produtos Alimentares), owner of the leading Saludaes brand. Also in 2000 the company became the leader of the cookie and cracker market in the Iberian Peninsula with the acquisition of Cuétara and Bogal Bolachas (Portugal). The 2001 merger of Sos Arana Alimentación and Cuétara gave birth to SOS-Cuétara, followed by the acquisitions of majority stakes in Koipe (owner of the Carbonell olive oil and Koipesol sunflower oil brands) and Aceica Refinería (a company dedicated to the bottling and commercialization of oil seeds), and of one-third of Aceitunas y Conservas (ACYCO).

Perhaps the boldest acquisition was that of American Rice in 2003–4 for $35 million, one of the largest US rice makers, and the owner of successful regional brands such as Comet, Adolphus, Blue Ribbon, and Wonder. American Rice owned Cinta Azul in Puerto Rico and Abu Bint in Saudi Arabia. According to its top executive at the time, this acquisition provided an "insuperable distribution platform for the launching of other products" (Salazar 2009: 247). In 2005 the company acquired Minerva Oil, one of the four main Italian olive oil producers (owner of the Sasso brand) for €62.72 million, followed in 2006 by the purchase of Sara Lee's rice assets in the Netherlands, a company with renowned brands such as Lassie and excellent production facilities, and Carapelli Firenze, owner of the Carapelli

brand and leader in the Italian virgin olive oil market, in a deal worth
€132.48 million. This acquisition turned SOS into the world's largest olive oil company with a 15 percent global market share. Also in
2006 an agreement was reached with Unilever to acquire Friol Italia
for €33.25 million, the largest Italian seed oil company. In 2008 the
company signed an association agreement with Rasoi Group to com-
mercialize olive oil in Asian markets, and sold its Cuétara cookie
division to Nutrexpa for €215 in order to buy Bertolli, the world's
largest olive oil company, from Unilever, in a transaction valued at
€627 million. With this acquisition, SOS commanded 22 percent of
the global olive oil market, and 30 percent of the overall cooking oil
market in the United States as of 2008 (Salazar 2009: 247).

As of mid 2009 Grupo SOS had food-processing factories in
Portugal, Holland, the United Kingdom, Italy, Germany, Australia,
Mexico, Guyana, Tunisia, Brazil, and the United States, as well as
Spain. It exported to seventy-two countries on all five continents.
The company imported significant volumes of rice and olives from
northern Africa. Grupo SOS has mainly grown via acquisitions, and
moved swiftly to integrate new brands into its production and distribution network. It relied on strategic alliances in order to reach into
foreign markets, as in the case of its agreement with Wal-Mart in
the United States. It is also a company that invests heavily in R&D,
especially in the development of highly nutritional new products
and quality control equipment. All in all, however, Grupo SOS has
relied more extensively on acquisitions and alliances than on greenfield investments in order to build capabilities, attain economies of
scale, and reach new markets.

As of the end of 2008 Grupo SOS resembled Ebro Puleva in
ownership structure in that the Salazar brothers, Jesús and Jaime,
owned directly or indirectly nearly 26 percent of the equity. Caja
Madrid, the large savings bank, owned 10.5 percent. Other regional
savings banks based in Spain's olive-producing areas accounted for
about 27 percent, and Banco Santander an additional 5 percent. In
early May 2009, however, the board of directors removed the Salazar

brothers from their executive positions in the wake of a scandal over a loan in the amount of €212.7 million extended in 2008 by SOS to a company owned by the two brothers with the ultimate goal of buying shares and selling them to Middle Eastern funds, in violation of the law. After years of rapid expansion via acquisition, the company now faces a period of financial restructuring with a former Caja Madrid executive at the helm.

FREIXENET

As in rice, pasta, and olive oil, Spanish firms in the sparkling wine industry did not rise to prominence internationally until the 1980s, although they tried from the 1930s onward (Mínguez Sanz 1994). French producers have traditionally dominated the premium end of the market, and shared the middle segment of the market with Italian and Californian producers. By the mid 1990s one Spanish firm, Freixenet (€383 million in sales, 1,258 employees), had rewritten the rules of competition in the industry, producing over 130 million bottles annually. Freixenet also became the leading exporter to the world's largest market, the United States, selling 12.6 million bottles, closely followed by Italy's Martini Rossi with 11.2 million and leaving far behind the traditional export leader, France's Moët & Chandon, with 8.5 million. The firm is the world's largest sparkling wine company, and one of the top ten wine groups overall.

Technically speaking, Freixenet does not make "champagne" but "cava," which is the official denomination for sparkling wines produced in Spain along the Ebro valley and, most importantly, in the Penedès county located to the west of Barcelona, where production first began in 1892. Thus, Spanish firms in the sparkling wine business have always had to surmount the comparative disadvantage of not being a producer based in the famous French champagne-producing regions, where the *méthode champenoise* was first developed some 300 years ago (Prial 1996). Up to the 1970s, the lower quality and weaker brand reputation of the Spanish producers could only be compensated by lower labor costs than in France – and by tariff barriers. Spanish cava output was mostly sold in the domestic market. By the early 1990s, however, 40 percent of Spanish production was sold in the United States, Germany, the UK, the CIS, Sweden, Switzerland, Canada, and other countries (Bonet 1993; Mínguez Sanz 1994). Freixenet accounts for 70 percent of total Spanish exports, even though it has traditionally been the second-largest Spanish producer. Codorníu, its bigger, neighboring rival, has been much slower than Freixenet at becoming an exporter, investor in distribution channels abroad, and acquirer of vineyards and production facilities in the United States and Latin America.

Freixenet is a family controlled and run company, now in the third generation. Its origins date back to 1889, and it started its internationalization fairly early. In 1935 it opened a short-lived US sales subsidiary. Beginning in the 1950s it pioneered exports to the United States and Europe, but by the late 1970s export levels were still rather small. It should be noted that the company was by then facing a great liability of foreignness due to the lack of a recognized brand and reputation, not only for the firm itself, but in terms of country of origin. However, the commercial efforts paid off in the end because little by little the company was gaining market share and reputation in markets such as the UK. In the words of Josep Lluis Bonet, Chairman and CEO of Freixenet:

> our business vision has a keen sense of risk and has been
> very tenacious. A clear example was our approach to the
> UK market, where we opened our first branch in 1960, and
> we never thought about shutting it down even in the face of
> continuing losses, because we knew that it was a difficult
> market to enter, one in which we had to have a presence.
> Nowadays it is our second most important export market.[2]

The big push came in the 1980s, with the creation in 1980 of Freixenet USA and in 1984 of Freixenet Alemania GmbH, located

---

[2] *El Exportador Digital*, September 2002.

in the two large export markets for sparkling wines. Germany is Freixenet's most important export market. It first entered the restaurant business through a distribution agreement with a juice company, Granini. In the early 1990s this firm was acquired by a larger rival, Eckes. Freixenet had to either discontinue the relationship or think about new ways to grow its presence in the market. The decision was made to conduct a consumer survey, which revealed that Freixenet could increase its market share by repositioning the product as one coming from Spain – a main destination for German tourists – and emphasizing feelings such as passion and happiness. The involvement of Eckes as the implementer of the new strategy was crucial. Freixenet's market share jumped from 3 to 10 percent (Ariño *et al.* 2000).

As in Germany, Freixenet decided to change its traditional approach to the US market. The new strategy included several key components. First, they studied the different market segments and decided to target the one for champagne bottles priced between four and nine dollars. Below that segment one could find the Californian low-quality competitors. Above it were the Italian and Californian high-quality producers, while the French premium champagnes dominated the uppermost end of the market. Then Freixenet introduced a new brand specifically for that intermediate segment, the *Cordón Negro* or "black bottle," which was supposed to appeal to the young professional class. They supported the launch of the new label with a massive advertising campaign, eventually turning the firm into the third-largest sparkling wine advertiser in the US market. Freixenet became the US market leader in volume within a short period of time, selling more bottles than all of the French producers combined (Adams/Jobson 1996: 71–4). The *Cordón Negro* was, still, a wine produced and bottled in Spain, and exported to the US and other major markets, thus suffering from a reputation disadvantage relative to the French labels.

In spite of spending about 12 percent of sales on advertising, however, massive and astute marketing is not enough to account for Freixenet's success. Technological choice also played a decisive role. Freixenet was torn between adopting industrialized methods of sparkling wine production using large metallic containers, and emulating the traditional *méthode champenoise*. The former is very efficient, but the quality of the wine suffers greatly. Understanding that its success depended on producing champagne of medium-to-high quality at low cost, Freixenet began spending 1 percent of revenues on R&D, and developed an automated procedure based on *jaulas* or "cage-like" racks for the second fermentation of the wine in the bottle, which produces its characteristic sparkling character. These devices hold a great number of bottles, making it possible to automate the daily operation of turning each bottle so as to shake the sediment of dead yeast cells that accumulate in the neck of the bottle. This operation was traditionally performed by hand. For a high-volume firm producing 130 million bottles annually, automation represented a major advantage, especially at a time when labor costs in Spain were rising quickly. This production innovation has allowed Freixenet to mass produce sparkling wine of consistent medium-to-high quality at low cost.

After developing its brand image and improving its production methods, Freixenet transformed itself into a full-fledged multinational firm. In 1985 it founded Freixenet Sonoma Caves in California (1.7 million bottles of the Gloria Ferrer label), and acquired the third oldest (1757) French champagne house, Henri Abelé of Reims (400,000 bottles), in a clear attempt to learn about new trends and technologies in the industry as well as to gain the right to include the prestigious "champagne" label in its catalog of sparkling wines. In 1986 it created the Sala Vivé vineyard in Mexico (700,000 bottles). These and other domestic acquisitions allowed Freixenet to almost double its production capacity in a matter of two years and position its new brand offerings in the higher segments of the market.[3] In

---

[3] In 1984 Freixenet acquired three domestic producers being privatized by the government after the nationalization of the Rumasa business group: Segura Viudas (eleven million bottles), Castellblanch (thirteen million bottles), and René Barbier (ten million bottles).

the late 1980s and early 1990s Freixenet opened marketing and sales subsidiaries in France, Russia, Mexico, Australia, Japan, and China, in addition to its grape- and wine-producing facilities in the United States, Mexico, and France. Its latest acquisitions have focused on still wines, including Yvon Mau in Bourdeaux, the Wingara Wine Group in Australia, and several wineries in the Spanish grape-growing regions of Ribera del Duero, Rias Baixas, Priorat, and Penedès. Freixenet nowadays has a presence in terms of production or distribution companies in more than 120 countries.[4]

Freixenet's Japan strategy illustrates how a firm lacking resources and facing strong competitors can establish itself in a key market. The firm started exporting its products to Japan in the 1980s. In 1991, it formally established a subsidiary. Back then the Japanese market for sparkling wines was very small and dominated by French brands. Freixenet sold only 180,000 bottles. The Japanese wine market, however, was growing quickly due to demographics, high purchasing power, and taste for Western products. The high population density in urban areas made distribution cheaper and more effective. However, high land costs as well as complicated distribution networks dominated by great wholesalers made any new entrant's life very difficult. Freixenet therefore opted for a strategy based on the minimal fixed capital costs possible, establishing itself with companies such as Suntory and Itochu, which are large, diversified beverage groups with extensive distribution networks. The firm presently sells six million bottles of sparkling wine in Japan, its fifth-largest market after Spain, Germany, the United States and the United Kingdom. It ranks second after Moët & Chandon. In still wines, Freixenet has managed to become the market leader, especially with the Lágrima Real label. Overall, Freixenet commands 16 percent of the Japanese wine market in volume, and 6 percent in value.

---

[4] *Wall Street Journal* (December 29, 1994, pp. 1, 5); *Dinero* (June 21, 1993, pp. 70–1, 74–6); *Expansión* (August 27, 1993, p. 3); *El País Negocios* (June 4, 1995, p. 10); *El País Negocios* (December 7, 1997, p. 6); *Advertising Age International Supplement* (June 29, 1998, p. 13); *Cinco Días* (November 27, 2002); *El País Negocios* (October 1, 2001).

Freixenet illustrates the use of greenfield investments, alliances, and acquisitions as means for emerging multinationals to enter new markets and build capabilities. The firm had originally developed strong capabilities in production and marketing in a fiercely competitive domestic market in which it was only the second-largest player. It then exploited them through exports, using alliances in distribution in order to overcome barriers to entry into certain international markets and to reinforce its own brands. Greenfield investments followed in countries such as the United States and Mexico, where it leveraged its internal capabilities. Lastly, acquisitions of high-end wineries helped the firm access new capabilities.

VISCOFÁN

Founded in Navarre in 1975 by a group of industrialists from the Basque Country, Viscofán is the world's leader in artificial casings for the meat industry, with a 36 percent global market share, dwarfing Scotland-based Devro and US-based Viskase. In the specific category of cellulose casings it commands a 60 percent share. In the United States, roughly two of every three frankfurters are manufactured using cellulose casings made by Viscofán. The firm started as a spin-off from Papelera Guipuzcoana de Zicuñaga (presently known as Iberpapel), a paper company active since 1941, with a presence in Europe, North Africa, and South America.[5]

Meatpackers use artificial casings to make sausage products by pumping a meat emulsion into the casing. The meat-filled casing is twisted at certain intervals to make individual sausages, and then cooked. The cellulose casing is removed and the final product packaged and sold as "skinless" sausages or frankfurters. During the interwar period, food companies around the world realized that natural casings were not ideal for mass production given their lack of homogeneity and standardization. Collagen casings made with cow skin became a viable alternative, pioneered by a German firm,

[5] The information on Viscofán was gathered through secondary sources and an interview with Jaime Echevarría, President of Viscofán, Madrid, May 8, 2009.

Naturin GmbH. They are especially appropriate for sausages, salami, and other similar meat products.

Artificial casings have clear advantages over natural ones. The raw material for the cellulose casing can be produced at will using well-understood technology, and it is easy and cheap to transport. The manufacturing process, however, is complex, and involves three steps:

(1) making viscose from natural cellulose fibers, which is a chemical process;
(2) extrusion or regeneration of the cellulose while simultaneously making cellulose tubes, which requires drying the extruded casing under carefully controlled conditions and winding it onto reels of semi-finished material called "flat stock," which are easily and cheaply transported over long distances; and
(3) shirring, a finishing operation during which reels of flat stock are pleated and compressed into tubular sticks, later used by the meatpackers.

Thus, vertical integration is required in order to produce quality casings at low cost. It should also be noted that the first two stages are capital intensive, while the third is more labor intensive. Given that the reels are easy and cheap to transport over long distances, the firm can actually locate each activity separately.

Papelera Guipuzcoana de Zicuñaga was engaged in the manufacturing of cellophane wrappings for candy and other foodstuffs. However, plastic-based products displaced cellophane by the late 1960s and early 1970s. Wishing to continue supplying the food industry, the management of Papelera saw an opportunity in artificial casings. They had decades of experience at cellulose manufacturing for other purposes. Moreover, demand for frankfurters and other types of fast food was predicted to grow vigorously. In the 1970s the cellulose casings business was dominated by Viskase, at the time owned by Union Carbide, and Teepak, originally owned by Johnson & Johnson, and later sold to Devro, a Scottish firm traditionally focused on collagen casings. Viscofán's founders thought that they could innovate in production technology so as to be more efficient than the incumbent firms, but they lacked a reputation in the market and access to customers. They decided to approach Naturin GmbH, the German firm that pioneered collagen casings back in the 1930s and was the world market leader. Viscofán gave Naturin 5 percent of its equity in exchange for business contacts. "Our alliance with Naturin was fundamental to our becoming a major global producer of artificial cellulose casings," asserted Jaime Echevarría, the President of both Viscofán and Papelera Guipuzcoana de Zicuñaga.

Viscofán grew fast during the early 1980s, entering several export markets. Union Carbide, then owner of Viskase, and Teepak felt threatened and filed a complaint with the International Trade Commission arguing that Viscofán had infringed on their patents and misappropriated trade secrets. Effective January 1985, Viscofán was barred from selling in the US market for a period of ten years. In 1986 the company went public in order to obtain resources to fund its ambitious plans for diversification and internationalization. In 1988 it entered the canned vegetables industry with the acquisition of Industrias Alimentarias de Navarra (IAN), Muerza, and Comarro.

Viscofán's internationalization process began in 1990 with the acquisition of its equity partner, Naturin, and the building of a greenfield asparagus-processing plant in Peru (another facility was being added in China in 2009). The families who owned the German firm were eager to sell, and Viscofán seized the opportunity. In addition to Naturin's valuable customer base, Viscofán came to own production facilities in Germany and a finishing facility in Detroit, Michigan, all focused on collagen casings. Given that the ten-year ban to sell collagen casings in the United States market was four years away from expiring, in 1991 the company established Viscofán do Brasil and set up a cellulose casings finishing plant in the world's second-largest market for sausages. In 1995 it acquired the Brazilian cellulose casings business of Germany's Hoechst, which included a vertically integrated plant. In 1996 Viscofán acquired Gamex in the Czech Republic, to which part of the the German and Spanish finishing operations were transferred due to lower labor costs. After the expiration of the ban, Viscofán moved the Detroit facility to Alabama, adding a cellulose casings manufacturing facility in 1998.

Rapid expansion, however, depressed profitability. After cutting costs through the shifting of more production from Germany and Spain to Brazil and the Czech Republic, the company resumed its international growth with the 2005 acquisition of Koteksprodukt in Serbia for €3.9 million and the 2006 purchase for €65 million of its erstwhile competitor and nemesis Teepak, which had been sold by Johnson & Johnson to Devro, and then to a financial group. With this purchase came facilities in both the United States and Mexico. The other main cellulose casings producer, Viskase, was burdened with antiquated facilities and high costs, and has moved in and out of bankruptcy protection for the last ten years.

In 2008 Viscofán reported revenues of €552 and employs 3,976 people around the world, has casings manufacturing plants in Spain, Germany, the United States, Brazil, Mexico, the Czech Republic, and Serbia, and canned vegetable facilities in Spain and China. It has commercial offices in Canada, China, Costa Rica, Poland, Russia, Thailand, and the United Kingdom. The Costa Rica and Thailand offices act as regional headquarters for Central America and Asia respectively. Eurasia is currently the firm's most important market, generating €226 million euros in revenue, followed by North America (€159 million) and South America (€72 million).

Viscofán became the world's largest firm in cellulose casings thanks to its streamlined operations, commitment to R&D, and strategy. The global market for cellulose casings is large: about 15,000 million meters, with each meter on average being enough to produce ten sausages. Thus, economies of scale and the experience curve are essential. Viscofán grew organically and through acquisitions to the point that it has a strong cost advantage over its competitors.

The company spends the equivalent of 5 percent of sales on R&D. It designs and assembles its own machines and equipment with the aim of speeding up the capital-intensive extrusion process and redesigns the labor-intensive finishing operations so that they can be conducted more efficiently. It has not been unusual for Viscofán to increase the speed of the extrusion lines significantly. Another key area of research involves improving the quality and reducing the thickness of the sheets. Finally, the firm also invests in new product development.

Thus, Viscofán's distinctive capabilities, those not matched by any other present or past competitor, include:

(1) proprietary machinery and equipment;
(2) size, which offers economies of scale unique in the industry;
(3) the ability to continue cutting costs incrementally thanks to its cumulative experience or learning curve;
(4) facilities in several locations around the world, which give it flexibility in meeting customer requirements and insurance against unforeseen labor, transportation, or other disruptions; and
(5) decoupled capital-intensive extrusion and labor-intensive finishing operations, which enable the firm to locate each in the optimal country depending on labor costs, and also to prevent present or potential competitors from understanding the intricacies of the overall manufacturing process.

Therefore, its commanding global market position is to a very large extent the result of proprietary technology and rapid deployment of plants around the world. And in a market that grows steadily between 4 and 5 percent a year, and is not subject to sharp downturns. "Sausages are the cheapest form of protein," asserts its President, Jaime Echevarría. "Moreover, it appeals to the young, and it respects cultural and religious preferences because they can be made of beef, pork, chicken or turkey and vegetables."

BUILDING CAPABILITIES IN FOOD AND BEVERAGES
Spanish multinational firms in the food and beverage sectors have pursued the path of capability building through entry into more

developed markets as opposed to the path of entry into less developed markets (see Figure 2.1). Ebro Puleva, SOS, Freixenet, and Viscofán started out by developing strong capabilities in a relatively large domestic market. Exports to more developed markets followed, thus bringing them into contact with more sophisticated competitors. Alliances and acquisitions in such markets helped them gain market share and build new capabilities. Over time, they engaged in greenfield investments. Most of their sales and assets are in developed markets (Europe and the United States), although they have built an important presence in some emerging economies. They have managed to become the largest firms in specific product categories – rice, pasta, olive oil, sparkling wines, cellulose casings for frankfurters – mainly because they built the necessary capabilities to succeed in developed food and beverage markets, which are the largest in the world. Having established themselves there, they can now more easily tap into the rapidly growing emerging markets of Asia and Latin America.

This pattern of expansion is quite different from the one followed by firms like Bimbo or Gruma of Mexico and Arcor of Argentina. These Latin American food multinationals built important capabilities at home, but decided to focus their international expansion on other emerging markets, and have made very few acquisitions. As shown in Table 3.1, the Spanish firms tended to integrate vertically, and also to diversify their product offerings (except for Freixenet). This pattern of growth was implemented through both greenfield investments and acquisitions. Before comparing them more systematically to their Latin American counterparts, let us analyze each of them in turn.

Grupo Bimbo is the world's second-largest bread company. With sales of $6.6 billion, it is the biggest food-processing multinational based in an emerging economy. Founded in 1945, it is majority owned by the Servitje family. It sells 5,000 different products under 100 brand names. After securing a dominant position in the Mexican packaged bread market, and becoming the sole supplier to

McDonald's, Bimbo expanded first throughout Latin America during the 1990s: Guatemala, Chile, Venezuela, and Peru. Later came the Czech Republic, and the 1998 acquisition of Fort Worth-based Mrs. Baird's, the largest family-owned bakery in the United States. A year later it purchased the bakery business of Four-S in California. Further acquisitions in Mexico, Latin America, the United States, and Europe turned Grupo Bimbo into a giant. In 2006 it acquired a baking facility in Beijing from Panrico of Spain. The company expects China to be its fastest growing market in future years. Mexico still accounts for two-thirds of sales. Bimbo has become a marketing powerhouse, but its most important skill is in efficient production. Daniel Servitje, the CEO, explains: "We know best practices in baking. We travel around the globe looking closely at all practices in baking plants. We can compare everywhere, and we can detect a good number of opportunities to raise productivity" (Siegel 2008: 13).

Gruma is also a considerably larger company than either Ebro Puleva or SOS. With $3.3 billion in sales, it is the world's largest corn flour and tortilla maker. Like Bimbo, it started its international expansion in Latin America. Unlike the Mexican bread giant, it is less diversified, and this has meant using greenfield investments as opposed to acquisitions (see Table 3.1). In recent years it has expanded vigorously into Europe, North America, and Asia, with acquisitions in Italy, the Netherlands, the UK, the United States, and Australia. In 2007 it established a greenfield tortilla plant in China. It has a 60/40 joint venture with Archer Daniels Midland that mills wheat flour. The Chairman and CEO is Roberto González Barrera. He and his family own 51 percent of the company, and Archer Daniels Midland about 23 percent.

Arcor of Argentina is smaller than Grupo Bimbo or Gruma ($1.8 billion in sales and 20,000 employees). Founded in 1951, it is the largest candy company in the world and Latin America's biggest cookie maker. It has thirty factories in Argentina, five in Brazil, four in Chile, and one each in Mexico and Peru. It exports to 120 countries on five continents. It is vertically integrated upstream into sugar and milk production and downstream into packaging. Its first export activities date back to the 1960s, first to Latin America and later to Europe and the United States. In the late 1970s it established distribution offices in Paraguay and Uruguay, in 1981 in Brazil, and in 1989 in Chile. In 1993 the second generation of the founding Pagani family took over at the helm. Aided by the stability of the Argentine economy thanks to convertibility, Arcor intensified its foreign expansion (Kosacoff et al. 2007). In 1995 it opened its first foreign plant, in Peru, and in 1998 acquired Dos en Uno, Chile's candy and chocolate market leader. In 1999, it set up a chocolate factory in Brazil. Sales subsidiaries were established in Mexico, Colombia, Canada, and Spain. In 2001 they reached a distribution agreement with Brach's for the US market, and acquired several Nestlé brands for the Brazilian market. In 2005 Arcor signed an agreement with Danone to jointly manage their cookie and cereal bar businesses in Argentina, Brazil, and Chile, and in 2006 started to collaborate with Bimbo to produce and sell confectionery and chocolate products in Mexico. Arcor is nowadays a multinational company with a strong presence in the largest economies of Latin America, and exports to other parts of the world.

The new multinationals in such a traditional industry as agrofoods have followed a common growth pattern. They started out in one line of business, expanding domestically from one region to the entire country, setting up several scale-efficient factories in the process. Several of them engaged in related product diversification domestically and in exports before pursuing foreign investments. Under pressure from domestic competitors and foreign multinationals with a local presence, they invested in new product development, improved production techniques, quality control, and brand recognition, building important manufacturing and marketing skills in the process. As they grew, they reorganized themselves into pseudo multi-divisional companies, though maintaining a relatively high degree of centralization in decision-making. They acquired some of their less successful domestic competitors, or drove them out of the market. They engaged in foreign investments after their home countries achieved some measure of macroeconomic stability and the exchange rate made it possible to engage in acquisitions (and started to discourage exports). They also used alliances with multinationals to enter some developed markets.

The biggest differences among the new multinationals in agro-foods have to do with ownership and with the sequence of foreign market entry. While there is a strong family connection in most of them – and certainly in the cases discussed in this chapter – they differed in terms of their strategy to fund growth. Some of them decided early on to go public, and some have even listed in the United States (e.g. Gruma). Others, like Arcor and Freixenet, remain family-owned. In terms of market sequence, the Latin American firms established themselves first in neighboring countries with similar levels of purchasing power. By contrast, the Spanish firms targeted more developed markets first – where strong brands are required – and then entered Latin American countries. Whereas SOS and Ebro opted for international acquisitions as a way to gain access to strong brands and market share, Freixenet chose to mainly develop its own brands when this strategy was feasible.

One important aspect of the strategy of the new multinationals in agro-food is their focus on a relatively narrow category of products when compared to the giants in the industry, namely, Nestlé, Unilever, or Danone. In addition, some of the new multinationals in these industries can take advantage of the customers' perception of the home country, as shown by the case of Freixenet. Each of the firms discussed in this chapter has become the number one in the world: Ebro Puleva in rice and in pasta; Grupo SOS in olive oil; Viscofán in artificial casings; Freixenet in sparkling wines; Bimbo in bread (actually, the number two, but with a good chance of becoming the number one); Gruma in corn flour and tortillas; and Arcor in candy. In this respect, they are very different from the likes of Nestlé, Unilever, or Danone, which through internal development and acquisitions have amassed a portfolio of several hundred product brands sold throughout the world. The fact that the new food and beverage multinationals are family owned, controlled and/or managed is intrinsically related to their desire to stay product focused.

4 Market access and technology in durable consumer goods

> The fact that a number of companies (such as Wal-Mart, Zara, Dell and Toyota) have managed to record extraordinary success while doing quite ordinary things (such as running supermarkets, selling clothes or making computers or cars) has made managers more fully aware that what their organizations produce can matter a lot less than the way that they produce it.
>
> *The Economist* (April 6, 2009)

> We can make any style at any price for any market.
>
> Sever García, Sales Director, Pronovias USA[1]

Competition in durable consumer goods – clothing, appliances, electronics, and so on – is driven by technology, design, economies of scale, and brands. Until recently, firms from the richest countries dominated the landscape. According to Interbrand (2009), all but three of the 100 most valuable brands in the world as of 2009 were from such rich industrialized countries as the United States, Japan, the United Kingdom, France, Germany, Italy, Canada, Finland, the Netherlands, Sweden, and Switzerland. The three exceptions are Samsung (ranked no. 19 in terms of value) and Hyundai (no. 69), both of South Korea, and Zara (no. 50) of Spain. Although emerging economies represent an increasing share of the global economy, their brands are still not well-known around the world. In its list of the 100 "global challengers" from emerging economies, the Boston Consulting Group identified only twelve companies in durable consumer goods, including clothing, appliances, and electronics (BCG 2009). Similarly, of the 104 emerging-market multinationals on the Fortune Global 500 ranking, fewer than five are firms in these industries (see also Accenture 2008).

---

[1] *Women's Wear Daily*, August 6, 2003.

Table 4.1. *Four types of durable goods industries*

Barriers to distribution channels in foreign markets	Importance of proprietary product technology	
	Low	High
High	Lighters	Household appliances
Low	Clothing, traditional toys	Electronic toys

In this chapter we examine the rise of new multinationals in fashion, simple assembled goods, and household appliances. We begin by outlining the cases of Spanish companies that have made a dent in global competition. We draw on examples from emerging economies to ascertain the extent to which the pattern of international growth of Spanish multinationals exhibits commonalities with their counterparts in other countries. We consider two types of strategies for international growth: internal capability development and external capability acquisition through alliances and takeovers. We analyze the extent to which four different product categories – clothing, toys, lighters, and white goods – differ from one another in terms of the importance of product technology (as opposed to design and process innovation), and access to distribution channels in foreign markets (see Table 4.1).

THE FASHION INDUSTRY: INDITEX AND PRONOVIAS

Until fairly recently, competition in the clothing industry was driven by cost, design, and brands. Production and distribution technologies, however, have come to play an increasingly important role. Perhaps the best illustration of this process of change is the rise of Spain's Inditex (Industria de Diseño Textil) as one of the world's foremost apparel companies credited with inventing the "cheap-chic" fashion segment. As of the end of 2008, Inditex was a huge company: €10.4 billion in sales, about 89,000 employees, and the owner of several world-renowned brands, including Zara, the world's second most valuable clothing label ($6.8 billion) after Sweden's H&M ($15.4 billion). The company had 4,264 stores in seventy-three countries around the world, although 44 percent were in Spain and 39 percent in the rest of Europe. Inditex had just forty-one stores in the United States, twenty-five in Brazil, ninety-eight in Rusia, twenty-seven in China, and none in India, countries that represent enormous future growth opportunities. Foreign stores generate on average more sales than European stores: nearly 11 percent of total sales come from the Americas and 9 percent from Asia. Only 12 percent of the stores are franchised, mostly in Asia and the Middle East. Inditex makes and commercializes over 600 million pieces of clothing per year. In 2003 *Wired* magazine included Inditex on its list of the twenty most innovative firms in the world.

Inditex's IPO in May 2001 caused a sensation, and turned its founder and majority owner, Amancio Ortega, into the world's tenth wealthiest person, with a net worth of $18.3 billion, about one-third of Warren Buffet's, according to *Forbes* magazine. Ortega was born in the northwestern province of León into a modest family. His father was a railway employee. The family moved west to A Coruña, in the region of Galicia, when he was young. In 1963 he set up a lingerie workshop with his first wife, Rosalía Mera (no. 246 on the Forbes ranking with a net worth of $2.6 billion). They opened their first store in 1975. They chose the name "Zorba," but it was already taken, so they settled for Zara. The firm is not merely run like a family firm, it is a family. The founder and most of the executives are locals and eat regularly with the workers, many of whom own shares.[2] Amancio Ortega is the largest shareholder with 59 percent, and Rosalía Mera the second-largest with 5.8 percent.

Inditex's just-in-time manufacturing and distribution capabilities have become legendary in the industry. The firm sells about 11,000 different types of clothing items and accessories every year.

---

[2] *Cinco Días* (May 9, 2003); *El País* (February 28, 2003).

Roughly half of them are made in-house, unlike most of its competitors, which rely on outsourcing for the overwhelming majority of their collections. Inditex outsources 80 percent of the fabrics and virtually all sewing activities. Its logistics and vertical integration are so well coordinated that the firm can respond to market trends in a mere two weeks.[3] The stores, most of which are company-owned, are electronically linked to headquarters. Inventories run as low as 7 percent of revenues. The strategy of highly coordinated vertical integration makes perfect sense given the firm's need to cut costs and generate flexibility by reducing the potentially harmful impact of uncertainty and asset specificity along the value chain. Much of this technological wizardry is attributed to José María Castellano, the CEO until 2005, a former professor at the local university, who worked for a couple of foreign multinationals before joining Inditex. In a fashion world characterized by extensive outsourcing and massive advertising expenditures, Inditex seems to be a stark reminder of the competitive power of integrated manufacturing and logistics. The company is growing fast on the basis of those capabilities while its main competitors (Benetton, Gap, The Limited) are stagnating or deeply troubled. The international financial media have fallen in love with the company.[4]

Almost 90 percent of Inditex's 89,000 employees work at the stores, 3.5 percent at headquarters, 5.8 percent in logistics, and a mere 1.3 percent in manufacturing. The most important company-owned manufacturing base is in Spain (about half of total capacity), with smaller facilities in Portugal, Morocco, and Turkey. At its twenty-plus Spanish factories, Inditex pays factory workers eight times what the comparable Guandong Province worker makes. Still, the company continues to be competitive in price across global markets. Inditex relies on a network of 1,200 suppliers in Spain, Portugal, Morocco, China, India, Bangladesh, Cambodia, and Vietnam. The

[3] *The Economist* (June 16, 2005).
[4] *The Economist* (May 19, 2001: 56); *Forbes* (May 28, 2001: 98); *Wall Street Journal* (May 18, 2001: B1); *Business Week* (October 20, 2008).

company has established seven supplier clusters employing 30,000 workers in Tangiers, Morocco; 53,000 in Istanbul, Turkey; 212,000 in Dhaka, Bangladesh; 22,000 in Delhi, India; 31,000 in Guimarães and Porto, Portugal; 3,200 in Galicia, Spain; and 14,000 in Phnom Penh, Cambodia.

Perhaps the only competitor with the ability to match Inditex's growth and profitability is H&M (Hennes & Mauritz AB). Although it has fewer than half as many stores as Inditex, the Swedish company generates as much revenue. Unlike Inditex, it outsources most of its production, predominantly in Asia. Founded in 1947, it did not enter a market outside Europe until 2000, when it opened its first US store. It entered the Middle East in 2006 and China in 2007. It has no presence in Latin America or India. Although analysts tend to compare H&M to Inditex, the companies could not be more different in terms of vertical integration and competitive strengths. Inditex seems poised to overtake H&M as the world's leading apparel brand.

Another stark difference between the two companies has to do with the pace and sequence of foreign market entry. While H&M has established a presence in fewer than thirty countries over sixty years, Inditex has opened stores in more than seventy countries over a period of just thirty-five years. H&M expanded first in Northern Europe, and later entered Southern Europe, the United States, Eastern Europe, the Middle East, and Asia sequentially. Inditex has expanded throughout Europe, the Americas, the Middle East, Africa, and Asia almost simultaneously, entering several new countries each year. For instance, in 1998 it established a first Zara store in countries as diverse as the UK, Turkey, Kuwait, Argentina, and Venezuela; in 2006 it went for Serbia, China, and Tunisia; in 2007 it opened stores in Guatemala, Colombia, Croatia, and Oman; and in 2008 it opened its first stores in the Ukraine, South Korea, Montenegro, Honduras, and Egypt. Thus, Inditex's sequence of foreign market entry has departed from staged models of international expansion (e.g. Johanson and Vahlne 1977). Another important feature is that

Inditex has used from the very beginning a combination of wholly owned and joint venture entry modes. In India, for instance, it operates in collaboration with Trend of the Tata Group.

Albeit much smaller and more focused, an equally innovative firm in the Spanish clothing industry is Pronovias, the world's largest maker and seller of bridal wear with approximately €175 million in sales and 738 employees. The company started out in Barcelona, on the segnorial Paseig de Gràcia, back in 1922. It languished until it presented its first prêt-à-porter wedding collection in 1964. It was perhaps the first company in the world to hit upon the idea of creating a chain of exclusive shops for brides. With annual sales of 480,000 gowns (the equivalent of a 5 percent worldwide market share split between the Spanish and foreign markets), it leads US firms Mori Lee and Alfred Angelo, British Brackenbridge and Brides International, and French Pronuptia. A staff of 70 designers comes up with as many as 650 different wedding and party dresses every year, and about 2,000 accessories that go with them. Most of its branded items are made in a factory outside Barcelona, while the accessories and intimate apparel are outsourced in China. It distributes worldwide through a network of 150 company-owned stores and 3,800 points of sale in 75 countries. It has franchised stores in Spain, Portugal, Greece, Turkey, Saudi Arabia, Egypt, Mexico, and Japan. The company has established distribution subsidiaries in several countries. Sever García, the sales director at Pronovias USA, points out what his company's competitive advantage is all about: flexibility and responsiveness. "We can make any style at any price for any market."[5] The ability to adapt to the local peculiarities of each market is indeed essential because of differences in physiology, custom, tastes, and average age at which women marry.

Like Inditex, the success of Pronovias is not only the result of a keen understanding of markets around the world. There is much design, production, and distribution know-how accumulated over

[5] *Women's Wear Daily*, August 6, 2003.

decades of experience. Spain in general, and Catalonia in particular, have relatively high labor costs. And yet, Pronovias offers sophisticated wedding and party dresses with all manner of laces and flounces at relatively affordable wholesale prices ranging from €150 to €3,000. Its current plans are to shift to the €600–10,000 price range, and to integrate forward into the distribution channel by substituting company-owned or franchised stores for arm's-length points of sale. The firm is fully controlled by the second generation of the founding Palatchi family, and is increasingly using professional managers.[6]

The cases of Inditex and Pronovias illustrate the importance of manufacturing skill and flexibility, seamless distribution logistics, and marketing savvy (though not necessarily massive advertising). Historically, Spanish firms did not play a prominent role in the global apparel industry. But firms like Inditex, Mango, and Pronovias are rewriting the rules of competition in their respective market segments.

SIMPLE ASSEMBLED GOODS: TOYS AND LIGHTERS

Like clothing, simple assembled goods are relatively traditional and mature products in which barriers to entry are low and product technology widely available. Therefore, competition tends to revolve around design, branding, and the ability to produce reliably and at low cost. Firms in these industries come in two types. Large multinationals from the advanced countries continue to rely on their design and marketing capabilities decades after their manufacturing advantage vanished. Outsourcing of production to Asia and Latin America has created opportunities for new companies to emerge, although so far they have only succeeded in the lower segment of the market.[7]

---

[6] *Actualidad Económica* (May 26, 2003); *Expansión* (February 23, 2001; February 28, 2003; September 17, 2003); "Pronovias Previews Spring," *Women's Wear Daily* (August 6, 2003: 12).

[7] The information on the toy and lighter industries comes from various Euromonitor's reports. The data refer to 2003, unless otherwise noted. Company information on Famosa and Flamagas was obtained through interviews

Like in the rest of Western Europe, the Spanish toy sector underwent a long crisis beginning in the 1970s, followed by somewhat of a recovery at the turn of the twenty-first century. The largest firm, Famosa, epitomizes many of the successes and the failures of the Spanish toy industry. It was born in 1957 as a confederation of family-owned toy workshops in the so-called Valley of Toys in Alicante, on the southeastern Mediterranean coast of Spain. Presently it sells in over 50 countries, employing 450 workers (250 of them based in the town of Onil) and generating sales of about €170 million by commercializing 1,500 products and 50 brands. In 2007 Famosa held a 19.8 percent share of the Spanish market for traditional toys and games, followed by Hasbro (18.6) and Mattel (17.4). The company had sizable market shares in the rest of the European Union, and an important presence in Chile, Mexico, and Puerto Rico. One-quarter of its sales are dolls, followed by stuffed animals (about 25 percent), figurines (14), pre-school toys (12), and battery-powered toy vehicles (30). It commercializes toys under license from Disney, Warner Bros., Marvel Comics (Spiderman), and several local designers.

New technologies have enabled toy companies, including Famosa, to introduce numerous process and product innovations, but they also represent a major source of substitute products, especially in the domain of video and other electronic games, which have partially displaced traditional toys. Still, the industry is relatively fragmented worldwide, with the three largest firms accounting for about 27 percent of total sales. The two largest are Mattel and Sony (10 percent world market share each), followed by Hasbro (7), Nintendo (6), and Microsoft, Electronic Arts, Bandai and Lego (each with about 3 percent). Famosa has a 0.5 percent world market share, 1.6 percent in Europe, and about 18 percent in Spain.

While traditional toys account for about two-thirds of the total toy market in value, electronic games are growing at nearly 8 percent annually, compared to 3 percent for traditional toys. Moreover,

conducted in 2006 under the auspices of the Centro de Estudios Comerciales (CECO) of Spain's Ministry of Industry, Tourism, and Trade.

in many markets, eight-year-olds already display a preference for electronic over traditional toys. Sales of traditional toys are concentrated in the most affluent markets. The United States accounts for 41 percent of the world's total, followed by Japan (10) and the UK (8). Since 1998, the markets with the largest growth rates are China, Spain, and South Korea. Other important trends in the industry include: the growth in outdoor equipment like slides, swings, and playhouses; the increasing demand for educational toys, often electronic in nature; the growing nostalgia for traditional dolls; growth in board games and puzzles; and the rise of the Internet as a major distribution channel for electronic games. Roughly 70 percent of new product introductions in traditional toys and videogames alike fail.

Even the largest firms in the industry are under stress. Mattel, whose Barbie dolls account for one-third of total sales, depends on the US market for half its sales, where it is struggling to keep up with the growth of videogames. In 2006 it acquired Hong Kong-based Radica Games for $230 million in an attempt to diversify away from traditional toys. The second-largest traditional toy firm is Hasbro, which brought to the world one of the best-selling products of all time, Mr. Potato Head. Hasbro has moved more resolutely into the licensing and videogame business than Mattel. They make most of their toys in China and Mexico. Half of their products are sold at Wal-Mart, Toys 'R' Us, and Target.

Even without globalization and technological change, traditional toys companies would be under pressure for a number of reasons. First, barriers to entry are generally low, especially in the rapidly-growing Asian markets. This is the case because economies of scale and capital requirements in traditional toys are relatively low. By contrast, barriers to entry into videogame consoles are quite high because of the large R&D investments and economies of scale. Moreover, the key players in this segment (Sony, Nintendo, and Microsoft) are large, resourceful, and highly profitable firms. Second, in the affluent markets, the rise of large distributors such as Wal-Mart, Carrefour, or Toys 'R' Us has reduced their bargaining power, unless they successfully invest in product differentiation through brands. Third, traditional toy manufacturers do not possess much bargaining power relative to their key suppliers, including raw-material produ- cers and intellectual-property owners such as Disney or Warner Bros. Lastly, traditional toys are subject to ever stricter safety regulations, especially in the American and European markets, although many see these constraints as a protectionist barrier against the Chinese manufacturers, who often have trouble meeting the standards.

The Spanish toy sector has evolved along lines similar to those outlined above. According to the Spanish Association of Toy Manufacturers (AEFJ), as of 2007 there were 215 firms in the industry, providing employment for some 5,000 people. Most firms (115) are micro-enterprises with fewer than ten employees. Exports amount to 388 million euros, overwhelmingly destined for European markets (78 percent). Imports reached one billion euros, 61 percent of which are from China. The appreciation of the euro relative to most world currencies has spelled trouble for European toy exporters ever since 2005. Spanish exporters, however, have suffered much less than their French and German counterparts, who have seen toy exports decreased 10 and 28 percent respectively until 2007.

The Spanish toy market continued to grow until 2008 due to increasing fertility and incomes. Despite recent improvements, demand remains extremely seasonal, with 66 percent of shipments to distributors taking place between October and the end of December, and 71 percent of sales to final consumers between December 1 and January 6. Like elsewhere, demand growth for videogames is out- pacing traditional toys. The largest firms in the Spanish traditional and electronic toy market are Sony (18 percent), Mattel (10), Famosa (9), Hasbro (9), and Nintendo (8). In the traditional segment, Mattel (20), Famosa (18), and Hasbro (17) dominate the market. Large retail- ers like Carrefour, Alcampo, Eroski, El Corte Inglés, Hipercor, or Makro already account for one-third of sales, but specialty stores continue to be the most important channel (65 percent).

Industrial toy production in Spain started after 1875 in the town of Onil, province of Alicante, at the hands of a retired Civil Guard, Ramón Mira Vidal. At the time dolls were made out of clay, porcelain, or cardboard, and all other toys out of tin. The Foya de Castalla, the so-called Valley of Toys, including the counties of Ibi, Onil, Biar, Tibi, and Castilla, soon became the epicenter of Spanish toy manufacturing. In 1957, after plastic had become the most important raw material, twenty-five small firms based in Onil realized the importance of gaining scale and decided to create Fábricas Agrupadas de Muñecas de Onil SA, or Famosa, with Isidro Rico Juan from the firm Isidro Rico Miralles as general manager and Ramón Sempere as president. The first products launched by Famosa included Güendolina, Paulova, Pierina y Yamita, followed by the Telerín figurines after signing a licensing agreement with the state-owned television monopoly in 1963.

As in the case of many other toy firms, Famosa's growth owed much to a couple of blockbuster products. In 1968 the firm launched the Nancy doll, its greatest success, of which more than one million units were eventually sold. In 1972 the firm came up with a popular Christmas song ("Las muñecas de Famosa se dirigen al portal...") which radio stations broadcast for free because they consider it to be part of the Christmas tradition. In 1978 Jaime Ferri took over from Isidro Rico as general manager, and Famosa launched Nenuco, a baby doll that would become a best-seller in Spain, France, and Italy.

Famosa and the rest of the Spanish toy industry started to feel the effects of the economic crisis during the early 1980s. The downturn coincided with the arrival of Mattel, Hasbro, and Lego, increased competition from Asia, and the introduction of the first videogames. This combination of factors threw several firms into bankruptcy (Eko, Paya), forcing others to sell themselves (Exin) or merge (Educa and Borrás). In spite of the wave of consolidation, the Spanish toy industry still included more than 200 manufacturers as of the late 1980s.

In spite of the writing being on the wall, Famosa took years to react to the new competitive environment. In 1991 it established a purchasing unit in Hong Kong in order to coordinate outsourcing in China. The same year it founded Onilco Innovación SA, a design and product launch center. Nowadays, Famosa outsources slightly more than 80 percent of its products to China. In Onil it makes only the battery-powered toys. According to General Manager Manuel Rubiales, "Famosa has not suffered as much as other firms because it has assumed the reality that Asia represents." Only two other firms (Falca and Injusa) have joined Famosa in sourcing from China.

As a result of outsourcing by US and European firms, China has become the toy manufacturing center of the world. There are more than 6,000 toy and videogame factories, of which 4,500 are located in Guangdong Province. China exports $15 billion in toys, accounting for 70 percent of worldwide production; Spain is the ninth most important destination for toys manufactured in China. Each year China manufactures 1.5 million different toys and games. Toy manufacturing costs are about 30 percent lower in China than in Spain, enough to justify the relocation of production. Roughly 80 percent of Chinese-made toys are outsourced by multinational firms.

Famosa has established commercial and technical outsourcing offices in Hong Kong. This office selects suppliers, handles orders, undertakes quality control, and manages shipments. Famosa relies on Shanghai suppliers for its stuffed animals, and on Guangzhou firms for dolls and figurines. In total, the firm outsources most of its toys to four or five suppliers, given the cost advantages associated with bigger orders. A network of sales subsidiaries in Nottingham, Paris, Milan, San Juan, Lisbon, Madrid, and Mexico City enables Famosa to distribute its toys in major markets. Outsourcing in China and sales subsidiaries in international markets have enabled Famosa to overcome the challenges of globalization and technological innovation.

An important aspect of Famosa's transformation has had to do with corporate governance and the entry of private-equity investors.

In 2002 the 27 families (220 individual stockholders) then owning the various firms associated with Famosa agreed to sell 100 percent of the capital to an investor group led by Inveralia, a private equity firm associated with Banco Pastor – a mid-sized bank – and the former owners of Larios, an alcoholic beverages group. Inveralia acquired a 31 percent stake, while Torreal (millionaire Juan Abelló's investment arm), and Ahorro Corporación (the private equity division of the Confederation of Spanish Savings Banks) took 24.5 percent each. General Manager Jaime Ferri and his team took the remaining 20 percent. The new investors' strategy was precisely to expand outsourcing in China and set up sales subsidiaries in major markets. In 2003 the Caja de Ahorros del Mediterráneo (CAM), based in the Alicante region, acquired 10 percent of the equity equally from the three existing investors, for 17.3 million euros. In 2005 Vista Capital de Expansión, a financial holding owned by Banco Santander and the Royal Bank of Scotland, acquired 100 percent of the equity for a sum between €140 and 150 million in cash, which meant a big capital gain for the three original investors, though not for CAM. Vista gave the new managerial team led by Manuel Rubiales 10 percent of the equity.

The new management team embarked on an ambitious series of acquisitions. In 2006 it bought Play by Play (€15 million in sales, 30 percent outside Spain), which owned the licenses to Super Mario, Garfield, Snoopy, and Pokémon. A few months later, Famosa acquired Feber (€30 million in sales), a manufacturer of slides, swings, playhouses, outdoor toys and, most importantly, battery-powered toy vehicles. 2006 also saw the acquisition of Plush Games. The managing director, Rubiales, has been quoted as saying that outside toy equipment is "a product that will never migrate to China" due to transportation costs and the possibility of automating production. The company carries a debt burden on its books, and Vista Capital had to inject a further forty-six million euros in 2008. As of the end of 2009, Vista was looking for an exit.

Famosa faces formidable challenges, including the need to speed up the innovation process, lower manufacturing costs, and ensure seamless distribution. Of the firm's 1,200 product offerings each year, 350 are new products. Disloyal competition from producers that do not meet safety regulations or pay licenses continues to harm the industry, reducing its profits by 17 percent annually. Local manufacturers insist that outsourcing is not the answer to the industry's problems, and that several categories of toys (outdoors equipment and tricycles, for instance) continue to be profitably manufactured in Spain. Some firms, like Juguetes Picó, have optimized their manufacturing operations by making certain toy components at facilities also used to supply local automobile assembly plants, such as Ford España, with exhaust tubes. Famosa and the rest of the Spanish toy industry still need to demonstrate that they can overcome the competitive challenges in an ever-changing marketplace through design and innovation.

Competitive challenges similar to those found in the traditional toy industry are also faced by companies in other types of simple assembled goods, although barriers to entry (and hence profitability) are not always low. For instance, branded lighters are a highly profitable product, with margins as high as 30 percent, thanks to effective product differentiation through design and branding. In addition, sharp differences in dominant distribution channels across countries, which are tightly linked to cigarette consumption, force companies to adapt to local peculiarities. In the United States, gas stations account for nearly half of sales, while in Western Europe tobacconists, frequently licensed by the state, are the most important channel, representing nearly 25 percent of sales. In Asia and Latin America food stores and street vendors dominate.

Spain's Flamagas, which sells lighters and other accessories under the "Clipper" brand, is the fourth-largest firm in the industry. The biggest firms are Bic of France, Tokai of Japan, and Swedish Match (owner of the "Cricket" brand). Flamagas was founded in 1959 by the Puig family, whose stronghold is in cosmetics. Antonio Puig started his business activities in 1914. His first commercial success was the Milady lipstick, launched in 1922. In 1940 it introduced its most famous product, Agua Lavanda Puig, an eau de cologne. Puig Beauty & Fashion is among the largest cosmetics firms in the world with a 2 percent market share (the number one is L'Oréal with 9 percent). In 2000 it acquired Myrurgia, and a year later Gal. Puig has agreements to develop Zara's and Mango's cosmetics lines.

Flamagas employs about 1,300 people and generates annual sales of about €100 million. It makes several types of lighters: stone or electronic, and rechargeable or disposable. It also makes kitchen lighters, and all associated spare parts, filters, and recharging equipment. The modern pocket gas lighter dates back to 1948, a product first manufactured by Flaminaire, a company acquired by Bic in 1971. Roughly 40 percent of Bic's capital is owned by founder Marcel Bich's successors, who have more than half of the voting rights. One-quarter or 470 million dollars of Bic's sales are lighters, which the company makes in Europe, the United States, and Asia (on a subcontracting basis). Tokai Corporation, part of the Itochu conglomerate, was founded in 1972, and has factories in several Asian, European, and Latin American countries. It also subcontracts in China. Swedish Match is a publicly listed firm, though controlled by AB Volvo. It has factories in sixteen countries, but only 4 percent or eighty million dollars of its total sales are lighters. Flamagas ranks just behind, with sixty-four million dollars in sales of lighters. Besides the big four, there are hundreds of small lighter manufacturers, 300 of them in China, mostly in Wenzhou, Zhejiang Province, just south of Shanghai.

China makes between 60 and 70 percent of the world's lighters, although few Chinese firms sell them under their own brand. In 2006 the cost of making a stone lighter in China oscillated between €0.04 and €0.06, and the cost of making an electronic lighter between €0.06 and €0.10. In Europe, costs were three to four times higher. Competition in the marketplace, however, is not primarily driven by cost. Design, branding, safety standards, and distribution channels are key to commercial success, and they ultimately represent barriers to entry that only a few, sophisticated firms manage to overcome.

Flamagas's international growth was initially driven by exports of lighters made at its Llinars del Vallès factory, just outside Barcelona. In some markets it signed exclusive distribution agreements with large tobacco companies, as with Imperial Tobacco in the United Kingdom. In other major markets it established sales subsidiaries (Portugal, Russia, Poland, Turkey, and Brazil). Exporting, however, was limited as a strategy to sustain growth. The appreciation of the local currency during the 1980s reduced the company's international competitiveness, precisely at the time that Chinese manufacturers started to export. The currency crisis of 1992–3 offered some breathing space, but Spain's adoption of the euro in 1998 meant that bolder steps would need to be taken. Flamagas decided that the time had come to establish foreign factories in low-cost locations. In 2000 the firm set up a plant in India, which makes thirty million lighters per year, of which about 70 percent are exported. In 2004 it established a wholly owned factory south of Shanghai, where it makes 70 million lighters per year, and could easily manufacture 200 million without enlarging the plant. The Barcelona plant continues to be the sole maker of two key components: the fixed valve and the burner, which are shipped to the Indian and Chinese facilities for final assembly. The valve, in particular, is a sophisticated component consisting of a metal cylinder with a membrane that ensures a constant flow of gas regardless of the pressure in the container.

Flamagas reports that the production cost at its Chinese plant is similar to that at its Barcelona plant. The former is very labor intensive, while the latter is fully automated. The big difference has to do with flexibility. It takes more time and money to switch models at the automated Barcelona plant than at the Chinese plant. Thus, Flamagas plans for production runs in ways that optimize the use of its three facilities, in a nice illustration of the kind of operational flexibility that multinational firms with a global production network benefit from relative to purely local competitors (Kogut and Kulatilaka 1994).

While the most important customer group – smokers – is dwindling, lighter firms from developed economies such as Flamagas have managed to continue growing through product differentiation and global expansion. Unlike in the toy industry, barriers to entry allow established firms to attain high levels of profitability, in spite of the cost advantages of emerging-market producers.

HOUSEHOLD APPLIANCES
Household appliances are also profitable products. Both R&D and barriers to entry into distribution channels can pose serious challenges to all but the most resourceful firms. Moreover, local firms tend to enjoy an edge in product adaptation and in distribution. Thus, the household appliances industry is a good example of what Ghemawat (2007) calls "semiglobalization." In spite of the common technologies at the core of many appliances, important cross-national differences in infrastructure, housing, and consumer preferences force companies to engage in local adaptation. In addition, there are strong local competitors in each of the major markets, all with well-established brands and distribution channels (Paba 1986). In fact, the industry was described years ago as a case of frustrated globalization (Baden-Fuller and Stopford 1991): local players tend to be more profitable than global firms. Although local differences persist, the industry is now more global than twenty years ago due to international consolidation through mergers and acquisitions (Bonaglia et al. 2007). At the global level, the industry was once dominated by European and US firms, but has witnessed successive waves of new international competitors, including Japanese, Taiwanese, South Korean, Turkish, Chinese, and Indian firms. The Spanish firm with the most staying power has proven to be Fagor Electrodomésticos, nowadays among the world's top ten.

Fagor Electrodomésticos was the starting point of Mondragón Corporación Cooperativa (MCC), the largest worker-owned cooperative group in the world. Its origins can be traced back to 1955 when a group of entrepreneurs and workers led by Father José María

Arizmendiarrieta, a Jesuit priest, acquired a firm located in the Basque Country's capital of Vitoria, a producer of oil stoves with a license to manufacture household appliances. At the time, the Spanish economy was heavily regulated, and the license was perhaps more valuable than any other of the acquired firm's assets (Ormaechea 1993). In 1956 the business was renamed ULGOR, an acronym standing for the initials of the last names of the five founders, and moved to Mondragón, about than 100 kilometers away. The company was incorporated as a cooperative and started to produce stoves and heaters (Ormaechea 1993). In 1957 an electronics division was added, and was later spun off as Fagor Electrónica. ULGOR, later to be renamed Fagor Electrodomésticos, hired many graduates of the technical and management school for the youth founded in 1943 by Father Arizmendiarrieta (Ormaechea n.d.). Several former students of the school formed other cooperatives over the years, including Arrasate (1957), a machine tool company, and Funcor (1956), a forge and foundry (Clamp 2003). The development of the cooperatives was fostered by the founding of Caja Laboral Popular in 1959, a savings bank. The motto "libreta o maleta" (either a savings bank account or a suitcase), attributed to Father Arizmendiarrieta, captured the spirit of self-reliance that informed the leaders of the cooperatives. The bank serves not only as a source of funds but also of managerial expertise for the cooperatives, which must sign a contract of association (Arrieta and Ormaechea n.d.).

As of the end of 2008, Mondragón Corporación Cooperativa (MCC) had 92,700 employees (16 percent outside Spain) and €16.8 billion in revenues (57 percent outside Spain), making it one of the ten largest corporations in Spain, and among the 500 largest business groups in Europe.[8] Cooperatives belonging to the group are engaged in everything from chips, appliances, automobile components and furniture to machine-tools, robotics, elevators, heavy machinery,

---

[8] The corporate information on MCC comes from its 2008 annual report, available from www.mcc.es.

and large construction projects. Mondragón also includes Spain's fifth-largest retailer (Eroski). Although it remains a worker-owned cooperative, Mondragón has become a multinational enterprise with 65 manufacturing plants in foreign countries and nearly 100 distribution operations in Western and Eastern Europe, the Americas, Northern Africa, and Asia. After 15 years of intense growth in which the number of employees has almost quadrupled from 25,000 in 1992 to the present 92,700. Only slightly over half of them are worker-owners. The manufacturing cooperatives account for slightly more than 40 percent of employees and revenues. Some of the sixty-five foreign manufacturing plants were acquired from other companies, especially in Europe. Most of the foreign plants represent horizontal investments seeking to overcome trade and other types of barriers, reduce transportation costs or supply customers' foreign-based assembly plants. Only a few of the plants are vertical investments intended to reduce costs. None of the foreign operations are incorporated as cooperatives; they are either fully or partially owned by one of the cooperatives in Spain.

Fagor Electrodomésticos is Europe's fourth-largest producer of "white goods" or household appliances such as cookers, ovens, extractor fans, microwave ovens, air conditioners, refrigerators, freezers, washing machines, dryers, dishwashers, water heaters, boilers, storage heaters, kitchen units, and kitchenware. It sells in over 100 countries and runs manufacturing facilities in Spain, France, Poland, Morocco, Italy, and China. Its strategy of dealing with different markets in slightly different ways while exploiting certain cross-border efficiencies is in line with the characteristics of the industry. Fagor and Bosch Siemens of Germany are the market leaders in the Spanish market, followed by Electrolux, Indesit, and Whirlpool. Taken together, these five companies account for 70 percent of sales. Fagor is the sixth-largest brand in Europe and the fifth-largest manufacturer. Worldwide, the industry's landscape has shifted with the rise of Haier of China and LG of South Korea as global competitors, although GE, Electrolux, and Whirlpool continue to be the largest firms.

Fagor's competitive strategy was originally shaped by the democratic principles that inspired the Mondragón cooperatives and the associated concern for offering workers higher wages and better working conditions relative to other firms in the area (Ormaechea 1993). In order to be competitive, the cooperatives committed to improving worker skills and using state-of-the-art machinery (Quevedo n.d.). Initially, this strategy translated into licensing product technology from established European firms, and focusing innovation efforts on process and production technology in order to increase productivity (Clamp 2003; Quevedo n.d.). Fagor realized by the 1970s that this strategy limited its growth and ability to become a market leader, since only relatively mature technologies were available through licensing (Ormaechea n.d.; Quevedo n.d.). In addition, licensors prevented Fagor from entering the most attractive markets. Mondragón undertook its first R&D projects in 1968. The first self-standing R&D center was founded in 1974, Ikerlan, to which each cooperative contributed funds proportional to its number of employees. Thus, in the first year, Fagor Electrodomésticos contributed 52 percent of the budget. In 2005 the firm decided to establish its own R&D lab, Hometek.

In spite of these early developments, the path to technological self-sufficiency was far from easy for Fagor Electrodomésticos. The most critical period in the history of the cooperative was in the mid 1980s, when the company faced the consequences of Spain's entry into the European Economic Community (nowadays European Union). The disappearance of tariffs meant that the domestic market was no longer protected. Foreign multinationals intensified their presence in the Spanish market, both via imports and acquisitions. In fact, Fagor was the only local appliance firm that survived the shakeout, and it decided to acquire other local firms (e.g. Fabrelec) in order to gain scale. Focusing on the domestic market, however, was a recipe for disaster. In the words of one manager, "internationalization was probably the only way not just to be competitive, but indeed to survive" (García-Canal *et al.* 2002: 100). The company came up with a plan focusing on basic products, redesigning them, and reorganizing manufacturing processes with a view to entering Latin American, North African, and Western European markets. The plan, however, could not be implemented without help from other firms because Fagor lacked technology and access to foreign markets.

Negotiations led in 1990 to the establishment of the Eurodom alliance with France's Thomson Electroménager. Britain's General Domestic Appliances (GDA) joined in 1992, and Italy's Ocean in 1993. The alliance sought to help these relatively small and locally based firms compete against such major players as Bosch, Electrolux, Zanussi, and Whirlpool. At first, the goal was to coordinate the purchasing of key components. Eventually, Thomson and Ocean merged, leaving Fagor and GDA as the sole partners. Years later, in 2002, Fagor would acquire the French and Italian brands with the purchase of the troubled Groupe Brandt, thus becoming the fifth-largest European household appliance maker. During their alliance, the joint development of R&D activities on specific technical projects allowed Fagor and GDA to share risks and avoid a duplication of efforts. In 2001 Italy's Merloni acquired a 50 percent stake in the equity of GDA and subsequently the alliance fell apart.

Fagor also established a 50/50 joint venture with German firm Vaillant in 1996 to manufacture water heaters at a plant in the Basque Country. The products were then branded, distributed and sold by each firm separately (García-Canal et al. 2002). Further acquisitions and greenfield investments in Latin America and North Africa gave the firm a firm foothold in emerging markets, where it now faces stiff competition from newcomers such as LG and Haier. For instance, in 1994 it established a greenfield refrigerator plant in Morocco together with a local partner, and a year later a joint venture with a local Egyptian partner to make washing machines and heaters. In parallel, it opened two plants in Argentina, which remained idle since that country's economic and financial debacle of 2001–2. Fagor's Eastern European expansion was boosted with the 1999 acquisition of a majority stake in Poland's Wrozamet, a maker of cooking appliances with whom it had a distribution alliance for refrigerators and washers. In 2000 the cooperative set up sales subsidiaries in Thailand, Malaysia, and China. In 2002 it established its first manufacturing operation in China, a rice cooker plant, becoming the second-largest firm in the world. In 2004 it invested in manufacturing facilities for commercial refrigerators in Poland and Turkey, and entered into a distribution alliance with Gazmash in Russia, a consortium of eleven local appliance manufacturers led by Gazprom. Fagor Electrodomésticos also invested abroad in order to reduce costs. In 1992 it set up a joint venture with a local Thai firm to produce semiconductor components for its different products, a facility later transferred to another Mondragón cooperative, Fagor Electrónica.

In spite of its strong presence in the Spanish and European markets, Fagor Electrodomésticos finds itself between a rock and a hard place. Companies such as Bosch, Electrolux, or GE possess better technological and design capabilities, while emerging-market firms such as Haier of China, Mabe of Mexico, or Acelik of Turkey are more competitive in price. It is interesting to note that these firms also used partnerships to access foreign markets and external resources, although they could ally with larger firms due to their larger bargaining power as local partners, and hence have managed to extend their reach throughout the world (Bonaglia *et al.* 2007).

CONCLUSION: INTERNAL VERSUS EXTERNAL
CAPABILITY BUILDING IN DURABLE GOODS
The cases analyzed in this chapter illustrate that new multinational firms in durable consumer goods develop their capabilities internally or externally depending on two key characteristics of the industry, as displayed in Table 4.1. New multinationals in industries in which neither proprietary product technology is important nor access to foreign markets is restricted can grow internationally through the internal development of capabilities such as design, process innovation, and distribution logistics, although they might increasingly

rely on outsourcing strategies as home-country manufacturing costs rise. Inditex and Pronovias in the clothing industry, and Famosa in traditional toys illustrate this pattern.

At the other extreme, when possessing proprietary product technology is crucial to remain competitive and significant barriers to foreign market entry exist, new multinationals from emerging and developing countries tend to grow internationally on the basis of technological and distribution resources and capabilities secured through alliances and acquisitions. The international growth of Fagor Electrodomésticos in the household appliances industry from the 1970s to the 1990s illustrates this situation.

As shown in Table 4.1, electronic toys and lighters are mixed-type industries. Competing in electronic toys requires possessing product technologies that are not necessary in traditional toys. However, access to distribution channels in foreign markets is not overly problematic if the firm makes a functional product with the required technology. Traditional toy firms have engaged in alliances and acquisitions in an attempt to secure such technological capabilities. Lighters have the opposite features: the technology is widely available, but access to foreign markets is problematic because of regulation and differences in distribution channels.

Following the appropriate internal or external capability development strategies, Spanish firms in these industries have catapulted themselves among the very largest in the world. However, they continue to be challenged by new entrants from both more and less advanced countries. Their future appears to be far from certain. Even in the clothing industry, the success and global reach of Inditex should not divert attention from the fact that firms in this industry succeed and expand globally only to find it difficult to sustain their position. The examples of Gap and Benetton represent a stark reminder that challengers abound when product technologies are not proprietary and entry barriers to foreign markets are low.

5 Serving global customers in producer goods

> It is impossible to study the economic growth of the developing
> countries in modern times without considering the mutual
> interactions between these economies and those of the advanced
> countries.
>
> K. Akamatsu (1962: 3)

> Once upon a time, I didn't have to do R&D. Now I do research, design
> and development; I have to be a leader and to rack my brains. These are
> costs, but thanks to them the relationship between the manufacturer
> and the supplier has become very difficult to be broken.
>
> Tarragó Pujol, Vice-President of Ficosa International[1]

Producer goods historically played a prominent role in the rise of the
newly industrialized countries beginning in the 1960s, including
South Korea, Taiwan, Thailand, Brazil, Mexico, and Spain, among
others. Sectors such as steel, metals, automotive components, and
machinery became the target of the government's development
efforts. In this chapter, we analyze selected examples of Spanish
firms that benefited from such policies and pursued strategies of global growth, albeit with different degrees of product diversification
and vertical integration. We also draw comparisons to Indian and
Chinese firms in the same industry.

One common policy to jump-start producer goods manufacturing is to attract investments by foreign multinationals. In the
automobile sector, for instance, governments frequently offer assemblers favorable conditions with a view to fostering the development
of local suppliers. Governments can speed up industrialization by
attracting inward foreign direct investments oriented to exports that
also entail local sourcing of components and support services. Under

---

[1] *El Mundo*, June 20, 2005.

these circumstances MNEs act as "instant transplanters of industrialization" (Ozawa 1996). For instance, in countries with low labor costs the establishment of a somewhat integrated value chain linking MNEs producing final products with local firms supplying intermediate goods can contribute to the economic development of the country and create huge growth opportunities for domestic firms. Over time, economic development may eventually raise salaries, eroding the basis of comparative advantage. By that time, however, some of the manufacturers of producer goods may have developed their own technology and/or other competitive advantages to replace their original labor cost advantage, allowing them to pursue new opportunities in foreign markets as well as domestically. As a particular case, some domestic suppliers with the required capabilities may be asked by their MNE clients to become a supplier in other parts of the world.

This process of upgrading and shifting direction of foreign direct investment was captured by Dunning and Narula (1996) as one of the building blocks of the "investment development path," a theory that describes the evolution of countries from being net recipients of foreign investment to net senders. It shows that incoming foreign investment may generate windows of opportunity for local manufacturers of producer goods to grow and become multinational firms as they pursue foreign growth opportunities. Catching this wave is one of the key ways in which some of the new Spanish MNEs in producer goods have grown internationally.

The best illustration of the internationalization of domestic producer goods companies is to be found in the automobile industry. According to the International Organization of Motor Vehicle Manufacturers (OICA), in 2008 Spain ranked eighth in number of automobiles produced, of which more than 80 percent were exported. Virtually the entire assembly industry is foreign-owned. There were at the time thirteen assembly plants of cars and all-road vehicles owned and operated by Renault, Ford, General Motors, Peugeot Citroën (PSA), Volkswagen-SEAT, Mercedes-Benz, Nissan, and

Suzuki. Spain is also a big market for automobiles, ranking ninth in size. From the 1950s to the 1970s, Spain attracted foreign investment because of the potential growth of the domestic market and the steep tariff and non-tariff barriers to trade erected by the government. During the 1980s and 1990s, foreign assemblers continued to invest in new and existing facilities, taking advantage of relatively lower labor costs than in the rest of the European Union, looking toward exporting small cars (Guillén 2001).

The switch to export-oriented assembly proved to be of enormous consequence to the domestic suppliers. They had to improve their technology and quality in order to survive. Specialization helped attain economies of scale. Big assemblers such as Renault, Ford, and General Motors started to make sourcing decisions at the European level. Suppliers were organized into hierarchical tiers, for ease of coordination. The expectation was that the best suppliers for a specific component or subsystem would stand ready to set up production facilities wherever needed. Spanish suppliers like Ficosa, Grupo Antolín, Fagor Ederlan, Gestamp, Zanini, and CIE Automotive took advantage of these opportunities, followed their customers abroad, and became multinational corporations in their own right. As a result of their foreign expansion, their future no longer depends on a comparative wage advantage. Naturally, dozens of other major suppliers disappeared or were acquired by other firms.

In this chapter we analyze four cases of Spanish companies in the producer goods industries that grew domestically, riding successive waves of inward foreign direct investment from the 1960s to the 1990s, and catapulted themselves internationally by extending their ties to multinational companies with operations in the Spanish market. Three of them started in the automotive components industry – Zanini, Ficosa, and Corporación Gestamp – while the fourth, Gamesa, was founded in 1976 to pursue opportunities in metal-based components for automotive firms and the military, and later entered aerospace and, more famously, the wind turbine industry. As noted in Table 5.1, these four companies chose to pursue opportunities for

Table 5.1. *Growth strategies in producer goods industries*

	Vertical integration	
Product diversification	Low	High
High	Ficosa	Gamesa
Low	Zanini	Corporación Gestamp

growth in very different ways. Ficosa diversified into a wide array of small automotive components, but without integrating vertically, while Corporación Gestamp vertically integrated to become a supplier of bulkier metallic automotive components such as chassis and body stampings. By contrast, Zanini decided to focus entirely on one single component, hubcaps. After several years actively involved in automotive and aeronautical components, Gamesa chose to become a diversified and vertically integrated group in the wind power generation industry.

FICOSA INTERNATIONAL

Ficosa International supplies command and control, underhood, door, seat, and rearview systems to the most important vehicle manufacturers, including Volkswagen, General Motors, Renault-Nissan, Ford, BMW, Fiat, PSA Peugeot Citroën, Toyota, Honda, and Daimler-Benz, among others. It is one of the world's main suppliers of rearview mirrors. In 2008 its sales amounted to 897 million euros and employed 7,174 people. Although dwarfed by giants Bosch, Denso Corporation, Delphi, and Magna International, the company has carved out a profitable niche for itself and established manufacturing facilities in nineteen countries on four continents.

The origins of Ficosa can be traced back to 1949 when eighteen-year-old José María Pujol Artigas and his friend José María Tarragó set up "Pujol i Tarragó," a small workshop to produce drive cables for the spare parts market in Barcelona. The venture had the financial support of Pujol Artigas' father. Drive cables needed to be specifically designed and produced for each type of car, which enabled them to compete in spite of their small scale. The initial years of Pujol i Tarragó were described by Mr. Pujol as "heroic" (Pujol Artigas 1998: 35). Ficosa took advantage of the growth opportunities associated with the development of the automobile industry in Spain. Barcelona was chosen as the site for the first large-scale assembly plant of SEAT, a joint venture between Fiat and the national government, and during the 1950s and 1960s, Ficosa managed to sign contracts with SEAT and the two other main manufacturers established in Spain, Citroën and Renault, which set up assembly facilities aimed at selling in the domestic market. Ficosa's strategy was to establish close links with the Spanish headquarters of its customers, and leverage their initial contracts to diversify into other components. This strategy was in part driven by the assembler's policy of sourcing parts from several suppliers in order to avoid disruptions, and encouraged by regulations that required assemblers to reach certain local content targets (Margalef 2005).

Ficosa incorporated a separate company to make each of the components, including Transpar Ibérica in 1962 for windshield washers and rearview mirrors, Technomatic in 1968 for sun-visors and window openers, Lames Ibérica in 1968 for flexible hoses, and Cables Gandía in 1966 for steel cables. All of these companies were controlled by Pujol y Tarragó, SA, which became the group holding company. Ficosa established its first foreign facility in 1971, a plant to supply drive cables to Fiat's assembly line in Porto, Portugal. The company was renamed Ficosa in 1976, two years after a proper holding company had been set up (Margalef 2005).

It was during the 1970s that Ficosa pursued opportunities with two other multinational assemblers that set up plants in Spain. Ford established a large assembly plant in 1973, followed by General Motors in 1979. Supplying different customers required considerable adaptations. For instance, export-oriented assembly was modular and just-in-time procedures were becoming the norm. In order to coordinate effectively, Ficosa started to use the holding company to manage logistics. The company also decided to set up new plants in less industrialized parts of the country, including the provinces of Lleida and Soria. As a consequence, the headquarters of Ficosa came to play a crucial role in managing the logistics for the entire group of companies (Margalef 2005: 314).

During the 1980s Ficosa prepared itself for Spain's eventual membership in the European Union. The company established its first foreign assembly plants outside the Iberian Peninsula. It also changed its name to Ficosa International and formulated a new strategy for growth based on the establishment of technological development centers located next to the R&D departments of the main assemblers. For each of these centers, Ficosa hired local technical staff to facilitate communication with the client. Naturally, the role of these centers was to perform not only technical functions but also commercial ones. In fact, their main role was commercial, as the bulk of the R&D efforts were made at corporate headquarters in Barcelona. Once a contract had been signed, Ficosa set up a new production facility or acquired a local company. The same pattern was replicated in several countries. The first center was established in the UK in 1988, near the engineering and purchasing department of Ford, followed by a wholly owned plant. Centers were also established that year in France, Germany, and Italy. In France, Ficosa took over Maurice Lecoy in 1989, a maker of cables, and in 1991 established Fico Co Cipa SARL, to manufacture mirrors, and Fico Co Triad to manufacture gearshift systems. In Portugal, where Ficosa was already present, Ficosa International Lda was established in 1992, also setting up a new plant.

Ficosa's strategy seemed to be paying off, as one European assembler after another asked the company to become their supplier. However, selling to assemblers in Europe was not enough to ensure viability in the long term. The industry was becoming increasingly globalized as assemblers grouped all of their models into worldwide families, implementing the concept of "global platform," which used the same underbody and suspension parts for all models of the same family across the world. This approach reduced product development costs and enhanced economies of scale. For the main suppliers, including Ficosa, platforms represented an opportunity to expand globally in order to reap the benefits of component development jointly with the assemblers.

So as to become a global supplier, Ficosa started to expand beyond Europe. In 1995 it entered the United States and Mexico, and in 1997 it set up operations in Argentina and Brazil. Also in 1997 the firm entered into a 50/50 joint venture agreement with Tata Group, although the Indian partner retained operational control (Porporato 2004). In 2001 Ficosa opened a technical and commercial office in Japan, and entered South Korea through a joint venture with a supplier of Daewoo. In 2002 it established joint ventures in China and in Romania. In the expanding European market of the turn of the century, Ficosa decided to increase its presence by acquiring in 1999 Metallwarenfabrik Wilke GmbH, a German manufacturer of mirrors for industrial vehicles and buses, and in 2000 the rearview systems division of Magneti Marelli, which enabled it to enter new countries such as Poland and Turkey.

The success of the initial joint venture with Tata in India led the partners to set up two new plants in 2005 and 2006. Two new facilities were also opened in 2005, in Turkey and Poland. In 2006 Ficosa established a wholly-owned subsidiary company and an engineering center in China, and another engineering center in Monterrey, Mexico. In 2007 Ficosa entered Russia via a licensing agreement with local firm Zavod Avtocomponent.

Automotive manufacturers ask their suppliers to be both innovative and efficient. Innovativeness is key to taking part in the design of the components for new models. Efficiency is necessary to meet the assemblers' cost reduction schedule over the life of the model as well as to deal with emerging competition from suppliers in lower-cost countries. Thus, in order to survive in this demanding environment, automotive suppliers must be prepared to deal with these two requirements that are based on different capabilities: cost and innovativeness. In the case of Ficosa, this ambidexterity forced the firm to become a technologically-oriented company and to be present in the main emerging markets.

R&D and innovation played a fundamental role in Ficosa's recent evolution. During the last years Ficosa has invested 4 percent of sales in R&D. Its efforts have been rewarded with more than 675 assigned patents. In the words of Mr. Tarragó Pujol, Vice-President of Ficosa, "once upon a time, I didn't have to do R&D. Now I do research, design and development; I have to be a leader and to rack my brains. These are costs, but thanks to them the relationship between the manufacturer and the supplier has become very difficult to be broken."[2] The company reinforced its R&D capabilities with the creation in 2004 of a large technological center in Mollet del Vallès, just outside Barcelona, which coordinates the activities of its technical and design facilities in the United States, Mexico, Brazil, France, Italy, Germany, Portugal, China, South Korea, Japan, and India. The company has entered into several R&D joint ventures in order to innovate in specific fields. For instance, they recently launched a joint venture with the Japanese automation systems maker Omron Corp to make advanced driver assistance systems.

The strategy of upgrading technological capabilities comes hand in hand with a relocation of production following shifts in comparative costs. Thus, Ficosa produces higher-value added components in its Spanish factories, where wages are no longer low, and labor-intensive ones in emerging economies. As Mr. Tarragó Pujol argues, making "a standard rearview mirror is labor-intensive so we were not competitive in Spain. We moved this activity to India and we are competitive again ... The bet in Spain is innovation. Spain has a well-prepared, qualified and very competitive labor force. We have to play in the league of technology and this requires universities, technical centers and a restructuring of what we do." Given that R&D is an expensive proposition, the firm has sought to grow

[2] *El Mundo*, June 20, 2005.

in size. "In this industry you either grow or you barely can cover your expenses. A technological center like the one in Mollet can be afforded because growth allows us to dedicate more resources to R&D," observed Mr. Tarragó.[3]

Emerging economies offer Ficosa not only a low-cost manufacturing base, but also growth opportunities. Ficosa is present in the main emerging economies, including all four BRICs. For instance, in India Ficosa participates in the development of the Tata Nano, the new low-cost minicar which Tata plans to sell for about $2,500. The firm will supply rearview mirrors, the washer system, and gear shifters.[4]

Ficosa faces an important challenge. As a family-owned firm, its financial muscle is barely sufficient to support its plans of expansion around the world. The company studied the possibility of launching an IPO at the end of the 1990s, but the initiative was shelved. Instead, Ficosa invited UBS of Switzerland and Landesbank Baden-Wüttemberg of Germany to acquire minority stakes of 6.67 and 5.2 percent, respectively. A related source of concern is the firm's continued reliance on alliances for international growth. The firm operates with partners in countries such as Russia, Turkey, India, China, Brazil, and Korea. Some important R&D projects are conducted worldwide also through joint ventures and other alliances. While the company has valuable experience in the management of alliances (Porporato 2004), collaborations are generally viewed as intermediate stages in the international expansion of a company. Ficosa has also diversified its activities in Spain through an alliance with Alcor to buy a controlling stake in Sacesa, a supplier to the aerospace industry which manufactures, among other components, the belly fairing of the Airbus A350. While the aerospace business is somewhat related to the automotive industry, this diversification lies somewhat outside Ficosa's traditional area of strength, a move that may distract its

[3] *El Mundo*, June 20, 2005.
[4] *El Periódico*, January 9, 2008.

attention from the threats facing the automobile industry. Another challenge lies in keeping the company adaptable. The ability to adapt was at the heart of Ficosa's expansion and growth. In the words of Mr. Tarragó Pujol, "Ficosa became what is today because there was a market in Spain not covered by other firms, and the assembler needed a supplier. For the sake of self-defense you have to satisfy the need of the client wherever they emerge."[5] At a time when assemblers are putting pressure on suppliers to deliver higher quality at lower cost, the abilities to innovate and adapt remain more crucial than ever.

ZANINI

While Ficosa International pursued domestic and international growth through diversification, other Spanish firms remained product-focused. Zanini Auto Grup is a Barcelona-based multinational firm devoted to the design, production, and sale of plastic automobile components. It is the world's leader in hubcaps (wheel covers or trims), of which in 2007 it made about thirty-two million units, a 12 percent global market share (35 percent in Europe and 15 percent in the United States). This product alone accounts for 80 percent of the company's total revenues. Zanini primarily sells in Western Europe and the United Sates. The firm employs about one thousand people and has factories in Spain, France, the Czech Republic, Mexico, Brazil, and the United States, where it also has a design center. It has an outsourcing office in China, and technological and commercial agreements with Indian and Turkish firms. It is the only maker of hubcaps with a sales presence around the world. Its main customers are Renault-Nissan, General Motors, Grupo VW, Ford, PSA (Peugeot-Citroën), Volvo, and Suzuki. About 10–15 percent of sales are replacement parts. Despite its leading position, Zanini was seriously affected by the recent production cuts in the automotive industry, with sales falling from €61.6 million in 2007 to €47.5 million in 2008.

---

[5] *El Mundo*, June 20, 2005.

Zanini was founded in 1965 in Parets del Vallès, in the province of Barcelona, where it still has its corporate headquarters and a factory. Initially, Zanini made plastic moldings for non-automotive customers. The founding family came originally from Italy, but it sold the company to a group of Catalan investors shortly thereafter. In 1976 the firm was acquired by the Torras family. Between 1997 and 2003 the British private equity and venture capital firm 3i owned 11.5 percent of the equity. Over the years, Zanini invested in the latest machinery and equipment in order to secure business from the world's leading auto-makers. Product technology is jointly developed with assemblers to specification, while process technology is essentially embedded in the machinery and equipment, and can be acquired from specialized machine-tool producers. Zanini's challenge was to train its workers to use them efficiently. Moreover, the Torras family owned another firm, Industrial Yorka, a maker of posterior lighting products for automobiles, which gave them experience in dealing with assemblers and running efficient manufacturing operations. In sum, Zanini was able to grow based on borrowed technology, and managed to obtain efficiencies through economies of scale and a steep learning curve, which eventually prevented competitors located in lower-wage countries from eroding its market share.

As mentioned earlier, the structure of the automobile components industry has changed considerably since the advent of lean production. Co-location between suppliers and assemblers is now a necessity given the emphasis on design collaboration, just-in-time delivery, and cost pressures. Economies of scale play a fundamental role. In labor-intensive plants, minimum efficient scale for hubcaps is about four million units, whereas in more automated ones it hovers around six million.

Zanini's most important competitors are Maier Sociedad Cooperativa (part of Mondragón Corporación Cooperativa) in the European market, and Lacks Enterprises and McKechnie in the US market. Asian manufacturers are not specialized and the market is very fragmented. Neither Maier nor Lacks or McKechnie have plants outside their respective home regions.

Zanini made its first foreign investment in 1997, acquiring the hubcap division of Peguform France, a subsidiary of a US company with sales throughout Europe. Two years earlier, Zanini had bought Wegu Ibérica, another troubled maker of wheel covers. In 1998 Zanini established its first plant outside Europe, in Mexico, a €3.6 million investment. In 1999 it set foot in Asia through a technical-commercial agreement with Polyplastics in Haryana, India. That same year the firm opened a factory in Curitiba, Brazil, some 350 km south of São Paulo. Entry into the large US market occurred in 2000 through a technical-commercial office in Southfield, Michigan, strategically located to secure contracts for its Mexican plant. In 2003 Zanini acquired Del-Met, a firm in Tennessee, not far from Toyota's assembly plant. In 2005 the company set up an outsourcing office in China to secure dice, ornamental parts, and chromate parts. In 2006 the firm invested seven million euros in the Czech Republic to build a plant.

Zanini's pattern of growth displays several key characteristics. The firm gained scale thanks to growing automobile assembly activity in Spain. It then pursued international growth opportunistically, engaging both in acquisitions, which gave it access to new customers, and in greenfield investments in order to satisfy the just-in-time delivery requirement of the assemblers in Mexico, Brazil, and the Czech Republic. Zanini is a product-focused company that leveraged economies of scale instead of economies of scope. Ficosa made a different set of decisions concerning product diversification, while our next case, Corporación Gestamp, chose to integrate vertically along the value chain as opposed to expanding into different types of products.

CORPORACIÓN GESTAMP

Corporación Gestamp is a vertically-integrated supplier of steel products for the automotive, electrical appliances, construction, and

wind power generation industries. It makes products such as stampings, road barriers, shelves, and tubular steel towers. Downstream,
the company also provides logistics services for its clients. Upstream,
the firm is also engaged in cooperative relationships with steel manufacturers, especially Arcelor-Mittal. In 2007 Corporación Gestamp
had revenues of €3,500 million and 15,228 employees.

The origins of Corporación Gestamp go back to the incorporation of Gonvarri in 1958 as a distributor of tin, piano strings,
and steel sheets. The company was founded by Francisco Riberas
Pampliega, a self-made man, and three friends of his who later left
the company. Riberas was keenly aware of the growth potential of
the steel sheet market, so the company established commercial links
with important clients and secured the supply of steel. However, to
fully exploit this growth potential Riberas realized the importance
of setting up a steel cutting line and becoming a steel service center instead of being a mere steel sheet trader. The business model of
steel service centers consists in manipulating and treating steel to
provide specialized finishing and processing services to industries
that need ready-to-use parts and components. Service centers play a
critical role within the steel value chain, as they buy large amounts
of structural steel directly from the mills, store it, sell it in small
batches with the processing services required by their customers,
and deliver it when needed in such a way that the steel is either
directly usable by the customer, or the customer's time required to
make the steel usable is reduced.

During 2007 steel producers in the EU-15 countries sold
33 percent of their production directly to Original Equipment
Manufacturers (OEMs), including automobile assemblers, 27 percent through independent steel service centers, and 40 percent to
steel stockholding companies, which are mere distributors (ECORYS
2008). These data show that steel makers are expanding downstream
either by setting up service centers or by taking over existing ones;
in some cases they are also entering into strategic alliances with
steel service centers. In 2007 Gonvarri was the leading service

center in Spain with annual sales of €1,800 million. Its main rivals were controlled by foreign multinationals: Thyssen Ros Casares, Arcelor Distribución Iberia (formerly Grupo Velasco), and Comercial de Laminados (controlled by Klöckner & Co AG). In fact, the industry is becoming globalized as steel players such as Arcelor-Mittal or Thyssenkrupp Steel have acquired a global presence and some of the largest US service centers, such as Reliance Steel & Aluminum Co. or Ryerson Inc., have also established operations in Europe and Asia.

Gonvarri's first processing plant was set up in Burgos in 1966, where Riberas was born. Burgos is a strategically important logistics area, situated in between four important automobile assembly sites: Valladolid to the west, the Basque Country, home of heavy industry, to the north, Barcelona to the east, and Madrid to the south. Despite the ups and downs in the steel industry, the Burgos factory has kept on increasing its capacity and adopting the technology necessary to meet evolving customer requirements in terms of quality, cost, and just-in-time delivery.

Mr. Riberas not only anticipated the market potential of steel services in Spain, but also the importance of establishing strong links along the entire value chain, from steel producers to steel users. For this reason, the expansion of the company started by building service centers close to the main steel mills in Spain, located in Asturias, the Basque Country, and Valencia. In 1972 Gonvarri acquired a majority stake in the equity of Hiasa, a small company located close to the plants of Ensidesa (nowadays Arcelor-Mittal) in Asturias. The management of the company remained in the hands of Manuel Álvarez, the founder, until his recent retirement. Gonvarri also set up Ferrodisa in 1978 in Sagunto (Valencia) close to Altos Hornos del Mediterráneo's mill. The company also had an equity stake of 60 percent from 1986 to 1996 in Laminados Velasco, a service center located in the Basque Country, close to Altos Hornos de Vizcaya. Naturally, Gonvarri ran the risk of downstream vertical integration by the steel manufacturers. To prevent that from happening, in 1992–3 Gonvarri sold 30 percent of its equity each to Sollac Aceros (the Spanish subsidiary of France's Usinor), and Ensidesa, its two main suppliers. Although the Riberas family ended up holding less than 50 percent of the equity, they retained managerial control. Ensidesa also took a 15 percent stake in Hiasa. Having both Ensidesa and Usinor as shareholders proved to be far from easy. Even though nowadays these two firms are part of Arcelor-Mittal, they were fierce rivals in the 1990s. After Ensidesa (by then called Aceralia), Usinor, and Arbed merged into Arcelor in 2001, the Riberas family repurchased part of the equity owned by Arcelor in such a way that they came to control 65 percent and Arcelor the remaining 35. They also repurchased the shares of Hiasa owned by Arcelor. The only significant change since then in the ownership structure of Gonvarri was the acquisition of a 5 percent stake by Caja Madrid (a large savings bank) in 2007. The Gonvarri group kept for several years a 6.67 percent stake in the equity of Aceralia (the result of a merger among domestic steel producers).

Gonvarri's most consequential vertical integration, however, took place downstream. The company set up its first service center in Barcelona in 1982, close to key automotive assemblers and component manufacturers. It also founded Gonvauto, a division for steel handling and cutting services for automotive clients. The first Gonvauto plant was established in 1991 in Barcelona to serve the needs of SEAT's assembly plant. A second facility, located in Navarre and dedicated to serving Volkswagen, opened in 2000. In 2004 the company created Gonvarri Galicia, a service center aimed at supplying Citroën's assembly plant and other clients in the area. As of 2007 61 percent of the revenues of Gonvarri have to do directly or indirectly with the automotive industry.[6]

The most important project launched by Gonvarri involved stamping and the subsequent creation of Gestamp Automoción. In

---

[6] The company also integrated downstream, albeit temporarily, by entering the shelving and storage industry with the 2000 acquisition of Esmena, which it sold in 2006 to Mecalux.

1986, the year Spain entered the European Union, Gonvarri acquired Estampaciones Arín (nowadays Estampaciones Vizcaya, SA), a bankrupt client of Laminados Velasco. The founder of the company thought that Gonvarri could turn the company around, taking advantage of its reputation among auto-makers. As Mr. Riveras declared in a book describing his business experience: "I believed that I would gain contracts for Estampaciones Arín once acquired, because I had good contacts and I convinced myself that this was our opportunity" (Lillo 2004: 320). The new stamping division started to supply PSA-Citroën and Renault. As business grew, Gestamp Automoción established two new stamping facilities, co-located with each of the assembly plants. The growth of the stamping business followed similar patterns to the initial expansion of Gonvarri in terms of technology adoption, co-location, and equity links with other firms. For instance, the large steel company Arcelor took a 35 percent equity stake in Gestamp Automoción.

Nowadays Gestamp's automotive division operates fifty-seven manufacturing plants and thirteen R&D centers in eighteen countries. The company has grown through acquisitions. In 1999 it bought Metalbages, a supplier to Opel (GM), and Matricería Deusto, a stamping firm facing a troubled financial situation. The acquisition of Metalbages was especially consequential as this company operated plants in Argentina, Brazil, and France. In addition, Aceralia had a 25 percent equity stake in Metalbages, so Gestamp Automoción became a partner of Aceralia in Metalbages at a time when Gonvarri was also partly owned by Usinor, by then Aceralia's main rival. Through this acquisition Corporación Gestamp consolidated its position as the main ally of Aceralia in stamping. Gestamp Automoción's main milestones in international expansion include full and partial acquisitions in Argentina (1999), Germany and Portugal (2001), Sweden (2004), and India and Turkey (2007). In 2008 Gestamp set up a greenfield stamping facility in China (in Kunshan), acquired a majority stake in a Korean firm, and entered into a joint venture with Severstal in Russia. Despite being the origin of the group, the international expansion of Gonvarri (the steel service center division) now depends on the decisions made by Gestamp Automoción.[7] As of 2008 Gonvarri had steel service centers in Portugal, Brazil, Mexico, and Slovakia. In the short term, Gonvarri plans to open new steel service centers in countries where Gestamp Automoción has manufacturing facilities, like India, Russia, and Argentina. The existence of manufacturing plants of Gestamp Automoción guarantee enough critical mass to open a new service center, although once established in an new country the company tries to gain new clients in the construction and domestic appliances industries, among others.

A final move downstream along the value chain was in the field of renewable energy. Corporación Gestamp entered first into the solar field as a turnkey contractor of solar power farms, with part of the photovoltaic infrastructure manufactured by the group at one of its facilities. In the field of wind energy the company is involved directly as a turnkey contractor of wind power farms, and as a manufacturer of towers used to install the wind power turbines. To accelerate its expansion in this field, Corporación Gestamp acquired the Spanish Ganomagoga Group in 2008, a firm specialized in the manufacturing of towers for wind turbines with manufacturing facilities in Galicia, northern Spain. In 2009 Gonvarri Infraestructuras Eólicas had enough capacity to build 600 towers per year, and was building a plant in Brazil with a capacity of 400 towers, with plans to set up similar facilities in other emerging economies.

Gonvarri thus transformed itself from being a small trader of steel into a vertically integrated group of companies. Like Ficosa, it replicated this model in other countries, following its main customers

---

[7] The first international project of Gonvarri took place in 1992, when acquiring Emilsider, an Italian steel services center, followed by the purchase of Cosider in Portugal one year later. In 1997 Gonvarri established a service center in Morocco, catering to the needs of the household appliances industry, and anticipating the establishment of automobile assembly plants. These early steps, however, were disappointing, and the company sold its facilities in Morocco and Italy in 2006 and 2007, respectively. For this reason, the international expansion of the steel service activities became conditioned by the existence of manufacturing plants of Gestamp Automoción.

in the automotive industry. Its policy of diversification and vertical integration gave the company vastly more growth opportunities than Zanini. Like Gonvarri, Gamesa, our next case study, also entered the field of renewable energy. However, unlike Gonvarri, Gamesa abandoned its initial focus on the automotive industry to embrace wind power.

GAMESA

Gamesa followed a somewhat parallel trajectory to that of Gonvarri. Originally an automotive and defense contractor, it emerged as a leading global wind turbine manufacturer and wind farm developer. Although successful globally, Gamesa is not a technology leader. It has become one of the three largest wind turbine manufacturers thanks to technological alliances and forward vertical integration into wind farm development. The company has an operational presence in nearly thirty countries across Europe, Latin America, China, and the United States.[8]

Given the scarcity of fossil fuels and the concern over global warming, the wind power generation industry is witnessing strong growth around the world. Together with Germany, Denmark, and the United States, Spain is at the forefront of the development of green energy, especially wind power (Dinica 2008). Iberdrola is the world's largest wind farm operator, Acciona the biggest wind farm developer, and Gamesa the third-largest manufacturer of wind turbines as well as a major developer of wind farms. These developments are in part a reaction against the country's dependence on foreign sources of energy, a favorable regulatory framework, and the innovative activities of these and other firms in the industry.

Between 1994 and 2008, installed wind power capacity worldwide increased at a cumulative rate of nearly 29 percent annually, from a mere 3,500 megawatts (MW) to 121,000. According to the Global

---

[8] This section relies on a case study written for the Centro de Experiencias of the Centro de Estudios Comerciales (CECO): Guillén and Tschoegl (2007).

Wind Energy Council, the United States, followed by Germany, lead the world in absolute installed capacity, and Denmark relative to the population. Spain ranks third in absolute capacity (16,754 MW or 14 percent of the world's total), just behind Germany. China and India are the next largest markets in absolute terms, with the former exhibiting the largest year-on-year growth rate. Still, wind power accounts for a tiny percentage of overall electricity consumption. In Denmark, the country that has invested the most on a per capita basis, installed wind power capacity barely suffices to light ten 60-watt incandescent bulbs per person, and in Spain just under six bulbs. Only ten countries in the world have enough installed capacity to light at least one bulb per person, per year. However, during especially windy days characterized by weak demand, wind generators in Spain account for as much as 25 percent of total electricity consumption.

Contrary to appearances, generating electricity from wind is an exceedingly complex activity involving turbine manufacturers, developers, constructors, operators, distributors, and regulators. The viability of wind power depends on a number of critical factors, ranging from technology to demand conditions, and from regulation to the structure of competition. In spite of its promise, wind power cannot presently compete in cost against conventional energy sources. Tax incentives and subsidies are thus of the essence. Another intriguing aspect of the industry is that it is growing quite rapidly in both rich and developing countries. Moreover, wind turbine manufacturers from China and India are making great strides internationally (Jacobsson and Lauber 2006; Kristinsson and Rao 2008; Lema and Ruby 2007).

Wind turbines consist of blades, a nacelle, a tower, and control systems. The nacelle is an aerodynamically-shaped structure that houses the gearbox, the drive train, a generator, a transformer, and a number of other components. The nacelle can rotate in order to orient the blades toward the wind. The design and manufacturing of blades is perhaps the most knowledge-intensive activity, followed by the assembly of the nacelle (which includes a gearbox, a generator, and a transformer, among other components) and the control systems. Turbine manufacturers differ from one another in terms of their degree of vertical integration – backward into component manufacturing and/or forward into wind farm development – and in terms of whether they possess their own technology or not. Given that minimum efficient plant scale is not large relative to the size of the major national markets and that transportation costs are high, wind turbine manufacturers prefer to organize production on a regional basis, setting up clusters of blade, nacelle, and tower factories in the major regions of Europe, North America, and East Asia, thus minimizing the need to export over long distances. Moreover, the long-term nature of the investments in wind farms and the need for government subsidies invites an active local presence.

The world's leading wind turbine manufacturer is Vestas Wind Systems A/S, a Danish firm that designs, manufactures, and sells wind turbines. Founded in 1945 as Vestjysk Stålteknik A/S, it originally made household appliances and began producing wind turbines in 1979. In 2003, when Vestas merged with the Danish wind turbine manufacturer NEG Micon, it became the largest wind turbine manufacturer in the world. Vestas has installed turbines in 63 countries and as of September 30, 2009 employed 20,256 people worldwide. Together with GE Wind of the United States and Enercon of Germany, it is perceived as being a technology leader in the industry because of the efficiency, reliability, and versatility of its turbines. Vestas developed a global manufacturing presence in the late 2000s. It makes blades in China, Denmark, England, Germany, and Italy; control systems in Denmark and Spain; nacelles in China, Denmark, Germany, India, Italy, Norway, Spain, and Sweden; and towers in Denmark and Scotland. It has installed turbines in sixty-three different countries. Unlike Acciona or Gamesa, the firm does not develop, own, or operate wind farms. Due to the strong growth of wind power in the United States and China, in 2009 Vestas was planning new manufacturing facilities in both countries.

Like Denmark, Spain is also a pioneer in wind energy (Dinica 2008). The first turbine was installed in the early 1980s by Ecotecnia. The most important turning point came in 1997 when the government passed a new electricity law requiring that utilities purchased all wind power generated and that they be compensated for the higher cost by a higher feed-in rate. Installed capacity grew and the industry came to employ as many as 30,000 people by 2007. Spain is home to the world's largest developer and builder of wind farms (Acciona, also the seventh-largest turbine manufacturer), and the largest operator (Iberdrola, followed by Acciona).

Gamesa was founded in 1976. Initially it produced metal parts for the automotive industry and ordinance for the military. The company quickly evolved an interest in the areas of aerodynamics and electrical machinery. During the 1990s it signed an agreement with Vestas whereby the Spanish company obtained technological licenses for the most sophisticated components in the wind turbines, although only for markets not serviced by Vestas, namely, Spain, Latin America, and Northern Africa. Vestas took an equity stake in Gamesa of 40 percent. In 2002 the two companies parted ways. Gamesa's engineers had managed to acquire enough experience at manufacturing and started their own design activities. By the end of 2008 the company had obtained or applied for 118 patents. Still, its R&D expenditures amounted to about 2 percent of sales. Gamesa also decided to become more active in wind farm development. While this move diverted financial and managerial resources away from R&D and manufacturing, it facilitated Gamesa's growth in Europe, the United States, and China. Gamesa's shares first traded in 2000. At the present time, the free float is 63 percent, and it is an Ibex-35 blue-chip component. The main shareholders are Iberdrola (17 percent), Lolland SA (owned by members of the del Pino family, 5 percent), Blackrock Investment Management (3.4 percent) and Barclays Global Investors UK Holdings Ltd (3.6 percent).

Gamesa sold its aerospace division in 2005 and its solar energy business in 2008 so as to focus its resources on wind power.

Aerospace presented some important synergies with blade design and manufacturing, but Gamesa's small scale as a supplier to Embraer, Bombardier, Airbus, Boeing, and Sikorsky made it difficult to operate profitably. As of 2008 Gamesa Eólica, the turbine division, ran twenty-eight manufacturing facilities, of which four were in the United States, one in China, and the rest in Spain. The firm assembles two types of turbines: 850 KW and 2 MW. Unlike Vestas, the company set up a wind farm division (Gamesa Energía), which develops, builds, and sells the farms to operators.

In its international expansion Gamesa resorted to greenfield investments, alliances, and acquisitions. In China, its entry strategy into manufacturing involved greenfield investments, while in the United States it combined greenfield and acquisitions. In some markets it has entered into alliances with local partners to develop wind farms (UK, Japan, India, China, and Australia). Gamesa is doing well in the two fastest-growing large markets, China and the United States. In terms of new capacity installed during 2007, Gamesa ranked as the largest foreign firm in China (after two local firms, Goldwind and Sinovel), and fourth in the United States after GE Wind, Vestas, and Suzlon. About 20 percent of Gamesa's total installed capacity is outside of Spain, and about 60 percent of new installations are taking place outside the home country.

Gamesa's entry into the United States illustrates the firm's strengths and weaknesses. The agreement with Vestas prevented the firm from entering the US market until 2002. Given that Gamesa was not known for being a technology leader, the firm decided to first establish a foothold in wind farm development. A big hurdle had to do with the administrative fragmentation of the United States, which, as far as electricity is concerned, is a collection of fifty state-level markets, each with its own regulator and licensing procedures. In order to surmount such an obstacle, Gamesa Energía decided to acquire Navitas, a small wind farm developer based in Minnesota which employed a mere dozen people. This state, bordering on Canada, was one of the top ten in terms of growth potential, and several other neighboring states in which Navitas operated were also classified at the time as attractive. Navitas did not have at the time a large portfolio of installed capacity. Its value to Gamesa lay in its knowledge about how to obtain licenses.

Given that in the United States the subsidy is not in the form of a higher feed-in rate but rather a tax credit, Gamesa Energía has an incentive to sell the wind farm to a company with large profits so that the tax incentive can be maximized. For instance, the firm acquired a wind farm under development from St. Joseph's University in the state of Pennsylvania and made arrangements for the electricity generated to be sold to First Energy Solutions Corp. Shortly thereafter Gamesa Energía sold the first phase of the farm, including forty 2 MW turbines, to Australia's Babcock & Brown Wind Partners, one of the top five operators in the world.

In 2004 Gamesa Eólica made the decision to set up wind turbine manufacturing facilities in the United States, driven by the rise in the value of the euro relative to the dollar, high transportation costs, and the political advantages of local production. After briefly considering Texas – the state with the largest wind potential – the firm opted for Pennsylvania, whose governor was firmly committed to green power. This state has committed to a ten-fold increase in the proportion of electricity generated from wind. Moreover, many large electricity consumers announced plans to switch up to 30 percent of their purchases to renewable sources, including the University of Pennsylvania, a private entity with an annual budget of €3,750 million. When the governor, Ed Rendell, agreed to treat Gamesa as a preferred provider, the firm moved its US headquarters from Minneapolis to Philadelphia, the state's largest city.

Gamesa Eólica has built four factories in Pennsylvania. The first is located at Ebensburg, Cambria County, some 400 km west of Philadelphia, and the other three at Fairless Hills, Bucks County, 62 km north, on a lot previously owned by US Steel. This location was eligible for a full exemption from local and state taxes until 2019. According to the company, Gamesa received approximately 7.6

million euros in subisidies, loans, and tax credits to start operations in Fairless Hills. The total cost of the plants was 9.2 million euros for the blades facility, 5.4 for the tower plant, and 19.5 for the generators and nacelles plant. Thus, the subsidies covered about one-fifth of the total cost. The plants became operative in 2006 and will eventually employ 530 people. The Ebensburg blades facility was inaugurated in 2005, employs 240 people, and cost some 19 million euros. These facilities have a capacity of 1,000 MW, or one-third of Gamesa's total. About 30 percent of their turbines are sold to Gamesa Energía and the rest to other developers. For instance, in 2005 Horizon Wind Energy – once owned by Goldman Sachs and presently part of EDP – signed a contract with Gamesa Eólica for 200 turbines or a combined capacity of 400 MW, and with an option for 100 more turbines. In the United States, Gamesa Energía developed and sold a wind farm in 2003 and another in 2006. It presently owns three under construction. Its goal is to sell 300 MW in the United States annually. The firm's most important challenge in the United States is to hire and retain technical personnel.

Gamesa has identified Spain, the United States, and China as its key strategic markets for the next decade or so. While in Spain it accounted for a commanding 48 percent of new turbines installed in 2007, it is has a mere 8 percent share of the US market and 15 percent of the Chinese market, where two local assemblers dominate, GE Wind and Windstar. Given that Gamesa is not a technology leader – like Vestas, GE Wind, or Enercon – its future will in part depend on how fast emerging-market turbine manufacturers grow. Perhaps the most adept challenger is India's Suzlon Energy Ltd, the fifth-largest in the world, which in 2007 surpassed Gamesa in the United States to become the third-largest supplier after GE Wind and Vestas, and was building a strong presence in China in addition to being the uncontested leader in India (Ramamurti and Singh 2009: 147–52). In 2007 Suzlon had made installations in over forty countries around the world – including Australia, China, Europe, India, New Zealand, South Korea, and the United States. Suzlon was founded in 1995 and is headquartered in Pune. It has manufacturing sites in India, mainland China, Germany, and Belgium, and design and R&D teams and facilities in Germany, India, and the Netherlands. Tellingly, it manages its international operations from offices in Denmark. In 2006 Suzlon acquired Belgium's Hansen Transmissions, the world's second-largest maker of gearboxes for wind turbines, and in 2007 it acquired a majority stake in REpower Systems AG, Germany's third-largest wind turbine manufacturer.

Suzlon illustrates a strategy of growth that is in some ways similar to Gamesa's, although in others it deviates significantly. Like Gamesa, Suzlon first established a strong presence in its domestic market, and then started to pursue opportunities in foreign markets. Suzlon, however, has used aggressive acquisitions in order to gain access to key components and technology, whereas Gamesa relied on alliances for both capability building and market access, making a very small acquisition in the United States in order to secure operating licenses, and quickly moving toward greenfield investments. Looking toward the future, Gamesa's challenge will be to remain competitive relative to two different types of firms: the technology leaders from Denmark, Germany, and the United States, and the low-cost firms from China and India.

EXPLOITING PROJECT EXECUTION CAPABILITIES AROUND THE WORLD

The four cases analyzed in this chapter illustrate different growth strategies in producer goods industries. The key strategic decisions involved vertical integration and product diversification, as noted in Table 5.1. Ficosa and Gamesa both opted for product diversification, while Gestamp and, especially, Zanini remained product focused. However, Corporación Gestamp and Gamesa also made the strategic choice of integrating vertically along the value chain. Each of these four strategies required different entry modes for international expansion, but were based on the same core toolkit of "project execution capabilities," that is, "the skills required to establish or expand operating and other corporate facilities, including undertaking pre-investment feasibility studies, project management, project engineering (basic and detailed), procurement, construction, and start-up of operations" (Amsden and Hikino 1994: 129). Starting from technology borrowed or acquired from others, each company establish itself as a supplier of choice for the automotive and/or wind generation industries in the domestic market, gaining a capability to undertake business projects for their clients.

The differences across the four firms lie in how they exploited this capability to take advantage of windows of opportunity. Corporación Gestamp and Ficosa, founded earlier than the other two firms and at a time when automobile production in Spain was taking off, found it easier to grow, horizontally in the case of Ficosa and vertically in the case of Corporación Gestamp. They took advantage of their reputation among automobile assemblers. Zanini, by contrast, managed to grow within one product category, relying on economies of scale as its main competitive advantage. Finally, Gamesa found it hard to grow in automobile components and diversified instead into aerospace and wind turbines. Project-execution capabilities are, thus, an asset that needs to be, in the words of Hamel and Prahalad (1993), "stretched and leveraged" in order to optimize the firm's growth opportunities. Successful relationships with large multinational clients in the domestic market helped Ficosa, Gestamp, and Zanini grow internationally. Gamesa, by contrast, left the automobile industry. In the wind power industry, its main clients were developers of wind farms. Given its lack of established relationships in this area, the company integrated forward to become a developer itself.

Another feature common to the four firms is that they have grown aggressively through acquisitions, a strategy that other firms from emerging markets have also adopted. Perhaps the two best examples are India's Bharat Forge and China's Wanxiang, which are the only two automotive suppliers included in the 2009 Boston Consulting Group list of the 100 New Global Challengers (BCG

2009). Bharat Forge is the world's largest chassis component manufacturer. After consolidating itself as a low-cost, high-volume maker of components for the domestic assemblers, the company embarked on a series of global acquisitions, first in Germany, by taking over Carl Dan Peddinghaus GmbH & Co. KG (CDP) in 2004, the leading German forging company, with a subsidiary specialized in aluminum forgings. In 2005 it took over Sweden's Imatra Kilsta AB, the leading manufacturer of front axle beams, which included a Scotland-based fully-owned subsidiary, Scottish Stampings Ltd. Finally Bharat Forge gained global reach in 2005 by acquiring Federal Forge, securing a manufacturing presence in the United States, which is now one of its largest markets. In 2005 they also established a joint venture in China with FAW Corporation. These companies gave Bharat not only market share but also technology, as in the case of aluminum forgings.

Wanxiang is China's biggest automotive supplier. Founded in 1969, it initiated foreign growth earlier than Bharat Forge. Once a supplier to big US autoparts companies like Visteon Corp. and Delphi, Wanxiang used acquisitions in the United States and Europe to expand its product lines and technology base. Emerging-market multinationals have often targeted firms in financial trouble. Their low-cost manufacturing skills tend to blend well with the technological capabilities of the targets.[9] Asian companies find in these deals an opportunity to upgrade their status as global suppliers, becoming "dual shore manufacturers," as they can produce with the low-cost advantages of emerging countries but with the design and reliability of developed-country suppliers. Firms located in China and India also have the advantage of their strong position in the domestic market, which offers them continued opportunities for growth, precisely the ones that European suppliers like Ficosa or Corporación Gestamp are attempting to tap into.

[9] See Reuters, April 9, 2008, "Asian Auto Suppliers Eye US Companies," www.reuters.com/articlePrint?articleId=USN0944744720080409.

Our analysis of cases in the producer goods industry would be incomplete without considering the role of the government. The development of the automobile components sector in the countries that industrialized during the 1960s owed much to selective policies of protection and export encouragement, which benefited suppliers in some cases but not others (Biggart and Guillén 1999). For instance, South Korea banned imports of assembled cars but established a tariff-free policy of imports of components, thus promoting the assembly sector at the expense of components manufacturers, which still to this day are not among the world's best. In Spain, by contrast, the shift in the 1970s from a policy of import-substitution to one of export promotion and openness to foreign direct investment both in final assembly and component manufacturing set into motion a process of natural selection among automotive suppliers. While some of them went bankrupt or were taken over by foreign multinationals, others became multinational firms in their own right, including Ficosa, Gestamp, and Zanini. In Taiwan, the government unsuccessfully tried to promote automobile assembly up until the 1980s; meanwhile, small local firms geared up to cater to the needs of foreign assemblers by specializing in plastic and electronic components that were easy to transport, turning the country into a major exporter of automobile parts. Finally, in Argentina, an import-substitution policy coupled with the requirement that local assemblers used at least 90 percent domestic components forced automakers to vertically integrate, rendering both assemblers and component manufacturers inefficient. Thus, the Spanish model of automotive development succeeded at attracting foreign assemblers and component manufacturers, and created the conditions for the rise of a few world-class Spanish-owned component multinational firms.

6 Learning by doing in infrastructure and financial services

> One cannot understand the economic strategies of former monopolies if one does not also take into account the related political strategies ... At the international level, these firms' political strategies have limitations related to the fact that not only the home government but also the host government plays an important role ... However, in spite of those limitations, political strategies still remain a key part of these firms' behaviors.
>
> Jean-Philippe Bonardi (2004: 116)

> Construction firms ... have diversified into activities requiring the same culture as that of the contractor ... entering services, infrastructure concessions and, more recently, energy.
>
> Florentino Pérez, Chairman and CEO of ACS[1]

Services account for two-thirds of the global economy. In high-income countries, the share hovers around 73 percent, and in low-income countries around 46 percent. Among the BRICs, Brazil's 65 percent and Russia's 57 percent are much higher than the corresponding share for China (40 percent) or India (52 percent).[2] Not surprisingly, only twenty of the BCG's ranking of the 100 most significant emerging-market multinationals are service-sector firms, although their size and international presence is likely to grow very quickly over the next two decades (BCG 2009). For instance, many firms in the field of business services outsourcing start by exporting from a home country with low wages and later establish operations abroad, as the cases of Tata Consultancy Services, Wipro, or Infosys illustrate.

---

[1] *El Pais*, December 24, 2006.
[2] World Bank, World Development Indicators database.

In the next two chapters, we examine cases of Spanish companies that have become major international competitors in the service
sector. In this chapter we analyze infrastructure and financial services, and in Chapter 7 we compare publishing, transportation, turnkey projects, and business education. The business model of firms
competing in fields such as banking, telecommunications, transportation, electricity, water, oil, and gas has changed dramatically over
the last two decades. Traditionally, they enjoyed what can be labeled
as a "quiet life" (Hicks 1935), thanks to natural and/or regulatory barriers to competition. However, the joint effect of globalization, technological change and market reforms and privatizations has progressively
removed the different shelters that protected these firms from competition (Boddewyn and Brewer 1994; Henisz 2003). As a consequence,
they have been forced to pay attention to new technological developments and market reform processes that not only allow the entry
by new competitors, but also expand the boundaries of the industry.
These changes, however, have brought about growth opportunities as
well as the threat of new competitors. As a consequence, in the early
1990s most firms in already (or soon-to-be) deregulated industries realized that, in order to maintain their competitive position, they needed
to have a presence in more countries and new businesses.

"Market-oriented" reforms have been the mechanism through
which corporate expansion was made possible. These reforms have
typically included at least one of these four elements: privatization
of state-owned firms, separation of regulatory authority from operating authority, regulatory depoliticization, and liberalization of entry
(Henisz *et al*. 2005). By the end of 1999, 144 out of 190 countries
for which there were available data had introduced at least one of
the four market-oriented reforms in their electricity and/or telecommunications industries. Each of these changes created windows of
opportunity to enter specific countries and activities, through processes that in most cases were led by governments that were shaping
the industry according to their needs or beliefs. This fact illustrates
one of the features of corporate expansion in regulated sectors: entry

is conditioned by decisions made by politicians and regulators. As a result, the international strategy of firms in these sectors is usually defined on a country-by-country or multi-domestic basis (Bonardi 2004; García-Canal and Guillén 2008). In regulated industries, decisions about where, when, and how to expand and invest fall to a great extent outside the control of the firm. In fact, the expansion strategy of these firms is most frequently based on taking advantage of whatever opportunities arise, even if the company is not fully prepared to take advantage of them, on the grounds that these opportunities appear only sporadically and to some extent unpredictably.

A superficial analysis could lead us to the conclusion that expanding abroad in regulated industries undergoing liberalization is all about being in the right place at the right time. In fact, firms in deregulated industries lack the capabilities on which conventional MNEs have grounded their international strategy, such as technology, brands, or a good reputation among its customers. In effect, incumbent firms in regulated industries tend to lack technological and marketing capabilities. They relied on other firms, such as equipment suppliers, for technology, and having operated in a protected domestic market for decades is not the best environment for developing marketing capabilities. In fact, they tended to abuse their monopoly position prior to liberalization and deregulation. However, their recent corporate expansion across the world is difficult to explain without acknowledging that the most successful firms in these industries have developed relevant capabilities that are not necessarily of a technological or marketing nature, in the classical use of those terms.

Among such capabilities, we highlight the following two: expertise in managing large-scale and complex operations, and expertise in dealing with governments and regulation (García-Canal and Guillén 2008). The more a firm develops these two capabilities, the higher the profitability of its domestic business and the greater the chances of making a profit in foreign markets, for three reasons. First, a profitable business at home can help finance international acquisitions. Second, learning how to operate the business efficiently is the key to adding value when acquiring a foreign company or setting up a business unit abroad, as the firm should be efficient enough to keep costs aligned with the price that can be charged for the service according to the existing regulations in the foreign country. Last but not least, the expertise in dealing with politicians and regulators is critical, not only in order to obtain a license to operate in the foreign market, but also to protect the firm against any subsequent regulatory change that could alter the status quo and profitability of the investment project. Political capabilities and industry expertise play a pivotal role in taking full advantage of the windows of opportunity associated with market-oriented reforms in infrastructure and financial services. Especially for any firm competing in a regulated industry, the ability to accumulate political capabilities is a necessary condition to survive because governments have the ability to dramatically alter the profitability of firms and investment projects by changing regulated prices, taxes, or other conditions (Henisz 2000; Henisz and Zelner 2001).

Since the mid 1980s, Spanish firms in the regulated infrastructure sectors became the country's largest foreign investors, accounting for 32.3 percent of the total number of foreign investments and operational establishments of Spanish firms (Guillén and García-Canal 2009). Seven firms alone – Telefónica, Banco Santander, Iberdrola, BBVA, Repsol-YPF, Unión Fenosa, and Endesa – account for 17.8 percent of the operations. According to the leading industry magazine *Public Works Financing*, seven of the ten largest private transportation infrastructure management companies in the world as of 2009[3] were Spanish: ACS (no. 1), FCC (no. 2), Ferrovial (no. 3), Abertis (no. 4), OHL (no. 7), Sacyr (no. 9), and Acciona (no. 10). In addition, as of September 30, 2009 Telefónica ranked as the largest telecommunications operator in Europe and third worldwide by market capitalization, and Santander was the leading bank in the

---

[3] This ranking is based on the cumulative number of transportation concessions (road, bridge, tunnel, rail, port, airport) over $50m capital put under construction/operation since 1985 by these companies. The ranking excludes design-build.

eurozone and eighth worldwide also in terms of market capitalization. Overall, Repsol, Endesa, and Telefónica are among the top 100 largest non-financial multinational firms, and Santander and BBVA among the fifty largest financial firms (UNCTAD 2009).

It is no coincidence that the industries in which Spanish firms have most successfully expanded internationally are regulated ones. Consolidation and an accrued expertise in managing regulated services in Spain prepared these firms to take over foreign companies, at a time in which there were no established multinationals, as in consumer or producer manufactured goods. Spanish firms benefited from years of heavy infrastructure spending by both the EU and the Spanish government. They attracted some of the brightest managers and engineers from the country's top business and engineering schools, and learned how to successfully operate large-scale, complex construction and engineering projects, telecommunication networks, and financial operations. They borrowed someone else's technology and, in Amsden and Hikino's (1994) terms, developed "project-execution" capabilities, which they could put to good use in a wide variety of infrastructure sectors. They eventually became among the most efficient and profitable firms worldwide.

However, this picture would be incomplete without taking into account the role played by governments, policymakers, and regulators. Business and politics have traditionally been a two-way street in Spain. Since the 1980s Spanish governments were very supportive of the international expansion of Spanish firms. Policymakers also shaped their corporate expansion. In this chapter we analyze the role played by politics, regulation, and learning in the cases of Telefónica, Santander, Unión Fenosa, and Agbar (Aguas de Barcelona). We include in our analysis two big firms, Telefónica and Santander, probably the best-known Spanish multinationals, and two other firms, Unión Fenosa and Agbar, which present interesting peculiarities: Unión Fenosa started its international expansion not in its main line of business, electricity generation and distribution, but in consultancy services, while Agbar based its overall corporate development on a long-lasting alliance with a French partner, Lyonnaise des Eaux, which is now in the process of taking over 75 percent of the equity of Agbar. Although each case exhibits its own distinctive features, they followed three common patterns in their corporate expansion:

(1) growth through participation in privatizations and license bidding, turning around formerly state-owned companies and/or efficiently executing new infrastructure investments;
(2) domestic and cross-border consolidation of their competitive position with a view to becoming global players in the industry; and
(3) diversification into related businesses, capitalizing on synergies stemming from technological developments and/or the firm's project-execution capabilities.

Two of these firms engaged in systematic attempts to explore and learn new capabilities shortly before and during the early stages of their international expansion (Santander and Agbar), while the other two focused on exploiting existing capabilities (Telefónica and Unión Fenosa). As shown in Table 6.1, Santander and Telefónica remained strategically independent from other corporations, while the international decisions made by Agbar and Unión Fenosa were subject to the influence of other firms with large equity stakes.

TELEFÓNICA

When it comes to global expansion, Telefónica is widely considered to be a trailblazer. Its international growth showed other Spanish and foreign firms that it was possible (and profitable) to expand abroad. The company's origins go back to 1924, with ITT as its main shareholder and technology partner. The government nationalized Telefónica in 1945 after purchasing ITT's 80 percent share. The company grew during the 1950s and 1960s, along with the expanding Spanish economy and rising standard of living of the population. The 31.86 percent equity stake that remained in the hands of the state was fully privatized in tranches during the 1990s, a process completed by 1997. Since its beginnings, the company had been granted a monopoly over all telephone services in Spain, with a view to developing

Table 6.1. *Four cases in infrastructure and financial services*

Exploration of new capabilities:	Strategic independence:	
	Low	High
High	Agbar	Santander
Low	Unión Fenosa	Telefónica

an integrated communications network across the entire country. This monopoly position lasted until 1998, when a new operator of fixed telecommunications obtained a license. Mobile telecommunications were liberalized earlier, in 1995.

Telefónica's first international steps took place in the late 1980s, and had Latin America as the destination. Back then, the company enjoyed a total monopoly of the domestic market. However, Spain's membership in the European Union meant that liberalization and deregulation would eventually arrive. In 1986, the year Spain entered the trade bloc, member countries agreed to create a single market for infrastructure services beginning in 1993. Telefónica realized that they needed to boost operational efficiency and expand internationally in order to maintain profitability over the long run. After years of international growth, Telefónica became one of the world's leading telecommunications companies, with a large presence in Latin America and Europe.

The company's main rivals in Spain are Vodafone and France Telecom (Orange). Telefónica has a market share of 75 percent in fixed telecommunications and 44.9 percent in mobile (CMT 2009). Within Latin America, its main rival is América Móvil, whose origins go back to the privatization of Mexico's national monopoly company (Telmex), and is owned by Carlos Slim. While as of September 30, 2009 Telefónica had 163.7 million customers in fifteen Latin American countries, America Móvil had 198.1 million customers in sixteen Latin American countries (58.3 million in Mexico). América

Móvil grew rapidly mainly through acquisitions and by following a low-cost strategy focused on pre-paid mobile services, a strategy that suited the needs of a wide range of clients in the area.

In Europe, Telefónica's main competitors are Vodafone and the domestic incumbent in each country. The competitive position of Telefónica within Europe has improved significantly after the acquisition of O2 in 2005, a mobile operator with a strong presence in the UK, Ireland, and Germany. When comparing the corporate expansion of Telefónica with that of the other main incumbents in Europe, a common pattern emerges. They all expanded abroad in anticipation of market liberalization (although Telefónica shows more of a focus on Latin America than the others), and their opportunities for expansion lie in offering an integrated bundle of services entailing, at a minimum, the so-called "quadruple play:" fixed telecommunications, mobile telecommunications, Internet access, and IPTV or TV services over the Internet (IDATE 2008: 67). The share of fixed telecommunications services in total revenue is shrinking, although the strategy of these firms is to quickly move to an integrated offering of fixed and mobile telecommunications. Telefónica is more internationalized than the rest of the European incumbents. In 2008, 63 percent of its revenues came from international markets, as opposed to 43 for France Télécom and 52 for Deutsche Telekom. As far as Asian markets are concerned, Telefónica entered China in 2005 through an alliance with China Netcom. Some of the Telefónica's rivals such as Vodafone, France Télécom, and Deutsche Telekom are also present in China. As far as the African continent goes, Telefónica is present in Morocco and South Africa. Vodafone, Deutsche Telekom, and Verizon are also present in South Africa.

Telefónica's corporate expansion has followed the three-pronged pattern described above: competitive bidding for local licenses, international consolidation, and business diversification. Initially, Telefónica's international activities were aimed at entering new countries through privatizations or license bidding for fixed and/or mobile telecommunications services. This is the standard means of entry into regulated industries and, given that opportunities arise as the political decision to liberalize entry or to privatize is made, it cannot be fully planned. Companies do not usually come to these bids on their own, but as members of bidding consortia. These consortia are formed by at least one telecom carrier, local partners that provide some local infrastructure and connections and, finally, financial partners. Telefónica's first international market entry took place in Chile in 1989 as part of the consortium that won the privatization of the long-distance carrier Empresa Nacional de Telecomunicaciones (Entel Chile). Telefónica also had the opportunity to acquire a controlling stake in the local Chilean phone carrier CTC. Under the management of Telefónica, CTC – nowadays known as Telefónica Chile – became an integrated provider of telecommunications services. One remarkable aspect of Telefónica's expansion is that the company took advantage of all of the opportunities arising in Latin America before even completing the process of improving its operational efficiency in the home country. In the words of former Telefónica president Cándido Velázquez (1989–96), "given that the beginning of our international expansion coincided with a time in which the company had yet to recover from its image of being an inefficient operator within Spain, the international development of Telefónica, frequently referred to as 'the American adventure', was poorly understood. Today, however, everyone in Spain and abroad understands that this strategy was one of the best decisions the company ever made" (Velázquez 1995). By the end of the 1990s, Telefónica had entered Argentina, Venezuela, Puerto Rico, Peru, Colombia, and Brazil, in that order, first with local equity partners and then increasing its stake to 100 percent.

The Latin American market had always been a strategic priority for Telefónica. The overall plan was to build an integrated Latin American network of telecommunications services. For this reason, the strategic value of a new license in a specific country was higher for Telefónica than for its main competitors. This caused Telefónica to overbid in most of the tender processes in Latin America during the 1990s, paying in some cases twice as high as the second-best offer. Despite some criticism encountered along the way, the fact remains that Telefónica's competitive position in Latin America became the company's foundation for further growth elsewhere in the world. In 2008 35 percent of Telefónica's profits stemmed from Latin America.[4] Telefónica's commitment to the region and to each market greatly enhanced the company's relationships with local governments (Guillén 2005). In fact, outbidding for privatized firms or licenses could be considered as a unilateral commitment aimed at establishing a long-term relationship with the local government (Gulati et al. 1994). Telefónica's main rival in Latin America, America Móvil, relied more heavily on acquisitions of companies owned by other firms to build its position in the region, partly due to their more recent expansion. Its dominant position in Mexico constituted the basis for financing the purchase of telecommunications companies that were sold by US firms like AT&T or Verizon, who wished to withdraw from Latin America (van Agtmael 2007).

Another reason for Telefónica to overbid was its confidence in being capable of turning around the privatized or acquired companies. In fact, the strategy of Telefónica when entering into a new country was aimed at improving the operational efficiency of the acquired company as well as the quality and reliability of the service. In fact, this was labeled as a "turnaround strategy" by former president Velázquez (Velázquez 1995). Telefónica could count on linguistic affinities and good relationships with local governments. But its main capability had to do with the know-how accumulated in Spain and each successive country entered as to how to improve service and make investments to meet demand that had gone unsatisfied after decades of underinvestment under state ownership. Telefónica had successfully tackled similar problems in Spain during the early 1980s, while North American firms from a more mature market were less prepared to do so. As former Telefónica Internacional chief executive Iñaki Santillana said in 1994, "we have the best ditch-digging

---

[4] "A Good Bet?" *The Economist*, April 30, 2009.

technology around ... When it comes to installing a million access lines in record time, no one can beat us."[5] In another interview he argued that, in Latin American countries, "we were facing problems of unsatisfied demand that we had solved not long ago in Spain. These problems required short-term project management expertise. North American firms ... were not used to installing so many lines at the same time, as their market had become saturated a long time ago."[6]

While the strategy of overbidding for Latin American privatizations proved fruitful for Telefónica, it led to an abject failure in the case of the European UMTS (third generation) licensing bidding process of 2000. In partnership with other firms, Telefónica won licenses in Germany, Austria, Switzerland, and Italy. In the midst of the technology bubble, the companies grossly overestimated the future returns stemming from new value-added telecommunications services such as video calls or phone TV, and underestimated the investments in infrastructure required to provide such services. In addition, in each of those countries the market was dominated by a national champion, the telecommunication network was fully developed, and the local government was not looking for a long-term relationship with a foreign firm, in sharp contrast with Latin America. Telefónica paid €6,280 million, representing 23.3 percent of its debt burden at the time.[7] Telefónica never made use of these licenses. The company sold the Austrian license in 2003 and lost its licenses in the remaining countries, without the option to resell, due to its failure to meet investment commitments.

Over time, it seems that Telefónica learned to adjust the premium paid in bids, as in Morocco in 1999, when it competed for the second mobile license through MEDITEL, a joint venture with Portugal Telecom and local partners.[8] In the 2005 privatization of

---

[5] *New York Times*, April 4, 1994.

[6] Interview transcript in *Bit*, no. 128, July–August, 2001. Online, available at: www.coit.es/publicac/publbit/bit128/perfil.htm.

[7] Telefónica, 2000 Annual Report.

[8] In August 2009 Telefonica and Portugal Telecom sold their equity stakes to their local partners.

Cesky Telecom, Telefónica's bid was just 4.3 percent higher than the second-largest bid. This somewhat reduced premium contrasts with the $2,000 million bid made in 1994 for 35 percent of Peru's telephone companies, Compañía Peruana de Teléfonos and Entel Perú, which was nearly twice as much as the next highest bid.

In addition to market entry, Telefónica has actively participated in the global consolidation of the telecommunications industry through alliances. During the 1990s, expectations were raised on the formation of global alliances to develop multi-country projects (Garcia-Canal and Sanchez-Lorda 2007). These projects were aimed at providing global services to multinational corporations, such as end-to-end, multi-country communication systems. The first global alliance in which Telefónica took part was Unisource, created in 1992 by the Dutch operator PTT Telecom and the Swedish operator Telia AB. Swiss Telecom and Telefónica joined the alliance in 1993. The alliance became truly global with the addition of AT&T in 1994. However, it never worked well and, at the beginning of 1997, coinciding with the appointment of Juan Villalonga as President of Telefónica and the subsequent replacement of senior executives after the electoral victory of the Conservative Party, the Spanish company decided to leave Unisource. At the same time, Telefónica started to negotiate a new global alliance with BT and MCI, which were planning a merger. However, the project was aborted when the North American firm WorldCom took over MCI in November 1997, prior to the actual merger between BT and MCI. Given this new scenario, Telefónica reconsidered its agreements with BT and MCI, choosing WorldCom as its main partner. The alliance came to an end in 2000, having accomplished none of its original goals.

Telefónica is not alone in its failure to form global alliances, as no firm in the telecommunications industry has been able to implement one successfully. Global alliances are part of a global strategy of acquiring presence in the most important markets in order to provide value-added services to large multinational firms (Bonardi 2004; García-Canal et al. 2002). However, in order to succeed, these alliances require not only that all of the partners cooperate (as in any alliance), but also that each of the partner's other alliances are compatible with the global alliance being pursued, and, most importantly, that all governments involved are willing to collaborate. The difficulty in meeting this last requirement makes it clear that global alliances in the telecommunications industry would have failed even if the partners had been fully committed to them. For this reason, telecommunications companies gradually abandoned the idea of pursuing global strategies, adopting instead multi-domestic, one-country-at-a-time approaches to foreign expansion (Bonardi 2004). As Telefónica's top executive since 2000, César Alierta, once said, "in this company, we always say that we are not a multinational firm, but rather a multi-domestic company, and the message conveyed to each executive is precisely this: we are a company that is deeply rooted in each of the countries in which we operate."[9] Although some of Telefónica's former presidents tried to follow a global strategy, over time the company learned that it was better to have a sound multi-domestic strategy than an ambitious global strategy built over weak global alliances.[10]

Building on this multi-domestic approach, Telefónica developed a policy of mergers and acquisitions to fill in gaps in its international network. The company entered Mexico in 2001, acquiring Pegaso Telefonía Móvil. In Brazil, they merged their assets with Portugal Telecom through the creation of the Vivo joint venture. The leadership position of Vivo in Brazil was reinforced in 2007 with the acquisitions of Telemig Celular and Amazonia Celular. However, the most important acquisition in Latin America was the purchase of BellSouth's operations in 2004 for $5,850 million. As mentioned above, in Europe, the most important acquisitions were O2, which gave the firm an increased presence in the UK and Germany, and Cesky Telecom in the Czech Republic. In November 2009 Telefónica

---

[9] César Alierta, President, Telefónica, *Diario de Sesiones del Senado*: Comisión de Asuntos Iberoamericanos 155, June 26, 2001, p. 21.
[10] "La Multinacional Multidoméstica", *El País*, March 26, 2006.

acquired Hansenet, a German mobile telecommunications operator. Telefónica also holds some minority stakes in other operators, such as Portugal Telecom and Telecom Italia. In Asia, the company has an equity stake in China Netcom since 2005 (now China Unicom, after the merger between China Netcom and China Unicom in 2008). Both companies have several projects underway, such as the development of a virtual private network on a global scale. Recently, both companies have cemented their relationship through a minority equity exchange, in which Telefonica raised its stake from 5.38 percent to 8.06 percent, and China Unicom acquired a 0.87 percent stake in the equity of Telefónica.[11]

In addition to privatizations and acquisitions, Telefónica has expanded its business through diversification. The most recent move was the acquisition in December 2009 of Jajah, the Silicon Valley Internet phone company that offers voice over internet protocol (VoIP) services. However, Telefónica entered into less related business through acquisitions, just like other global telecommunication companies and, like all of the others, failed to create value in a majority of the cases. The most important deals were the acquisitions of the Internet portal Lycos in the United States, the media producer Endemol, and the Internet bank Uno-e. The logic behind these investments was the supposed convergence among the media, financial services, and telecommunications industries. Telefónica president Juan Villalonga (1996–2000) was directly responsible for this strategy.

Telefónica originally entered the Internet content business in 1999 by acquiring an Internet portal in Spain, renamed Terra, which became the number one portal in the Spanish language after establishing subsidiaries in all of the countries in which Telefónica was present as a telecommunications operator. With the aim of complementing the international presence of Terra and enriching its

---

[11] Information disclosed by Telefónica to the Comisión Nacional del Mercado de Valores (relevant fact number 115173, October 21, 2009).

contents in English, Telefónica acquired Lycos in 2000, perhaps the most ruinous investments it ever made. Even though Terra-Lycos became the number three Internet portal in the world at some point, virtually none of the expected synergies materialized, and the portal never turned a profit. Lycos (excluding the Internet access business and Terra USA) was sold in 2004 to Daum Communications of South Korea for about 1 percent of what Telefónica had originally paid.

In the TV business, Telefónica was a shareholder of Antena3 TV, a Spanish TV channel from 1997 to 2003. During this time, the company led a platform to build a digital satellite TV channel named Vía Digital that in 2003 merged with Sogecable, a company belonging to the media group PRISA, which provided an alternative digital platform (Canal Satélite Digital) to launch a joint platform, Digital+. This merger was motivated by the poor results of the satellite pay-TV business. As of December 2009, Telefónica had a 21 percent stake in Digital+ and offered TV services over ADSL (IPTV). Telefónica's most important move in the media industry was the acquisition in 2000 of Endemol, the company that generated some ideas for reality TV shows like *Big Brother*. Endemol was sold in 2007 for nearly half the original price paid by Telefónica.

One of Telefónica's most controversial diversification moves was the equity alliance with BBVA, the second-largest Spanish bank. This was an extremely complex alliance aimed at exploiting the synergies between telecommunications and banking, one that involved a minority cross-shareholding, interlocking directorates, and joint ownership of an online bank (Uno-e). The alliance was formed in 2000, just one month before the general election in Spain that returned the Conservative Party to power for a second term. The alliance did not bring about any tangible benefits, and Uno-e is currently 100 percent owned by BBVA. The companies still maintain an equity position in each other.

The main lesson that Telefónica learned from diversification is that there is no need to have a wholly-owned subsidiary or an equity position in a company in order to exploit the synergies with businesses related to the telecommunications industry. Each of the acquisitions mentioned above were geared toward gaining exclusive rights over contents or services. However, like other telecommunication companies around the world, Telefónica fell victim to the rosy predictions common during the technology bubble of the late 1990s, which led them to pay exuberant premiums. Telefónica finalized the Endemol, Lycos, and BBVA deals in 2000, at the peak of the bubble. Adding to the complexities and imponderables, each acquisition or alliance was scrutinized by antitrust authorities in order to prevent any dominant position in the new markets created by technological innovations. For instance, the Telefónica–BBVA alliance was carefully examined and closely monitored in order to prevent putting other banks at a disadvantage.

In spite of these failures and difficulties, Telefónica remains the biggest Spanish multinational and the second-largest in its industry worldwide. Its international expansion is not only important per se, but also because it was the first company in the regulated sectors to put in practice a model of international expansion based on a strong position in the domestic market on the one hand, and the exploitation of the experience and political capabilities developed at home in foreign markets, on the other. This model was replicated by other main players in regulated industries, and lies at the heart of the success of Spanish multinationals in infrastructure and financial services. Over the years, Telefónica became a master at exploiting its project-execution and political capabilities. Operating in risky countries, especially Latin America, was not always easy (Ontiveros *et al.* 2004). However, Telefónica clearly illustrates that making profits in Europe can be more complicated than in Latin America, and that diversifying into other business can be even more difficult. There are some important parallels between Telefónica and América Móvil, its main rival in Latin America. Both companies had a strong position at home, and both took advantage of windows of opportunity for growth in Latin America through privatizations and/or the corporate restructuring of US companies with operations in the region. Both have been far more successful in their expansion into Latin America than in other regions of the world, suggesting that their political capabilities are not equally valuable across the world.

UNIÓN FENOSA

The internationalization of Unión Fenosa, an electrical utility, also followed a logic based on the exploitation of project-execution and political skills. However, what makes Unión Fenosa's case particularly interesting is that it is probably the company that has made the most intensive use of management expertise in its international expansion. In fact, the company's foreign growth could be considered as the outcome of a process of internal change aimed at boosting the efficiency of its businesses and internal processes.

Unión Fenosa is the third-largest firm in the Spanish electricity industry, after Endesa and Iberdrola, whose revenues more than double those of Fenosa, which in turn is twice as big as the fourth firm, Hidroeléctrica del Cantábrico, a subsidiary of Portugal's EDP. These firms are all vertically integrated from electricity generation to transport and retail distribution.

Since 1980 the electricity industry in Spain has undergone important changes. Two waves of restructuring can be identified, one domestic and the other European in scope. The first wave, domestic consolidation, consisted of mergers and acquisitions, and a process of liberalization, both driven by politicians and regulators. As a result, a national champion emerged, Endesa, which included the state's interests in the electricity industry plus some acquired regional companies. The second and third players in the industry emerged from two mergers: Iberdrola (the outcome of the 1991 merger between Hidroeléctrica Española and Iberduero) and Unión Eléctrica Fenosa (the result of the 1982 merger between Union Eléctrica and Fenosa). During this process, Endesa was fully privatized and the market witnessed a level of liberalization that allowed large electricity customers to choose their suppliers, as well as the setting up of a wholesale market through which energy producers could sell the electricity they generated. The effects of this liberalization, however, were limited by the market power associated with the size and degree of vertical integration of the two largest players in the industry, which curbed the efficiency gains from these reforms (López Milla 2003), as well as the possibility of further domestic mergers.

Consolidation at the European level started in the year 2000 and has yet to conclude. The coming of the European single market for electricity, among other factors, boosted cross-border mergers and acquisitions (Ortiz de Urbina and Montoro 2007). Friendly domestic mergers between electricity firms were replaced by hostile (or, at least, comparatively less friendly) cross-border and/or cross-industry takeovers. Attempts at domestic intra-industry mergers like Fenosa-Hidrocantábrico or Endesa-Iberdrola were effectively blocked by the regulators when they imposed onerous conditions for the approval of the deals. The 2001 acquisition of Hidrocantábrico by a consortium led by Portugal's EDP was the deal that kick-started the consolidation wave in Spain. Other competing bids for Hidrocantábrico were made by American TXU, German En-BW and Fenosa. Despite being the largest Spanish firm, Endesa was also a target. Gas Natural and E.ON both unsuccessfully attempted a takeover, and later Acciona and Italy's ENEL came to control it.[12] There were also some failed attempts to control Iberdrola, one of them part of the proposed merger between Endesa and Gas Natural. Spanish electricity firms also took over other European firms: Iberdrola acquired French Perfect Wind SAS in 2006 and Scottish Power in 2007. These, however, had not discouraged attempts to take over the company. In fact, ACS, the world's largest infrastructure management group and the main shareholder of Iberdrola, attempted in 2009 to gain a controlling stake in the firm. ACS, until 2008 Fenosa's largest shareholder, agreed to sell

---

[12] Enel had acquired recently the Acciona shares, gaining full control of Endesa. Ironically the Enel bid was supported by the Spanish government because of the presence of a Spanish company in the bidding group.

its stake to Gas Natural and planned to invest part of the money in Iberdrola. ACS is not alone in the contest for Iberdrola, as French EDF is also interested. The whole European electricity industry is undergoing consolidation. The firms emerging as the main players are E.ON, EDF, Suez and, with the acquisition of Endesa, Enel. The process of international consolidation is in many ways driven by politicians and regulators. In fact, most of those firms are still state-owned, at least in part.

Unión Fenosa also had a presence in the gas industry, where the main players were Gas Natural (which in 2009 successfully bid for Fenosa, although it had previously entered the electricity industry as a producer and seller in the free market), Cepsa (in which Fenosa had, until recently, a minority equity stake), and Naturgas. Gas and electricity are industries with huge synergies, not only because gas is the fuel used in combined-cycle turbines (the most advanced technology in power generation nowadays), but also because both are network industries in which the experience accrued in one business can be capitalized in the other and because the customers to be served may be the same.

At the time of their merger in 1982, Unión Eléctrica and Fenosa were under financial stress. Due to their commitment to large investments in power-generation plants, both of them were heavily into debt. Given the economic crisis that Spain was facing at that time, with unemployment above 20 percent, these investments generated lower cash flows than expected. To make matters worse, interest rates were on the rise. The merger between both companies should have alleviated this problem. However, it posed several challenges. First of all, the companies had different corporate cultures and different geographical scopes. In addition, they had excess personnel, but it was expensive and unpopular to lay off workers at the time. In order to boost efficiency levels and to overcome these obstacles, Unión Fenosa launched the so-called "Fénix" project to improve operational efficiency by taking advantage of new technologies in order to redefine internal processes and make them more reliable, efficient, and capital-intensive. This project, in fact, featured some of the ideas that flourished in the 1990s under the label of business process re-engineering, such as the use of information technologies and quality teams to redesign business processes, as well as other tools to achieve organizational change and engage in knowledge management.

One of the most important outcomes of this project was a new corporate culture whereby the know-how generated inside the company had to be fully exploited. As stated by the former General Manager of Unión Fenosa Internacional, José Manuel Prieto Iglesias, "one of the principles of Union Fenosa's business strategy is the capability to turn into value the knowledge and experience accrued by all the people belonging to the organization" (Prieto Iglesias 2002: 189). In order to fully exploit this knowledge base, the company set up Norsistemas and Norconsult, two companies providing consultancy services to Spanish firms in the fields of systems development, human resources, and change management.

The most immediate outcomes of the Fénix project were some state-of-the-art information management systems to manage two key processes, the Sistema de Gestión Comercial (commercial management system), and the Sistema de Gestión de la Distribución (distribution management system). Word quickly got around other companies, especially outside Spain, which contacted Unión Fenosa to buy a license to use them. However, selling these systems was not like selling turnkey software. In order to guarantee ease of use to other firms abroad, a lot of adjustments were required to adapt these systems to the requirements of each client, as well as to the legal norms, including tax rules, and the business and banking practices of each country. Thus, each and every project involving technology transfer required a joint team in which people from the client company adapted and improved the systems with the help of Unión Fenosa's experts. In addition, the systems sometimes required a complete turnaround of the company, which meant that their transfer also entailed some additional services such as power projects engineering, business processes re-engineering, and change management. For this reason, the company set up a consultancy branch, the Departamento de Acción y Consultoría Externa, which grew quickly during the 1990s. The company even acted as a consultant for foreign governments and regulators, advising them on the design of privatization processes. This department became an integrated, full-service consultancy for utilities firms. The success in these technology transfer initiatives, at a time when the company was burdened by heavy debts, offered an alternative path to internationalization, one that consisted in exploiting its managerial and organizational knowledge for the provision of customized consultancy services.

Unión Fenosa's first international foray into technology transfer began in 1988 with a project for the improvement of management systems at the state-owned Uruguayan firm Usinas y Transmisiones Eléctricas (UTE). Unión Fenosa created its first foreign subsidiary, Ibersis, which later expanded into the main countries of Latin America. In 1991, Fenosa entered Eastern Europe with the formation of Energoinfo. Since then, Unión Fenosa has advised the Slovakian Ministry of the Economy and Energy as well as several local companies. In 1994 the company set up Iberpacific as the vehicle for its expansion into the Asia-Pacific area, with Manila Electric Railroad and Light Company (MERALCO) as their first client. In 1995 it established Iberáfrica to serve the African market with the Kenya Power & Lighting Company Ltd (KPLC) as their first client.

Despite its success in the international transfer of knowledge, there were a number of reasons why it remained unclear whether Unión Fenosa was fully exploiting its competitive advantages by acting only as an exporter of services. First of all, not all of the clients were licensing the company's entire set of systems and practices, so not all of their know-how was being transferred to each client, meaning the company was not maximizing the use of its intangible assets and knowledge. In addition to this, even if the client were using all of Unión Fenosa's systems, their exploitation required some managerial know-how that was more difficult to transfer to the client.

For instance, Unión Fenosa's systems allowed the user company to identify losses of energy in distribution networks, as well as to quickly calculate the power consumption of each customer in order to charge for these services. Thus, it was easy to locate illegal connections to the electricity distribution network and consumers who were failing to pay for energy consumption – two very widespread problems in Latin American markets and in emerging markets more generally. However, fixing these issues required some decisions that Unión Fenosa's consulting clients were not used to making, such as canceling service to non-payers (something that usually requires a complex legal process) or suppressing every illegal connection to the network, which in some instances could mean leaving entire neighborhoods without electricity, as in the cases of the Argentinean "villas" or Brazilian "favelas." These decisions were especially difficult in the case of state-owned companies that were largely considered to be part of a welfare state of sorts. Thus, a licensee of Unión Fenosa's systems could not be exploiting the transferred know-how in the same way a subsidiary under Unión Fenosa's equity control would, and for this reason the price to be charged for the systems could not be based on all of the potential gains that they could generate.

The wave of electricity and gas privatizations of the 1990s led other operators, including Spain's Endesa and Iberdrola, to expand abroad as foreign direct investors, thus limiting the potential market for consulting, and leading to some paradoxical situations in which the main beneficiary from the transfer of Unión Fenosa's knowledge to a state-owned company in an emerging economy would be the foreign investor. In fact, during the early 1990s, the evolution of Unión Fenosa's share prices was worse than Iberdrola's and, especially, Endesa's. Investors were rewarding international expansion through foreign direct investment in the electricity business, not international consulting. As a result, Unión Fenosa turned to foreign direct investment, guided by several principles: selective investment in countries with development potential, geographic diversification in order to reduce regulatory and macroeconomic risk, synergies with the consultancy branch, and leverage of experience and relationships developed in the past (Prieto Iglesias 2002). The strategy of the company translated into bids for public concessions and privatizations through alliances in which local, technical, and financial partners participated, but with Unión Fenosa retaining managerial and operational control. In order not to compromise its financial stability, Unión Fenosa initially took small equity stakes.

The first country in which Unión Fenosa invested was Argentina in 1995, although the company had acted as an operator in an electricity project in that country in 1993 without taking an equity position. The company entered Bolivia and the Philippines in 1997, through a minority equity stake in Meralco. In 1998, Mexico became the next host country, which became its most important foreign market. In just two years, 1999 and 2000, Unión Fenosa made investments in Guatemala, the Dominican Republic, Nicaragua, Costa Rica, Colombia, Ecuador, and Moldova. It was at that time that the share price of Unión Fenosa rose relative to its domestic rivals, more than compensating for its underperformance during the 1990s.

From 2001 onwards, Unión Fenosa's international expansion entered a new phase. With most of the privatization processes already completed at that time and the financial crisis of Argentina cooling the expectations of foreign investors (Unión Fenosa had divested from Argentina in 1999), it was not the best time to make further investments in Latin America. Unión Fenosa focused its efforts on consolidating its position in Mexico, Central America, and Colombia. The company faced many challenges and had to exercise its political skills. For instance, in Colombia it pressed the government into negotiations over a subsidy to cover the cost of illegal connections to the grid in low-income neighborhoods. Unión Fenosa cut service repeatedly until social demonstrations forced the government to compromise. As a result of the settlement of the dispute, electricity counters were installed in the affected neighborhoods.

The consulting business kept on growing even as Unión Fenosa turned its attention to foreign investment. Within Spain, new demand came from new entrants into the telecommunications sector. Outside Spain, knowledge and systems were transferred to the firm's acquisitions in Latin America and elsewhere, and also to independent clients in Western Europe. Realizing that the dispersion of consulting activities across a number of companies within the group limited synergies and growth, the company created an umbrella brand and holding company called Soluziona.

Unión Fenosa sought to exploit synergies in other areas. Given the connections between electricity and gas, especially with the combined-cycle gas turbines (CCGT), the company signed long-term contracts with foreign suppliers such as the Egyptian General Petroleum Corporation in 2000 and the Sultanate of Oman in 2002. Unión Fenosa also invested, together with its suppliers, in LNG (liquefied natural gas) infrastructure. In 2003 the company signed a strategic alliance with Italy's ENI, which entailed ENI taking a 50 percent stake in Unión Fenosa Gas, as well as the development of several joint projects. Another alliance was signed with the Russian group ITERA in 2001, although no projects materialized. The policy of securing fuel supplies also led Unión Fenosa to acquire a coal mine in South Africa in 2006, aimed exclusively at meeting the needs of coal-based production plants in Spain.

Once fuel supplies were secured, the company built several CCGT power stations in Spain and entered the Spanish gas distribution industry. The company also entered the gas industry in other countries, such as Uruguay and the UK. Fenosa entered Uruguay's gas distribution industry in 1998. In the UK, Fenosa acquired Cambridge Water in 1999, a diversified utility distributor with interests in water, electricity, and gas. However, this company was mainly a water distributor with a recent involvement in the electricity and gas industries, and it was sold in tranches.

Unión Fenosa also diversified into telecommunications, though only in Spain. In collaboration with its main shareholders (Endesa and Banco Central Hispano), Unión Fenosa took part in several consortia aimed at developing new operators of fixed and mobile telecommunications in Spain (Airtel, Retevisión, and later Amena and Auna). These investments were highly profitable for Fenosa, as the company managed to sell its equity positions in Airtel and Auna with large profits, and also because these investments allowed the consultancy branch of the company to act as a provider of services for these companies.

Unlike Telefónica, the international expansion and corporate growth of Unión Fenosa was shaped by the presence of controlling shareholders. Even though the company enjoyed ample autonomy when it came to defining its strategy, the priorities of its shareholders also played a key role, as the diversification into telecommunications shows. In the early 1990s, Fenosa's main shareholders were Banco Central Hispano (BCH) and Endesa, who jointly controlled a holding company with a 14.36 percent equity position in Unión Fenosa. The chairman of the board of BCH was also chairman of Unión Fenosa, although the respective managerial hierarchies operated entirely separate from each other. Still, BCH frequently acted as the financial partner and advisor when it came to making major investments. In addition, BCH owned construction firms, such as Dragados, which frequently undertook projects for Unión Fenosa.

The 1999 merger of BCH and Banco Santander brought about significant changes. Under the leadership of Emilio Botín, the merged bank developed a more instrumental approach to equity stakes in non-financial companies (Guillén and Tschoegl 2008), treating its stake in Unión Fenosa as a financial investment. As Emilio Botín said in 2002, once the integration process between the BCH and Santander was completed, "we have actively managed our portfolio [of stakes in non-financial firms] with a single goal: to create value for our shareholders, which in some occasions entails selling and, in others when we see projects with potential, buying."[13] This strategy led the bank to raise its equity stake in Unión Fenosa to 22 percent.

[13] Emilio Botín's address at a press conference held in Madrid, January 22, 2002. Online, available at: www.acceso.com/display_release.html?id=4213.

In 2005 the Santander sold its stake to ACS, obtaining capital gains of €1,160 million. This deal took place in the midst of a high-stakes battle over Endesa, in which different groups of large firms tried to control the country's largest electrical utility. In the words of the Chairman and CEO of ACS, Florentino Pérez, constructing firms have "diversified into activities requiring the same culture as that of the contractor … entering services, infrastructure concessions and, more recently, energy."[14] A controlling stake in Unión Fenosa offered two benefits to ACS. On the one hand, the possibility to reduce its exposure to the cyclical nature of the construction business, and on the other the potential for playing a pivotal role in the restructuring of the energy sector in Spain. In fact, ACS was more proactive than Santander in guiding the strategic decisions of Unión Fenosa, especially as it built its stake to 45 percent. For example, ACS asked the company to sell Soluziona to Indra, a high-tech systems developer, in exchange for an equity stake. After the deal, Unión Fenosa became, to use Hennart and Reddy's (1997) terminology, more "digestible," i.e. easy to acquire and restructure by another energy firm. Moreover, ACS has also acquired a minority stake in Iberdrola, and could have orchestrated a merger between the two companies. But as regulators and the government balked at the idea, ACS sold in 2009 its stake in Unión Fenosa to Gas Natural, which had long waited for the opportunity to expand its electricity business. With this deal, ACS has pocketed €2,729 million in capital gains.[15] Unión Fenosa's lack of strategic independence has meant all along that its process of corporate expansion could not be fully developed because of the priorities of its main shareholders.

SANTANDER

Telefónica and Unión Fenosa illustrate a process of internationalization based on capabilities developed in the home country, barely

[14] *El País*, December 24, 2006.
[15] Information disclosed by ACS to the Comisión Nacional del Mercado de Valores (relevant fact number 96363, July 31, 2008).

using the process of international expansion as a way to explore and acquire new capabilities. Banco Santander represents the exact opposite. The bank systematically used foreign alliances, acquisitions, and greenfield investments to gain access to new resources with which to bolster its international competitiveness and stature.

Santander is one of the world's largest banks, and has a major presence in Latin America and the UK as well as the Iberian Peninsula. It is also a leader in consumer finance in Eastern and Western Europe, and owns a medium-sized bank in the United States. It was founded in 1857 as a local bank in Santander, a small city in northern Spain. It remained a tiny provincial player until the 1950s, when it grew organically and via acquisitions to become a bank of national stature (Guillén and Tschoegl 2008). International growth started during the 1960s in the form of representative offices in several Latin American countries during the 1960s. Between 1963 and 1982, Santander entered, through foreign direct investments, into Argentina, Mexico, Panama, the Dominican Republic, Costa Rica, Guatemala, Chile, Ecuador, and Uruguay. During the late 1970s and 1980s, however, Santander divested from most of these countries, except for Chile and Uruguay. After taking over from his father as chief executive in 1986, Emilio Botín led the bank from being the sixth-largest in Spain and 152nd worldwide to becoming one of the world's top-ten financial institutions and the largest in the eurozone.

Interestingly, the appointment of Mr. Botín to the presidency of the bank coincided with Spain's entry into the EU and a liberalization process of financial services in Spain that boosted competition and rivalry in an industry not hitherto used to them. It was a time of great uncertainty regarding the future of banking, and the only thing that was clear was that banking in Spain would never again be the same. For this reason, leadership and strategic direction were critical in the bank's expansion.

Three stages can be identified in its recent corporate expansion. An initial stage that started in 1986 with the appointment of Mr. Botín and lasted until 1994. The strategy followed by the bank during this period was a combination of commercial aggressiveness in the domestic business and a number of strategic alliances in the form of minority equity exchanges with other international banks and financial institutions. When Spanish banks started to compete, an increasingly intense rivalry started in which Santander most often acted as a first mover. For instance, it developed an aggressive marketing strategy, launching products like the "supercuenta" (a high-interest checking account) and "superhipoteca" (a low-interest mortgage), accompanied by massive marketing efforts. Other banks, especially the BBV (nowadays BBVA) reacted by launching alternative products. This strategy boosted organic growth in a context in which its main rivals were trying to react to domestic mergers, such as those between Bilbao and Vizcaya, and Central and Hispano. The growth in the Spanish market culminated during this phase with the acquisition of Banesto, a bank in financial straits.

In a second stage lasting from 1995 to 2003, Santander continued its strategy of alliances, but started to invest aggressively in Latin America through acquisitions in the most important countries, taking advantage of banking reforms and liberalization processes that opened new opportunities. At the end of this period, they acquired several banks in Argentina, Brazil, Chile, Colombia, Mexico, Peru, and Venezuela and consolidated their presence in Puerto Rico. During this stage, the bank also completed its consolidation in Spain via a merger with the Central Hispano Bank in 1999. This was the biggest merger ever in the Spanish banking industry and boosted the growth of the bank, as BCH had a significant number of international investments and alliances and numerous equity stakes in non-financial firms. In fact, the Latin American investments of BCH plus Santander's aggressive acquisition strategy reinforced its leadership in Latin America. However, despite being billed as a merger of equals, the process of integration proved dysfunctional, and ended with Emilio Botín regaining full control in 2002.

During the third stage, the bank began its consolidation as a global player, replacing its policy of alliances with a strategy of acquisitions in Europe and the United States. This stage started with the acquisition of Abbey in 2004 and implied the dissolution of Santander Bank's most successful alliance; namely, that with Royal Bank of Scotland (RBS). To some extent this (friendly) divorce also implied that the bank was strong enough to position itself as a global player. During this period, Santander also bought Sovereign Bankcorp in the United States, starting with 20 percent in 2005, an additional 5 percent in 2006, and the remaining 75 percent in the midst of the financial crisis of 2009. The bank also bought Alliance & Leicester and Bradford & Bingley in the UK, and took part – jointly with Fortis and Royal Bank of Scotland – in a consortium to buy ABN AMRO in 2007. In this deal, Santander gained control over Banco Real in Brazil and Antoveneta in Italy, although the Italian bank was sold one month after its acquisition with a €2,400 million capital gain.[16] This period represented a qualitative leap for Santander. A common feature of the acquired banks was that they were all either underperformers or financially troubled. The transfer of Santander's expertise in financial and risk management to the acquired banks made possible their turnaround. During this phase, Santander also divested its industrial group, most of it inherited from the acquisition of other banks. As in Unión Fenosa's case, the industrial group was never a strategic priority within the corporate expansion of the bank, although the bank had excelled in the fine art of buying and selling companies, obtaining hefty capital gains in the process.

As important as its competitive aggressiveness in the domestic market was, the seeds of Santander's rise to global prominence were planted during the late 1980s and early 1990s in Latin America and Europe through alliances and greenfield investments in strategic areas. Santander used equity and non-equity alliances with Cariplo, San Paolo di Torino (Italy), Commerzbank (Germany), Société Générale (France), Metropolitan Life (the US insurer), Kemper (a US fund manager), Nomura (Japan), and the Royal Bank of Scotland

[16] El País, November 9, 2007; Expansión, November 9, 2007.

(RBS) to learn about new marketing ideas and banking technologies, and to explore market opportunities.

The Santander–RBS alliance was by far the most successful partnership. It comprised a framework agreement specifying several activities to be jointly developed, an equity cross-shareholding, and interlocking directorates. Santander acquired 9.9 percent of RBS, and the latter 4.9 percent of Santander. The two banks became each other's largest shareholders. The framework agreement specified three areas of cooperation, namely, a coordinated investment policy in Europe, the interconnection of their branch networks in Spain and the United Kingdom, and the development of a technological agreement to facilitate international money transfers. Even though activity in the first two areas was not intense, the partners learned much from monitoring each other's activities. This was especially the case with Santander. A joint committee met every six weeks to exchange information. These meetings were crucial in developing trust between the two banks and exchanging know-how and information, which in the end was the most important outcome of the alliance. In fact, RBS provided Santander with advice, support and, in some cases, financing at critical junctures, including its 1999 merger with BCH and the 2000 acquisition of Banespa in Brazil. Even after the alliance was formally dissolved in 2004 as a prerequisite for Santander's acquisition of RBS's rival Abbey National Bank, the two banks continued to collaborate, as in the daring acquisition of ABN AMRO in 2007. Emilio Botín summarized the benefits achieved through this alliance: "Each time we met, we challenged each other, shared ideas and offered our support. We learned a lot from each other. And we were there to support each other when help was needed. Analysts cannot understand the importance of such relationships."[17]

A second way in which Santander used international expansion to acquire new resources and capabilities had to do with its

---

[17] "Botin Sees No Advantages from Cross Border Mergers," *Reuters News*, January 31, 2000.

investment banking operation, Santander Investment. Founded in 1984, it established operations throughout Latin America during the 1980s, in the wake of the debt crisis of 1982, at roughly the same time that Santander was itself selling some of its scattered minority stakes in small banks throughout the region. In 1988 Emilio Botín dispatched his daughter, Ana Patricia, who was working at JP Morgan, to help run Santander Investment. After some reorganization, in 1991 she became Director General of Banco Santander de Negocios, and in 1994 CEO. Although the actual profitability of the activities undertaken by Santander in investment banking and capital markets remains a hotly debated issue to this day, Ana Patricia Botín contributed to laying the foundations for the bank's extraordinary Latin American expansion into commercial banking during the 1990s. Specifically, investment banking contributed to gathering information and accumulating experience about a remarkably volatile part of the world. It also provided a training ground for a cadre of sharp young managers who came to know each other well and learned to operate as a team (Guillén and Tschoegl 2008). Unlike Telefónica and Unión Fenosa, Santander's international expansion entailed exploration of new capabilities and exploitation of existing ones, deploying a similar template in each market: learning through alliances or small investments, turning around acquired banks, organic growth, further acquisitions to gain critical mass, and transfer of the learning from one country to the next.

AGBAR

Sociedad General de Aguas de Barcelona (Agbar) is the head of a business group that leads the way in the business of water management and supply in Spain. Despite being in the process of becoming fully controlled by the French multinational group Suez-Lyonnais des Eaux (SLDE, which in 2009 became GazdeFrance-Suez), Agbar undertook a remarkable process of international expansion. Important growth opportunities presented themselves in the water industry, as many emerging, developing, and transition economies privatized water supply services. However, despite privatizations, water is not as globally consolidated as other regulated industries. There are two basic reasons for this: privatization has only occurred in developing and emerging economies, not in developed ones, and firms that have entered the industry diversifying from related business (such as construction or electricity) and/or that have expanded internationally in the field have obtained lower-than-expected results. As a consequence, multinational firms such as Bechtel, Bouygues or E.ON sold their water divisions after struggling for years (see Hall and Lobina 2007). Only Suez, Veolia, Berlinwasser, and Agbar stayed the course, although they have withdrawn from several countries. Firms focused solely on the water industry, such as Anglian Water, Severn Trent, or Vitens, have sold their international operations as well.

Spanish companies with interests in the water business have been an exception to this rule, as not only Agbar is active in international markets, but construction firms FCC and Sacyr Vallehermoso are also major global players. Comparing Agbar to Unión Fenosa and Santander is analytically useful because, like the latter, it used alliances to acquire new capabilities, although as in the case of Unión Fenosa, it is not strategically independent company.

The origins of Agbar can be traced back to the end of the nineteenth century, when foreign investors created a company to provide water supply services to the Barcelona metropolitan area. The company came under Spanish ownership at the turn of the century. Since then, it gradually grew by winning new service concessions, first in Catalonia and, after the 1970s, in the rest of Spain. Like other Spanish firms competing in regulated industries, the company began its international expansion in the early 1990s.

Agbar's foreign growth was fueled by financial and technological alliances. The main technological partner was Suez-Lyonnais des Eaux (formerly Lyonnais des Eaux, LDE), which has had an equity stake in Agbar since 1979. Endesa, with a 11.78 percent stake between 1994 and 2004, jointly developed with Agbar several water-related projects. For instance, in 1994 the two companies joined Argentaria, then a state-owned bank, to create Interagua, a vehicle used to participate in bids for foreign water projects and companies.

Lyonnais des Eaux also helped Agbar expand internationally, especially during its first steps in Argentina in 1992, and in Portugal, Chile, and Cuba in 1994. After creating Interagua, the company pursued new projects in these countries, especially in Argentina, and entered Morocco, Uruguay, Brazil and, more recently, Algeria. The company also entered the United States by acquiring a 20 percent stake in the equity of California's Western Water.

After 2000 the international strategy of Agbar underwent changes, as the company withdrew from some countries in which it faced increasing regulatory problems. The company is now present only in Chile, Cuba, and Colombia. In 2001 they sold their stake in Western Water. Instead, they turned their attention to Europe by taking over British Water in 2006.

The performance of most Latin American concessions was lower than expected. Indeed, Agbar was clearly the least successful of the firms analyzed in this chapter. However, this was not entirely Agbar's fault, as evidenced by the fact that many other multinational water companies have also withdrawn. The water business differs from telecommunications, electricity, or banking in that people are not used to paying for it, or at least paying for the true cost. Previous research has established that, among regulated industries, water is the hardest in which to turn a profit and one subject to frequent regulatory changes (Lobina and Hall 2007; Ontiveros *et al.* 2004).

As it wrestled with difficult conditions, Agbar gradually realized that their main asset was the ability to manage infrastructure, providing a quality service to their clients with efficiency levels that were higher than if the service had been undertaken by municipalities. Based on this capability and experience, the company decided not to emphasize the water business and to diversify instead into a number of other services such as tax collection, waste management, automobile safety inspections, health insurance, and even IT outsourcing. In fact, the company's diversification had already started before it expanded internationally in the water business, although its experience in the latter supported growth in the other activities. Agbar first diversified into waste management in Spain, acting in partnership with Suez-Lyonnais des Eaux. The company usually diversified via acquisition, following a trial-and-error tactic, with small investments acting as real options. As a former CEO of Agbar, José Luis Jove explains:

> We always start little by little, through small acquisitions and in good company. I wouldn't advise starting from scratch. In order to grow, we believe that it is a good idea to buy a small cell in the country or industry in which one is interested. This acquisition allows one to enter the industry and train people in the skills and idiosyncrasy of the new country or the new business from inside the company and, in case of a mistake, the economic damage is very greatly minimized ... We buy a small platform, relocate one, two or three people from the group there in order to get them to know the new business under real fire and, after that, we analyze this experience, examine the advantages and disadvantages and decide whether we go ahead in the business or abandon it.[18]

The most important industry into which the company diversified was certification and car safety inspection. Their first step was to acquire a small company in Spain, operating in the northern region of Galicia. Once they had analyzed the potential of this activity, Agbar created a division to perform these services throughout Spain and abroad. They either acquired companies or bid for concessions in countries such as Argentina, Portugal, and the United States. The company entered China in 2000 by forming a joint venture with the state-owned company Long Distance. In 2002 Agbar spun off all activities in this field by creating Applus+. Later, Unión Fenosa

[18] "El proceso de globalización es imparable, pero requiere control," *IESE Revista de Antiguos Alumnos*, September 2002, pp. 106–9.

and Caja Madrid, a large savings bank, acquired minority stakes in the company. Unión Fenosa merged its certification divisions into Applus+. The company kept growing in 2005 with the acquisition of the Danish network of vehicle inspection facilities, among others. In 2006, however, after taking into account the investment plan required to make Applus+ a leading company at a global level, Agbar's equity partners and shareholders decided to put the company up for sale. In 2007 it was sold to a venture capital firm. Another important diversification for Agbar was in the field of health insurance. The company is the main shareholder of Adeslas, in which French Mederic also has a 45 percent stake. Adelsas operates mainly within Spain.

Agbar's diversification and international expansion cannot be understood without taking into account the alliance with Suez-Lyonnais des Eaux, which, since the late 1980s, was the Spanish firm's reference partner for all its international projects, as well as Agbar's current main shareholder. At the outset of the alliance, Suez-Lyonnais des Eaux was a more experienced firm, not because it was older but because in France most water services were already privatized and the company was more diversified than Agbar.

In 1979 Suez-Lyonnais des Eaux bought shares in two of Agbar's subsidiaries, and later in Agbar itself. To cement the relationship, Agbar reciprocated with a 3 percent equity stake in Suez-Lyonnais des Eaux, becoming the fifth-largest stockholder of the French company, and occupying a seat on its board of directors. When Agbar started its international expansion in the early 1990s, La Caixa and Suez-Lyonnais des Eaux, the two main shareholders, agreed to set up Hisusa, a jointly-owned holding to pool their stakes. In this holding, Suez-Lyonnais des Eaux had 51 percent of the equity and La Caixa the remaining 49 percent. Both companies gradually increased their jointly owned stake in Agbar during the 1990s to a proportion just below 50 percent.

Following Endesa's withdrawal from the equity of Agbar in 2004, Suez-Lyonnais des Eaux acquired a more predominant role in defining the strategy of Agbar. A critical juncture occurred in 2006 when Suez and Gaz de France merged to create an integrated energy group. By then, there were some doubts regarding the future of Suez's involvement, but La Caixa and Suez confirmed their alliance in Hisusa and in 2007 launched a takeover bid to raise their stake in Agbar. Today, Hisusa controls two-thirds of Agbar's equity, while Suez and La Caixa separately control additional stakes of 12.02 percent and 11.55 percent, respectively. Agbar and Suez-Lyonnais des Eaux were never equal in size. However, this difference started to gradually become more pronounced in the 1990s. First, Lyonnais des Eaux merged with the French constructing firm Dumez in 1991. Then, Lyonnais des Eaux merged with the Compagnie de Suez in 1997, creating Suez-Lyonnais des Eaux. Finally, the merger with Gaz de France and the increasing equity control position in Agbar multiplied not only the control rights of Suez, but also the differences in size, in such a way that the current relationship between Agbar and Suez-Lyonnais des Eaux can be hardly defined as an alliance. In fact, most analysts now consider Agbar as part of the Suez group (Hall and Lobina 2007) and it is clear that Suez's influence has been critical in refocusing Agbar's strategy back on its core business. This control over Agbar has been reinforced through an agreement between Agbar's main shareholders, Suez and La Caixa, at the end of 2009. By virtue of this agreement, Suez will control directly 75 percent of the equity of Agbar and La Caixa will acquire the equity stake of Agbar in the insurance group Adeslas.

Obviously, the partnership with Suez-Lyonnais des Eaux was crucial in Agbar's international and corporate expansion. However, this expansion became truncated to some extent precisely for the same reason. This became clear when the development of its trial-and-error multi-domestic and multi-industry strategy yielded important businesses, such as Applus+, which could not be developed to reach its potential due to a lack of involvement among the main shareholders. As in the case of Unión Fenosa, Agbar's potential was both expanded and constrained by its strategic dependence.

CONCLUSION

Multinationals in regulated industries came of age in the late 1980s at a time when dozens of countries around the world initiated market-oriented reforms. Spanish firms willing to become multinationals in these industries did not have to face the disadvantage of being latecomers. There were no established multinationals, as in consumer or producer manufactured goods.

The four case studies indicate that the main asset Spanish firms had was their accrued experience in the home country. Experience in expanding network industries, building infrastructures, managing mergers and acquisitions, and/or operating in a deregulated financial environment proved crucial in taking over privatized companies or carrying out infrastructure projects abroad. However, in two of the cases (Agbar and Santander) international alliances and expansion became a major source of new capabilities.

The four cases also illustrate that project-execution and political capabilities were more valuable in Latin America than elsewhere, although not every project executed there was successful. These firms reacted quickly to every opportunity for international expansion that arose there, even when they were not fully prepared to do so, because these opportunities were unrepeatable. Over time, however, they became increasingly concerned about the political risks that they were facing. García-Canal and Guillén (2008) argued that political capabilities can reduce the hazards of operating under governmental discretion. However, it seems that these capabilities are not equally effective everywhere and that there is a limit to the amount of regulatory and policy risk that firms are willing to be exposed to. The behavior of the four firms was consistent with the following proposition: when it came to expanding into emerging countries, the Spanish firms entered basically into Latin America, and once they gained enough experience and/or expanded into the most profitable markets, they directed their efforts to more developed countries. Other emerging regulated firms such as Egypt's Orascom Telecom, with an outstanding record of profitability in challenging environments (Noland 2008), have entered into Africa, South Asia, and the Middle East. Thus, these firms do not try to do business in every emerging economy available, but only in those where their political capabilities prove valuable. In addition, firms willing to take risks in politically unstable countries tend to look for big markets, paying less attention to smaller ones (UNCTAD 2004: 46). This hypothesis would explain why MNEs in financial services and infrastructure industries turned their attention to developed countries once they gained a significant presence in emerging markets.

Taking into account the differences among the four cases, our analysis suggests that the best scenario is to be strategically independent and to use international expansion to explore new capabilities. Santander was the only firm that performed successfully along the three dimensions of corporate expansion in this type of industry: license bidding (including privatizations), diversification, and global consolidation. The main advantage of an exploratory approach is that the firm can learn from the experience accrued by firms in other environments. The main advantage of strategic independence is that the firm faces no restrictions in order to exploit its knowledge and resources. Our cases show that the international expansion of some Spanish-regulated multinationals was truncated by their controlling shareholders, as happened in the cases of Agbar and Unión Fenosa. In Agbar's case, the main shareholder increased its control and influence over time until it reached a majority equity stake. However, in Unión Fenosa's case international expansion was truncated by a series of attempts to gain control over the company staged by a number of large firms. While takeovers and the market for corporate control are within the rules of the game in market economies, acquisitions and corporate restructuring in regulated industries are greatly affected by the role of governments. Hardly any large, regulated company can be acquired against the will of the government. In the case of Spain, moreover, politicians played an active role. This became clearly evident in the case of Endesa's takeover by Italy's Enel, a firm partially owned by the state. Ironically, some Spanish multinationals have become victims of the regulatory environment in which they developed the political capabilities that sustained their international expansion.

7 Competing in hard and soft services

> Both the opportunity and the need for international delivery of a wide array of services have grown dramatically in recent years, either displacing or complementing parallel delivery of similar services by purely domestic operations. Some firms – such as hotel chains – follow their customers into new markets; others extend their geographic reach in search of new opportunities to increase their sales and expertise.
>
> Lovelock (1999: 278)

> Investing abroad changed our mentality, and enabled us to see other countries and firms, and to improve our competitiveness because it does away with many inferiority complexes. Going abroad opens up your mind.
>
> José Cosmen, President of ALSA[1]

Infrastructure and financial services account for the bulk of the dollar value of foreign direct investment from the service sector. In terms of the number of firms and of foreign operations, however, about half are engaged in a wide array of other service activities, including hospitality, the media, leisure, transportation, business services, consulting, education, healthcare, and so on. In the case of Spain, between 1986 and 2008 about 54 percent of all foreign operations established by Spanish service-sector firms fall under this heterogeneous category (Guillén and García-Canal 2009). This wide array of activities can be classified according to two key dimensions. The first one is the degree to which the production of the service can be separated from its consumption. "Hard" services are those that can be separated, with the important implication that it can be exported at arm's length (Erramili 1990). Media and consulting companies, for

---

[1] *La internacionalización de la empresa española* (Cátedra SCH, Universidad de Nebrija, 2003), p. 98.

instance, produce hard services. "Soft" services, by contrast, require simultaneous production and consumption, and thus the company and its customers must be co-located. Exporting is generally not an option (Vandermerwe and Chadwick 1989). This is the case of traditional educational services (excluding distance learning), transportation, many business services, hospitality, and healthcare.

The second dimension is the degree to which the substance of the service entails the transfer of professional or technical knowledge. For instance, companies engaged in consulting or education sell professional or technical expertise to their customers. In these activities, human and relational capital is by far the most important capabilities (von Nordenflycht 2010). Therefore, their most important challenge is to attract, motivate, and retain professional personnel (Greenwood 2005; Hitt et al. 2001, 2006).

In this chapter we compare four firms that exhibit different combinations of the two key variables (see Table 7.1). In the transportation sector, ALSA is engaged in land transportation services, which require joint production and consumption. In postgraduate education, IESE Business School offers professional services and mostly sells them in the classroom, thus also requiring joint production with the customer. In the media industry, Planeta produces hard services of a non-professional kind. Finally, in the engineering consulting sector, Duro Felguera also offers hard services – such as turnkey plants, engineering, procurement, and construction – but drawing on its professional and technical expertise. These four cases help understand competitive dynamics in some of the most rapidly-growing sectors of the economy.

ALSA

Automóviles Luarca SA (ALSA) was founded in 1923 in Luarca, a small fishing village in the northern region of Asturias. It focuses on the provision of regularly scheduled bus passenger transportation services. The company grew by gradually expanding the number and frequency of destinations. Given that transportation is a regulated

Table 7.1. *Hard versus soft service firms by type of service*

Separation of production and consumption	Type of service:	
	Non-professional	Professional/technical
Hard services (separable)	Planeta	Duro Felguera
Soft services (non-separable)	ALSA	IESE Business School

industry, growth required either obtaining new licenses or acquiring companies with licenses. After decades of organic growth, in 1960 ALSA tried to take over Empresa Cosmen, another company located in Asturias and owned by the Cosmen family. Instead of accepting the offer, the Cosmen family proposed a merger between both companies. This new proposal was accepted and the family received newly issued shares of ALSA in exchange for their transportation business. One year later, Mr. José Cosmen assumed the top executive position at ALSA, and the family purchased ALSA shares until they gained full control over the company.

Under the leadership of Mr. Cosmen, ALSA grew to become a multinational bus transportation service operating on four continents. This growth was facilitated by an expanding domestic market, with improvements in the highway infrastructure, and quantitative and qualitative changes in the demand for transportation services. Nowadays ALSA offers four types of service: urban transportation in twenty Spanish municipalities and in Marrakesh, Morocco; regional transportation within thirteen of Spain's nineteen autonomous communities; national transportation connecting virtually all parts of Spain and, finally, international transportation, operating sixty-five routes that connect Spain with continental Europe, the UK, and North Africa. ALSA also operates bus routes in Portugal, France, Belgium, Switzerland, and Germany, and is a member of EUROLINES, a network of thirty-two independent European bus companies that provide single-ticket services connecting routes operated by different companies. Outside Europe, it operates regional services in Chile and in China. ALSA merged in 2005 with National Express, a UK-based multinational transportation group with interests in bus and rail transport. As a result of the deal, the Cosmen family became the main shareholder of National Express and one of Mr. Cosmen's sons, Jorge, was appointed as a non-executive director and Deputy Chairman. The Cosmen family nevertheless retained ownership of the ALSA businesses in China (where the company has had a presence since 1984). Similar to what happened with the absorption of "Empresa Cosmen" by ALSA, the Cosmen family tried to gain full control over National Express in 2009 by launching a tender offer. At this time the company was in a dire financial situation coinciding with the resignation of the CEO. However, the Cosmen family withdrew the offer after completing due diligence. Nevertheless, the Cosmen family remains the biggest shareholder with a stake of 19 percent in National Express's equity. According to DBK, a consulting firm, ALSA is the market leader in Spain, with a 16 percent share as of 2008, followed by AVANZA with 9 percent, and Arriva with 5 percent.[2] ALSA has a small subsidiary active in rail transportation.

Acquisitions played a key role in ALSA's growth, starting with several small companies (Turytrans, Rutas del Cantábrico S.L., Viajes por Carretera SA), and reaching a climax with the 1999 purchase of Enatcar, a state-owned bus transportation company. In 2007 ALSA acquired Continental, the second-largest bus transportation group in Spain, and in 2008 it bought Transportes Colectivos, a city bus transportation firm.

A second factor in ALSA's expansion was operating efficiency. In order to standardize service and ensure safety, the firm invested heavily in training and bus maintenance. As Mr. Cosmen once pointed out, "our relative success in transportation is based on the

[2] "Las tres grandes del autobús superan por primera vez el 30% de cuota de mercado," *Cinco Días*, April 28, 2009.

establishment of effective, strategically distributed maintenance facilities" (Cosmen 1994: 166). The company trains its drivers at dedicated facilities in Madrid, Oviedo, China, Morocco, and Portugal (Fernández and Nieto 2008). As the driver is normally the only person of the company that is in touch with the client throughout most of the process, their behavior is critical to ensure customer satisfaction (in addition to a good use of the buses).

A third factor in ALSA's expansion has been the continuous innovation in services, not only to create more customer value (for instance by selling tickets on the Internet), but also to introduce customized services to specific types of customers. Even though bus routes are concessions in Spain, and bus companies enjoy a monopoly position over them, bus transportation is under threat of substitution by other means of transport like private cars, railways, or airlines. Over the years, ALSA developed several innovations in order to persuade customers to switch to bus transportation. An example is the so-called "Supra" service, a non-stop intercity route that incorporates certain attributes of business class in airlines using luxury coaches with larger seats, more leg room, and complementary services such as refreshments, newspapers and, more recently, Wi-Fi.

In terms of international expansion, the company first decided to operate bus routes originating in Spain, and later to extend the business model developed in Spain to other countries.[3] Their first experience in the international market was the Oviedo–Paris–Brussels route in 1964. This route was followed by Oviedo–Lyon–Zurich and Oviedo–Salamanca–Geneva, serving the Spanish immigrant communities in France, Belgium, and Switzerland. At the time, bus services were much more convenient than rail, and cheaper than flying. Nowadays, up to sixty-five ALSA bus routes connect Spain to other countries. These routes are usually based on agreements with companies in the countries along the itinerary so as to secure the

---

[3] See Fernández and Nieto (2008) for a detailed chronology of ALSA's international expansion.

necessary permissions and gain access to the local infrastructure. In some cases, ALSA established a joint venture with a local company. The company also set up travel agencies in Switzerland and Portugal to sell its tickets directly to the customer.

Despite the success of its international routes originating in Spain, the most important foreign expansion decisions had to do with direct investments. The idea was to exploit the accrued know-how from its Spanish operations to run local or regional bus routes in distant countries. The first important foray was in China, where the company established a series of fourteen joint ventures beginning in 1984. In 1999 ALSA started to invest more aggressively abroad because competition authorities barred it from further domestic growth after the acquisition of Enatcar. In 1999 ALSA won the bid for the concession for urban bus services in Marrakesh, Morocco, and in 2001 it won approval for regional services in the same part of the country. Also in 2001 ALSA took over 51 percent of the equity of Autobuses Lit, a leading Chilean transportation company. In 2003 ALSA acquired 49 percent of Tas Choapa, also in Chile, which enabled it to operate some international routes within Latin America, although ALSA withdrew from this area in 2005. ALSA also invested in several companies in Portugal (e.g. Rodoviaria do Tejo and Moreira Gomes e Costa), Germany (by taking over Deutsche Touring in collaboration with other investors, a company with routes in Eastern Europe), and France (by forming a joint venture with Keolis to exploit local rail routes).

China was a remarkable experience for ALSA. Initially, José Cosmen was interested in importing an innovative toothpaste made in China (Cosmen 1994). During the process of finding information about this business, he discovered that passenger transportation by bus presented a unique opportunity. China's infrastructure was underdeveloped, and transportation services backward. However, due to regulatory restrictions, foreign investors could only operate taxis, and only in specially designated areas. Thus, in 1984 the company launched a joint venture with local partners named Nanyio

Transportation Services Co. Ltd, operating in Shenzhen, a Special Economic Zone close to Hong Kong, where foreign investors were allowed to operate under certain conditions. ALSA held a 49 percent stake in the equity but considered this investment as a good platform to learn how to operate in China and adapt to local peculiarities and do business with a local partner. As Mr. Cosmen observed, "at the beginning we wanted to transfer all of our business systems and we realized that it wasn't possible. Changes ought to be introduced slowly, justifying each decision" (Cosmen 1994: 164). For a company with a long-term orientation, this early step became a first-mover advantage, as it is not easy to build business relationships with Chinese partners from scratch. Thus, when in 1990 the government allowed foreign investors to operate bus services, ALSA was fully prepared to take advantage of the opportunity. It created a new joint venture to exploit the route connecting Beijing with the rapidly industrializing coastal city of Tianjing. ALSA offered services that China had never seen, including regular schedules and modern coaches with comfortable seats. New joint ventures were set up to operate routes between Beijing and Shanghai. The company then moved to smaller cities, launching companies in Shijiazhuang and Nanjing. Step by step, ALSA replicated its business model introducing special services like the Imperial Class, the Chinese version of the Supra service offered in Spain. So as to overcome the difficulties associated with the subpar infrastructure, ALSA formed joint ventures to build bus stations, assemble buses (in collaboration with the Spanish firm Irizar), and develop and manage maintenance facilities. Over time, ALSA became an expert on the Chinese market, so the company also established an import-export subsidiary to help other companies operate in China. Andrés Cosmen, one of the sons of Mr. José Cosmen, has been running the company's operations in China since 1987. Summarizing the key factors of ALSA's success in China, Mr. Andrés Cosmen noted that "we have dedicated a lot of time and effort to developing relationships with both our Chinese partners and the Chinese administration ... It is also important to adapt the business concept to China's characteristics ... But it is even more important to know which aspects or processes of our business should not be changed" (Cosmen 2004: 92). Thus, ALSA's success illustrates the exploitation of home-country expertise in foreign countries that are very different.

IESE BUSINESS SCHOOL

Like ground transportation, education is a soft service in that it requires joint production with the customer (except in the case of distance learning). The business model of graduate business schools is to provide students with the technical knowledge, skills, and attitudes to succeed in executive positions, using teaching methods oriented towards the development of decision-making abilities. Given that the quality of the output depends on the motivation and personal abilities of the students, business schools compete among themselves to attract the most promising students. For their part, the students wish to pursue a graduate degree because of not only the training or education they will receive but also the signaling effect of the diploma. The reputation of the faculty is a critical attribute, and an indicator of the overall quality of the school. Thus, education is a soft service in which professional knowledge is key to success. There is a considerable barrier to entry because tuition fees are not enough to cover all of the expenses associated with offering an excellent education (Hawawini 2005; Iñiguez de Onzoño and Carmona 2007). Although new business schools are created every year, it is very difficult for newcomers to be leaders.

Modern graduate management education, and MBA programs in particular, are an American invention (Guillén 1989; Khurana 2007). Although business schools existed in Europe before the founding of the first US school – Wharton in 1881 – the MBA degree was pioneered at Harvard during the early part of the twentieth century. Not surprisingly, most of the best business schools to this day are located in the United States. During the last two decades, however, Asian and, especially, European schools have improved their quality and visibility. The international rankings now include London Business School, INSEAD, and IMD among the world's leading business schools. Surprisingly, Spain is home to three internationally ranked business schools, IESE Business School, IE Business School, and ESADE. While business schools have also flourished in emerging countries such as China (e.g. CEIBS), Brazil (Fundação Getúlio Vargas), or Costa Rica (INCAE), the case of the Spanish business schools is especially remarkable because until recently virtually nobody associated Spain with world-class management education, and the country continues to be a laggard in science and technology.

The first European graduate schools of business were founded after World War II thanks to the influx of US foreign aid, foreign direct investment, and technology transfer (Puig and Fernández 2003). The Marshall Plan provided not only funding but also a program of collaboration with US universities aimed at the creation of business schools in Europe modeled on those of the United States (Kipping *et al.* 2004). Although Spain had outstanding undergraduate schools of business like the Universidad Comercial de Deusto, founded in 1916, the first business school modeled on the US version was the Escuela de Organización Industrial (EOI), jointly founded in 1955 by the Spanish Ministries of Education and Industry with funding and expertise from the US technical aid program (Guillén 1989). While EOI continues to be a solid business school, it is not internationally ranked. IESE Business School (initially named Instituto de Estudios Superiores de la Empresa, Institute of Higher Business Studies) was founded as a graduate business school in 1958 by the University of Navarra. This university, founded six years earlier, was an ambitious educational project sponsored by the Opus Dei. IESE nowadays is a truly global institution with 32,000 alumni belonging to 105 countries. Although IESE's main campuses are in Spain (in Barcelona and Madrid), the school has a network of affiliated schools on four continents. In addition, IESE has offices in Munich and São Paulo, and a center in New York. IESE offers traditional programs such as the MBA, Executive MBA and PhD in Management, as well as customized executive education programs, continuous education, and innovative programs such as the Global Executive MBA, which combines residential sessions in Barcelona, Silicon Valley, and Shanghai with state-of-the-art distance learning. In 2009, IESE placed first in the world ranking of full-time MBA programs of the Economist Intelligence Unit. Without a doubt, this is an outstanding accomplishment for a school that is just fifty years old and located in a country not perceived as being at the leading edge of business, science, or technology.

The early years of IESE were not easy. Its first dean was Antonio Valero, an industrial engineer by training, professor of economics at an engineering school and partner of a consultancy firm. The case study method of teaching was introduced with the help of the Ecole d'Administration des Affaires, a school founded in Lille, France, by a Harvard Business School graduate. IESE's initial activities involved long, open executive education programs aimed at top managers of Spanish firms (see Canals 2009, for a more detailed account of IESE's history).

In 1964 IESE made its first qualitative leap by launching an MBA program, which would be overseen by a joint advisory committee consisting of faculty from Harvard Business School and IESE. It was the first two-year MBA degree program in all of Europe. In 1974 IESE started to offer executive programs in Madrid. In 1980 a bilingual English/Spanish MBA program was established. An executive (part-time) MBA program was launched in Madrid in 1982. In 1993, IESE offered short residential programs of one to three weeks for international executives. In 2001 the Global Executive MBA was launched. In parallel, the school developed its offerings of customized, in-company programs for international companies such as Boeing, Sun Microsystems, or Henkel as well as for Spanish multinationals such as Telefónica, BBVA, Santander, and Repsol.

IESE became a leading global business school thanks to four key factors: the development of a qualified full-time faculty; a

staunch international orientation; a pragmatic approach to executive education; and the support of the Opus Dei. The development
of a highly qualified full-time faculty was critical to IESE's success.
Its first full-time professors came straight from managerial positions
in businesses, but the school soon realized the importance of hir-
ing faculty with PhDs earned at the best US business schools, such
as Harvard, Wharton, or MIT. In order to lay the foundations of a
world-class faculty, the school offered some of its best MBA students
the opportunity to pursue a PhD in the United States and at its own
doctoral program. IESE's aim had always been that their faculty be
involved not only in teaching but also in research and consulting
activities. As former dean Carlos Cavallé once pointed out, IESE's
professors "have to do three things: teach at the highest possible
level of quality, carry out useful and relevant research ... and finally
be involved in business activities."[4] These principles guided IESE's
efforts to build a strong faculty, although for many years the school
lacked star professors, and lagged behind in publications in the most
competitive management journals. In order to overcome these problems, the school turned during the 2000s to the competitive job market in order to hire the best faculty it could attract.

A second key variable in IESE's success was its international
orientation. Since its inception, the school looked abroad, not only
by learning from foreign schools like Lille or Harvard, but also by
proactively attracting international students, partnering with other
schools, and establishing campuses abroad. The alumni association
was also designed as an international network, with chapters in
eighteen different countries. The 32,000 alumni participate in con-
tinuing education programs and meet once a year in some countries.
In the words of current IESE dean Jordi Canals, "American universities and schools have a limited and poor international vision,
although they are outstanding in research. We believe that we can
provide our experience as an international business school with a

[4] *El País*, September 8, 2000.

multicultural perspective, our teaching cases, and the outcome of our research."[5]

A third factor crucial to IESE's success was its approach to executive education, focused on providing solutions to the shifting problems that senior executives faced over the years. Puig and Fernández (2003: 663) proposed several examples to illustrate this ability to tailor educational programs to the specific needs of clients. During the early years, IESE helped companies address the shortcomings of an authoritarian managerial style predominant in Spain at the time, helping them incorporate the most advanced human-relations theories and practices. Another example was IESE's focus on the problems facing family businesses, a somewhat marginal field in the United States, but one that was of utmost importance in Spain in general and Catalonia in particular. Similarly, IESE's specialization in the field of entrepreneurship proved helpful in a country with a deficit of entrepreneurs.[6]

Last but not least, an important factor in IESE's rapid development was the support of the Opus Dei, a Catholic organization with some 87,000 members around the world (36,000 outside Europe). Even though the Catholic organization does not interfere in the management of the school, the Opus Dei helped IESE with the formation of a worldwide network of associated schools, as most of the partner schools belong to universities linked to the Opus Dei. However, according to Jordi Canals, the main influence of the Opus Dei has been in setting IESE's mission and values, which center around a humanistic vision of firms and society beyond mere economic efficiency. IESE's corporate culture, deeply rooted in an Opus Dei ethos that promotes perfectionism and service in work and everyday activities, encourages excellence and achievement (Casanova 1983), as well as a commitment to the common good of companies and society.

---

[5] *El País*, August 12, 2007.
[6] This focus on providing solutions for real problems is highlighted in a book that takes stock of the first fifty years of IESE, which is named *Sabiduría Práctica (Practical Wisdom)*. See Canals (2009).

As these values are shared by IESE's faculty and staff, IESE's commitment to service constitutes an important competitive advantage. According to Jordi Canals, IESE not only has a mission of service, but a sense of mission in such a way that an orientation to service is present "in any interaction between every participant in an IESE program and any person in the school's educational community."[7]

Like many service-sector firms, IESE's international expansion started with technology transfer. IESE built a network of associated schools that to some extent replicated IESE's model: IPADE (Mexico, 1967), Tayasal Escuela de Negocios (Guatemala, 1977), IAE (Argentina, 1978), PAD (Peru, 1979), AESE (Portugal, 1980), INALDE (Colombia, 1986), LBS (Nigeria, 1992), IDE (Ecuador, 1993), CEIBS China Europe International Business School (China, 1994), IEEM (Uruguay, 1994), School of Business Administration (Philippines, 1995), ISE (Brazil, 1997), ESE (Chile, 1999), IME Institute for Media Entertainment (United States, 2004), NTU (Egypt, 2004), and SBS (Kenya, 2005). IESE provided these schools with guidance, expertise, teaching materials, and visiting faculty, sometimes in collaboration with other schools like Harvard. Associated schools also have provided candidates for IESE's PhD program. IESE also organized an International Faculty Development Program, aimed at improving the skills of professors of other business schools.[8]

After IESE grew in size and sophistication, it entered a second stage of collaborating with schools such as Harvard, MIT, and Michigan on joint programs, and with London Business School, Kellogg, and Wharton on student exchanges. In a third phase, the school has established its own campuses abroad, including Germany (2005) and the United States (2007).

IESE's growth displays some of the features of the new multinationals, including learning alliances, the development of networks of collaboration, and specialization in market niches not served

---

[7] *La Gaceta de los Negocios,* September 8, 2007.

[8] This program is still being offered, with 35–40 professors from other business schools attending each year.

by the established leaders. Another successful Spanish school, IE Business School (formerly Instituto de Empresa) followed a similar pattern, though initially relying more extensively on part-time faculty teaching in one-year MBA programs. Founded in 1973, IE has 37,000 graduates. It founded SUMAQ, a network of business schools in Spain and Latin America. IE's lack of affiliation with a university forced it to take over Universidad SEK, a humanities university, to create IE Universidad. ESADE, the other top business school in Spain, was founded in 1958 as an undergraduate school of business and law with the support of the Jesuits, and is part of the Universitat Ramon Llull. ESADE has offered a two-year MBA program since 1964. This school has 35,000 graduates (including bachelor degrees), and campuses in Barcelona, Madrid, and Buenos Aires. The presence of three prominent business schools has positioned Spain in the international market of postgraduate studies in management, attracting greater numbers of international students each year. However, only IESE has taken steps to set up foreign centers outside Spain to serve specific niches. When discussing the school's new US center, IESE's dean observed that "we seek to do what American business schools will not."[9] As education is basically a soft service, business schools willing to make a dent in international markets need to either attract foreign students or establish campuses abroad. Spanish business schools show that the latter option is more difficult to put into practice, not only because postgraduate education is a field in which qualified faculty and reputation are paramount to success, but also because firms competing in soft services cannot take advantage of cross-country differences in personnel costs and other resources. In order to assess strategies of internationalization in the context of cross-border arbitrage of production factors and other resources, we next examine two cases of firms that sell hard services, which offer them a wider scope of options to profit from their accrued know-how and experience in foreign markets.

[9] *El País*, August 12, 2007.

PLANETA

While ALSA and IESE produce and sell soft services, other firms specialize in services that do not require the simultaneous production and consumption of the service. In the media industry, Planeta is perhaps the most successful Spanish firm, one that managed to make the transition from book printing to multimedia, riding successive waves of innovation. Like other media groups in Spain and around the world, Planeta is family owned. In its original business, books, the company leads the market in Spain, Portugal, and Latin America.

Planeta was founded by Jose Manuel Lara Hernández in 1949. The name of the company was chosen because, in his own words, it "was the biggest thing that I could think of."[10] In fact, Lara had an ambitious growth plan, first for Spain and, since 1966, for Europe and Latin America. The strategy of the company was based on four pillars: the proactive search for best-selling books written in Spanish; new commercial formulas to sell cultural products; acquisitions of other publishers to expand its title collection; and alliances with other firms in order to gain access to content for the Spanish-speaking markets.

To promote books written in Spanish, Planeta organized up to fourteen literary awards to attract the best authors. In 1952, just three years after establishing the company, Lara announced the Premio Planeta for unpublished novels originally written in the Spanish language. He named a jury stacked with outstanding academics and writers, and offered a large cash prize, which nowadays amounts to €601,000. Planeta would hold exclusive rights to the publication of the book, and use the award as a way to promote sales.[11]

---

[10] "Editorial Planeta, el origen de un gran grupo," *Cataluña Económica*, November 15, 2004.

[11] These prizes can be understood as some sort of backward vertical integration, as they were paid against the royalties of the book, so the author would only earn extra money when the accrued royalties exceeded the amount of the prize. Thus, these prizes guaranteed Planeta the availability of successful best-sellers each year.

The company also pioneered new formulas to sell cultural products. During the early years, it developed a sales force specialized in sales on credit to the final customer of pricey products such as encyclopedias. This sales force was the starting point of a division within Planeta devoted to direct sales which nowadays not only sells encyclopedias and luxury editions of books, but also a wide variety of items such as multimedia products, dining services, watches, jewelry, and fashion accessories, which are available over the Internet via the company's website. Another innovative formula introduced in the Spanish market was the sale of specialized dictionaries, encyclopedias, and other items in weekly or monthly installments, using newsstands as the distribution channel, and sometimes in collaboration with national newspapers.

The company also expanded through acquisitions of other publishers. The main goal was to gain control over an expanding catalog of books in print, but without integrating them into the same publishing firm. Planeta actually kept acquisitions separate, with their own personality, readership, and brand name, catering to a specific segment of the market. Over the years Planeta acquired Ariel (academic books), Seix Barral (innovative novels), Ediciones Deusto (business books), Espasa Calpe (encyclopedias and academic books), Destino (literature in general), and MR Ediciones (novels, and practical and esoteric books), among others. The only segment of the book market in which Planeta is still not present is textbooks in Spanish, where the main potential targets are not for sale. Planeta's presence in textbooks is limited to the French market, where it isthe second-largest publisher thanks to its acquisition of Editis Group.

Finally, Planeta entered into alliances with other publishers so as to gain access to other types of content. A key agreement was the one signed with Larousse in 1963, whereby Planeta published the Spanish edition of the famed French encyclopedia. Another important alliance for Planeta was the 1985 agreement with Italy's DeAgostini. This 50/50 joint venture focused on installment publications, interactive products, and comics. The company also entered into alliances with other publishing firms to jointly exploit specific opportunities. For instance, EDP-Editores was a joint venture between Bertelsmann and Planeta whose purpose is the joint distribution of luxury book editions. The company is now wholly owned by Planeta. Technological change offered Planeta myriad opportunities to pursue multimedia delivery of its contents. Armed with several decades of experience and a strong cash-flow from operations in Europe and Latin America, Planeta digitized its entire contents in order to sell them through the Internet and other channels. The company also entered the distance-learning industry in 2002 by taking over two companies, Centro de Estudios CEAC (a traditional mail-order learning company), and Home English (a distance language teaching company). Planeta and its Italian partner DeAgostini also invested jointly in the media and audiovisual industries, by promoting a new company, DeAPlaneta. Since 2003 Planeta owns a majority stake in the Antena 3 Group, a media group that comprises a leading TV station in Spain and a radio station named Onda Cero, among other companies. Planeta is the main shareholder in *La Razón*, one of Spain's six biggest newspapers, and the sole shareholder of *ADN*, a free daily newspaper. In January 2010 Planeta sold its participation in *Avui*, the main newspaper in the Catalan language. The company has also launched an online business school in partnership with the University of Barcelona, for which part of the contents are developed by Editorial Deusto (part of Planeta) and by EAE, a Barcelona-based business school which it acquired in 2007. In 2007 Planeta also entered the business of creating content for mobile phones by buying a 25 percent equity stake in Zed Worldwide. Thus, the corporate growth of Planeta has been a combination of diversification and vertical integration. Through the family office, Planeta has also diversified into unrelated fields such as low-cost airlines (Vueling) and banking (10 percent of Banco de Sabadell). Planeta group is currently run by José Manuel Lara Bosch, son of the company founder.

The international expansion of Planeta started in the 1960s through wholly owned subsidiaries aimed at commercializing cultural products developed in Spain. The firm also started to publish books written by Latin American authors. The company first established operations in Colombia, Mexico, Argentina, and Venezuela (1966), followed by Chile (1968), Ecuador (1981), and Peru (2005). Local sales forces were trained and hired to promote sales on credit. Planeta also made acquisitions in Latin America, including Editorial Joaquín Mortiz in Mexico (1985) and a minority stake in Editorial Sudamericana in Argentina (1984), which is presently owned by Bertelsmann. Its most important Argentine acquisitions were Emecé and Minotauro in 2001, and Paidós in 2003. Emecé is a large general publisher, Minotauro specializes in fantasy literature, and Paidós in social sciences and general interest books. In 2007 Planeta acquired Editorial Diana through a public offer in the Mexican stock exchange, which owns the rights to Gabriel García Márquez's books. These acquisitions consolidated the position of Planeta not only in the respective home countries of the targets, but also in the entire Spanish book market given that each purchase brought with it an expanded catalog of books. In Latin America, Planeta also acquired in 2007 Casa Editorial El Tiempo, a big Colombian media group with interests in newspapers, TV stations, book publishing, and Internet content.

Planeta's expansion was not limited to Spanish-speaking markets. The company entered Portugal in 1992 in collaboration with DeAgostini. Planeta also bought Editorial Dom Quixote in 1999, although this company was subsequently sold in 2007. Planeta entered Brazil in 2000 by acquiring Barsa International Publishers, a publisher of encyclopedias and luxury editions of books. In Brazil, Planeta also created Planeta do Brazil, acquired in 2007 Editora Acadamia de Inteligência, a publisher specialized in self-help books, and signed an alliance with Grupo Globo to launch a series of collectibles in Brazil. The entry into non-Spanish-speaking countries taught Planeta that language was not a relevant barrier for the firm. According to Mr. Lara Bosch, the language per se does not pose a barrier in these countries; the difficulties to find good local managers and editors do (Lara Bosch 2002). In order to tap into the Spanish-speaking market in the United States, Planeta signed an agreement with Random House in 1993. In 2006 the company entered into an alliance with Harper not just for the Spanish market in the United States but also for English translations of Planeta's book catalog.

In 2008 Planeta acquired Editis, the second-largest French publishing group, founded in 1835. With a turnover of €760 million the year prior to the acquisition, and twenty publishing companies, Editis positioned Planeta in the French-speaking countries thanks to both its catalog of books in print and its distribution and logistics infrastructure. Editis's distribution subsidiary, Interforum, with the largest coverage of points of sale in France, and branches in Belgium, Switzerland, and Canada, commercializes not only all of the Editis catalog but also the works of eighty other publishing companies in French-speaking countries. Finally, Planeta now sells collectible publications in Poland and Japan.

Planeta has thus evolved from book publisher to producing and selling a wide range of cultural goods and services through multiple channels, apart from the traditional ones, including the Internet, TV, newsstands, and mobile phones. It has also capitalized its expertise on Internet sales by launching online travel agencies and online marketing services. In so doing, the company leverages its reputation and expertise in direct marketing. In a context in which the traditional book loses market share to new distribution channels and platforms, Planeta has no option but to ride each new wave of technological innovation.

DURO FELGUERA
While Planeta sells hard services related to culture, but mostly unrelated to professional or technical knowledge (except in its relatively small business books division), Duro Felguera sells its expertise as a turnkey plant contractor. The increasing demand for infrastructure projects worldwide has boosted the expansion of the turnkey contracting industry. High demand, as well as some financial

innovations, has facilitated the entry of new competitors from emerging countries and from other related industries. In the specific context of Spain, the international expansion of large Spanish firms in regulated sectors created a unique opportunity for other Spanish firms (see Chapter 6), especially turnkey contractors.

Turnkey contractors are firms that take on the responsibility for setting up a plant, facility, heavy piece of equipment or infrastructure project for a specific client, and for bringing it to the point that it can start operations, all within specific time and budget constraints. Although many of these projects used to be undertaken by construction firms, recently engineering services firms have also participated in the industry. This process was in part fueled by heavy construction firms which have increasingly outsourced activities to specialized contractors. At the same time, engineering firms, which tend to be smaller than the biggest construction firms, started to undertake large-scale turnkey projects thanks to new financial innovations such as project finance or innovative ways of contracting like take-or-pay contracts. In both cases, firms operate on a project-by-project basis, performing the role of integrators within a network of specialized contractors, technology suppliers, and industrial customers. An increasing number of large-scale projects in industries such as transportation infrastructure, energy, oil, gas, water, or telecommunications have favored this process of convergence between construction and engineering firms. Economic reforms, privatizations, and liberalization have expanded the demand for infrastructure projects across the world, and a project-based organization allows these firms to manage the risks and financial constraints of each project individually.

Energy infrastructure is one of the highest-growth areas for turnkey projects. Despite the economic crisis of 2007–9, the most recent estimates of the International Energy Agency (2009), forecast that world electricity demand will grow 2.5 percent annually until 2030. The business model of turnkey contractors in the energy industry is to adapt its services to the needs of the customer (usually an electricity producer) using a standardized technological core provided by a partner such as Alstom, ABB, General Electric Power Systems, or Siemens Westinghouse. While these large firms contribute the hardware, the turnkey contractor manages the whole process, including engineering, procurement, and construction, precisely the reason why these contracts are also referred to as EPCs. Turnkey contracts usually include operation and maintenance of the facility during a certain guarantee period. As these firms do not develop their own technology, their competitive advantage lies in the ability to manage the project efficiently and on time, in a way that the various contractual clauses are met. Contracts are typically awarded on a competitive bidding basis and include penalty clauses in case of non-compliance. For these reasons, successful turnkey contractors need to be able to not only estimate a feasible and competitive price but also manage effectively the whole process.

Given growing demand, low entry barriers, and the rise of turnkey contractors from countries such as India and China, competition is stiff. The main Spanish players are ACS, Abeinsa/Abengoa, Isolux/Corsan, Técnicas Reunidas, Iberinco, and Duro Felguera. Each of these firms has a different background, although all resulted from mergers of long-standing construction and/or engineering firms, except for Iberinco, established in 1995 by Iberdrola as an independent company, Técnicas Reunidas, an engineering and turkey contractor founded in 1960, and Duro Felguera, a capital goods producer founded in 1858, which decided to reduce its original focus in the wake of mounting international competition in favor of the turnkey business.

Duro Felguera is organized into three main product lines: manufacturing of capital goods (its traditional business), specialized services, and turnkey contracts. The capital goods division makes mechanical metal components and heavy-duty equipment for various industries. The specialized services unit embraces, among others, mechanical and electrical erection activities and the maintenance of facilities in various industrial sectors. The execution of turnkey contracts is currently its main product line, accounting for 75 percent of sales. Its main area of specialization is the engineering, procurement, and construction of electric power stations with gas turbines. It has built thirty-two combined-cycle gas plants in Europe and Latin America. Despite the focus on power plants, the company is capable of providing engineering services and executing turnkey projects in the mining, material handling, steelworks, petrochemical and automatic warehousing areas, virtually in any country.

The trajectory of Duro Felguera illustrates how a capital-goods producer can manage to enter the business of turnkey contracts. The company was originally founded in 1858 as a coal and steel producer that went on to become a vertically integrated company in order to overcome the constraints and bottlenecks of early industrialization in a country implementing protectionist policies. In particular, it was forced to build the ships for transporting its production and power plants for its electricity needs. It also entered the coal storage and distribution business. Paradoxically, it was the accrued experience in a variety of industries that allowed this company to survive when the coal and steel business went into decline during the second half of the last century, as the theory of project-execution capabilities predicts (Amsden and Hikino 1994). Its early manufacturing experience allowed the company to reinvent itself as a manufacturer of capital goods. By doing so the company initiated a diversification strategy focused on catering to the specific needs of several industries, taking advantage of the resources and capabilities accumulated in activities such as manufacturing equipment for mining, boiler work, and foundry components, among others. However, the accrued experience of the company was only fully capitalized on when it started to execute turnkey contracts in the mid 1980s. With the entrance in this activity – coinciding with a crisis in the capital goods market – the company exploited not only its knowledge in manufacturing, but also its experience in bidding for contracts (most of the deals in the capital goods industry are based on competitive bids).

A key aspect of the competitive strategy of Duro Felguera in the field of turnkey contracts is that the company always uses well-established technological partners. Its main partners are Mitsubishi Heavy Industries (for desulphurization and denitrification plants, and for tunnel boring machines), Ishikawajima-Harima Heavy Industries (for fuel storage facilities), and Alstom, General Electric Power Systems, Siemens Westinghouse, and Mitsubishi Heavy Industries (for power plants).

Duro Felguera started its international expansion during the 1950s and 1960s while it was a manufacturer of capital goods. The company sold abroad via exports, and established two joint ventures in Mexico. After competition forced the company to diversify into turnkey contracts, the firm internationalized in earnest, with 36 percent of sales coming from abroad, and plans to reach 50 percent. Duro Felguera's foreign presence depends on whether it can undertake turnkey projects. In order to follow market trends and secure orders, the company has established subsidiaries and commercial offices in countries such as Mexico, Venezuela, Argentina, Peru, Italy, Japan, and India, relying on agents for the rest of the world. International expansion is a natural outcome for successful turnkey contractors, as the demand for projects where they can capitalize their experience is dispersed across the world. In turn, international experience also helped Duro Felguera gain experience in some areas of engineering to expand its activities in Spain. During the 1990s, for instance, demand for electric power stations with combined-cycle gas turbines was expected to grow. Duro Felguera lacked experience in this area. It seized the opportunities in Latin America as a way to build up its expertise. Its first project was the building of the power station Las Flores I, in Colombia in 1993, in partnership with Westinghouse. This was followed by five additional projects in that country with the same partner. The experience gained during these initial projects allowed the company to successfully bid for projects in other countries, including Mexico (three), Peru (three), Argentina (three), Italy (two), and Chile (one). In Spain it has undertaken nineteen projects since 2002. One peculiarity of the projects located in emerging economies is that the client tends to be an electrical utility from a developed country. In spite of the amount of experience gained as a turnkey contractor, Duro Felguera is still small in size. Growth is in part constrained by the scarcity of engineering and managerial talent. In the near future, the company could expand its in-house training center (founded in 2003), or engage in acquisitions.

Duro Felguera's main challenge is to reach enough scale to undertake a greater number of projects. The most important limitation it faces has to do with the size of its technical staff. In order to overcome this problem, the company set up a corporate training center in 2003, in which engineers obtain a master's degree. It is also considering acquisitions, although identifying a suitable target is no easy task.

CONCLUSION

The four cases of soft and hard service-sector companies demonstrate once again that the new multinationals expanded abroad on the basis of home-grown capabilities, frequently combined with other resources obtained through strategic alliances and partnerships. Thus, IESE tapped into Harvard's resources, Duro Felguera expanded into new fields thanks to its international technology partners, Planeta benefited from its alliance with DeAgostini, and ALSA secured knowledge from a French company in order to enter the rail transportation business.

Another common feature of these new multinationals in the service sector is that they focused their resources and attention on a well-defined market niche and geography. ALSA chose China because of its underdeveloped infrastructure and backward bus services. Planeta went to Spanish-speaking countries with the aim of expanding the market for books written in Spanish and enlarging its catalog. IESE transferred its know-how to Latin American business schools that replicated its business model. Finally, Duro Felguera specialized its international turnkey contracting activities in the area of power generation. In so doing, these firms managed to establish a reputation for themselves and to build their capabilities and experience.

There are also important differences, mainly driven by the nature of the service produced and sold. Whereas non-professional service firms such as Planeta and ALSA used acquisitions in their international expansion assiduously, professional service firms like IESE and Duro Felguera did not. One of the peculiarities of professional firms is that, whereas highly-qualified personnel is in fact one of the crucial resources, capturing the value generated by them is not always straightforward, and competition for attracting and retaining talent is strong (Collis and Montgomery 1995; Greenwood *et al.* 2005). When it comes to mergers and acquisitions, the task becomes even harder because of problems of information asymmetry (Coff 1999) or post-merger integration (Empson 2001). However, this problem is not specific to the new multinationals, but to all professional service firms regardless their country of origin. One important difference between the new professional services multinationals and the established ones is that, whereas the most competitive conventional professional multinationals go abroad following their clients (Hitt *et al.* 2006; Roberts 1999), the Spanish firms analyzed in this chapter had to create an international customer base from scratch. Both IESE and Duro Felguera proactively tried to position themselves within the customized executive education and turnkey contracting sectors, respectively, rather than following their clients. In fact, Duro Felguera, as we saw earlier, took its first steps in the field of turnkey contracting for the power generation industry in Latin America, instead of Spain. This is a common feature of the new multinationals in the field of professional services, perhaps best illustrated by Indian firms such as Infosys, Wipro, or Tata Consultancy Services. These companies grew abroad by offering business process outsourcing and by providing customized services to new international clients; they did not become global leaders by following abroad their domestic customers.

In the case of the non-professional service firms, the pattern was just the opposite. ALSA and Planeta grew internationally by replicating their existing business model in Spain. The innovative formulas developed in the home country (e.g. premium transportation services to attract new customers and cultural goods in Spanish sold through non-conventional channels, respectively) helped them expand abroad. However, Planeta found it easier than ALSA to enter into a large number of countries. This disparity may be attributable to the difference between soft and hard services. As the production of hard services is separable from consumption, new multinationals from emerging countries have more possibilities to expand abroad, especially by taking advantage of their lower cost advantages. Once again, the case of the Indian IT companies is paradigmatic, especially in hard professional services in which the wage differentials are significant. However, in the case of soft services, the new multinationals have encountered many problems when stepping outside of their original niche, as they cannot take advantage of wage differentials or specialization in competing against the established multinationals. In soft services, the new multinationals have to compete against the established ones having basically the same labor costs.

8 The new multinational as a type of firm

> I think it is fair to characterize [research on the multinational firm] as resting heavily on the multinational's ability to exploit know-how and expertise gained in one country's market in other countries at low cost, thereby offsetting the unavoidable extra costs of doing business in a foreign country.
>
> Michael E. Porter (1986: 15–17)

> Twenty years ago I would never have dreamt that we would be the ninth-largest bank in the world.
>
> Emilio Botín, Presidente del Grupo Santander (*Euromoney*, July 1, 2005)

The rise of new multinational companies from newly industrialized, emerging, and developing countries challenges our conventional assumptions not only about the ways in which firms overcome the liability of foreignness and expand around the world, but also about the distinctive features of the multinational enterprise. The new multinationals initially lacked the traditional advantages attributed to multinational corporations, namely, proprietary technology and brands. This disadvantage, however, did not prevent them from expanding around the world. In contrast to the classic multinationals, they found strength in their ability to organize, manage, execute, and network. They pursued a variety of strategies of vertical integration, product diversification, learning by doing, exploration of new capabilities, and collaboration with other firms. Over time, some of them have developed technological and branding capabilities or evolved from niche players to generalists, but only after gaining enough scale.

The rise of the new multinationals is not restricted to a few home countries or industries. Increasing numbers of Southern European, East and South Asian, Latin American, Middle Eastern, and African firms have catapulted themselves to global visibility in a wide array of activities, ranging from food-processing to consumer durables, producer goods, infrastructure, and financial services. In so doing, they have demonstrated that international expansion and competitiveness can be based on different combinations of resources and capabilities at the firm level.

The new multinationals are no longer a marginal phenomenon. They account for about 20 percent of the cumulative stock of foreign direct investment in the world, if one includes firms from Southern Europe as well as those from emerging and developing countries. Thus, the traditional emphasis on technological and brand-related intangible assets as the foundation of foreign direct investment (e.g. Caves 1996; Dunning 1979; Hymer 1960) needs to be revisited. The global economy of the twenty-first century is very different from the heyday of the classic European and American multinationals. Nowadays, a variety of multinational firms equipped with different capabilities – ranging from technology and brands to project-execution and political skills – coexist in the global economy, even within the same industry. In this chapter we take stock of the evidence presented in the previous chapters regarding the trajectories of several of the new multinationals from Spain and other countries. Based on this evidence, we develop a typology of corporate strategies and an integrative framework to analyze the process through which these firms accumulated and developed the resources and capabilities that sustained their international expansion. The chapter concludes with the implications of the rise of the new multinationals for the theory of the multinational firm.

THE EVIDENCE ON THE NEW MULTINATIONALS

The two dozen cases of new multinationals examined in the preceding chapters document different patterns of international expansion and capability building depending on the industry. In the traditional food and beverage sectors (Chapter 3), these companies generally started in one specific product category and region within their home country. It was only after they expanded nationally and experimented with some product diversification that they took their first steps at internationalization. We compared selected Spanish and Latin American firms such as Arcor, Bimbo, Ebro-Puleva, Freixenet, Gruma, SOS, and Viscofán. Although each became a global leader in its respective activity, the Spanish firms followed a very different path to internationalization than the Latin American ones. After gaining a strong position domestically, they pursued more developed markets, first with exports, and later with alliances and acquisitions. This process helped them upgrade capabilities and gain access to valuable assets such as brands and some production technology. Eventually, they also engaged in greenfield foreign direct investments in markets both more and less developed than Spain. The Latin American multinationals differed from this pattern in two key respects. First, they were less vertically integrated. Second, they first grew within Latin America, perhaps as a way to gain scale, subsequently expanding into Europe and the United States. However, they have been more successful than Spanish firms in emerging economies, especially China, perhaps because their capabilities are better suited for less developed economies. Moreover, the Spanish firms tended to develop capabilities externally through alliances and acquisitions, while the Latin American firms developed them internally.

We further analyzed the reasons underlying internal versus external capability building in Chapter 4 with cases from the consumer durable goods industry. We identified difficulties in foreign market access and the importance of proprietary product technology as the two key drivers. When access to foreign markets was easy and product technology was not proprietary, we found that the new multinationals grew internationally on the basis of internally developed capabilities in the areas of design, process innovation, and distribution logistics. The cases of Inditex and Pronovias in clothing and Famosa in traditional toys illustrated this pattern. By contrast, when

access to markets was difficult and product technology was proprietary, the new multinationals engaged in external capability building through alliances and acquisitions, as illustrated by the case of
Fagor Electrodomésticos in household appliances. We also analyzed
intermediate cases in which firms combined internal and external
capability building strategies, as in electronic toys and lighters.

We dedicated Chapter 5 to study the peculiarities of the new
multinationals in producer goods industries. Following domestic
customers to foreign locations represented the main motivation and
opportunity for international expansion in this industry. Accordingly,
adaptability and project-execution capabilities were the main competitive advantages of these firms. We analyzed four Spanish firms
that were suppliers to automobile assemblers with facilities in Spain.
Our analysis also highlighted the role played by vertical integration
and diversification as the key variables shaping the growth of these
firms. Vertical integration and diversification at home in order to
sell more components to the main customers allowed these firms to
strengthen the relationship and to develop their knowledge base, as
illustrated by Corporación Gestamp and Ficosa. Firms that failed to
develop a strong link to their main clients became niche players selling to the same customers abroad (e.g. Zanini) or forced to vertically
integrate at the international level (Gamesa). International acquisitions were a means to accelerate international expansion, diversify
into new subfields and/or gain access to new technology.

Chapters 6 and 7 dealt with the service sector. We analyzed
regulated infrastructure industries separately from other types of
services, given that in the former technology and brands play a secondary role when compared to project-execution, organizational,
and political capabilities. Privatization, liberalization, and technological change shaped the growth of these firms. Business expertise
in the form of project-execution capabilities and management of network industries was crucial in the expansion of infrastructure firms,
although our analysis demonstrated the importance of upgrading
capabilities through alliances even in these industries. Firms like

Santander or Agbar learned from partners with expertise in different environments and contexts. Political capabilities were also important in the expansion of these firms, although they were not equally useful across the world. Spanish infrastructure firms concentrated their bidding activity in Latin America, a sign that these firms considered it easier and more profitable to use their expertise in that part of the world. Our analysis also showed the importance of enjoying strategic autonomy in order to define the optimal scope of the firm. Infrastructure regulated firms are at the crossroads of several industries, and each of them followed a different path regarding geographical reach and product diversification in order to make the most of the bundle of resources. However, the international expansion of some firms like Unión Fenosa and Agbar was truncated by their controlling shareholders, who had different goals and priorities.

In Chapter 7 we analyzed the non-infrastructure service sector, taking into account two key dimensions. The first had to do with whether the production of the service could be separated from its consumption (hard services) or not (soft services), while the second focused on whether the service entailed the transfer of professional or technical knowledge (professional services) or not (non-professional). One important difference between the new professional-services multinationals and the traditional ones was that, whereas the latter typically expanded abroad by following their clients, the Spanish professional-services firms we analyzed (IESE and Duro Felguera) created an international customer base from scratch. They could only succeed at that by focusing on specific niches not well served by the established multinationals. Non-professional service firms like Planeta and ALSA expanded abroad replicating their business model in other countries, although soft services firms found more difficulties in competing against the established multinationals because the co-location of the supplier and the customer reduced the possibilities of taking advantage of cross-country differences in labor costs.

In sum, the case-based evidence indicates that the wide array of new multinationals analyzed in the preceding chapters built their international expansion on the basis of their know-how, project-execution, networking, and political skills, but that their specific strategies differed along certain dimensions that we analyze in the next section.

A TYPOLOGY OF THE INTERNATIONAL STRATEGIES OF THE NEW MULTINATIONALS

The new multinationals are a heterogeneous group, and precisely this heterogeneity lies at the heart of their increasing international success. The rising preference of consumers for product differentiation and multiple brand offerings supports the presence of a diverse set of competitors in the market, including those with weaker technological and marketing capabilities than the established firms. This process has been facilitated by globalization and the emergence of narrow market niches present in many different countries. Within this scenario of global segmentation, it is possible to identify the two key variables that drive the strategies of the new multinationals. First, some of the new multinationals opted for serving specific market segments while others became generalists. Second, some firms adopted a multi-domestic approach, adapting their strategy to the characteristics of each country, while others adopted a global approach, competing in each country with the same strategy. Figure 8.1 displays the four strategic configurations that result from cross-classifying these two dimensions. We also list in each cell the corresponding cases analyzed in the preceding chapters. Our distinction between generalist and niche players focuses on the segments covered by each firm in international markets rather than in the home market. A niche player offers goods and services in one niche only, while a generalist offers an array of goods and services positioned at different price-quality points.

Global niche players are companies focused on the same segment regardless of the country. They sell similar products or services at a comparable price across markets. The best examples of this type of strategy are Viscofán, Flamagas, Gruma, Arcor, and Zanini.

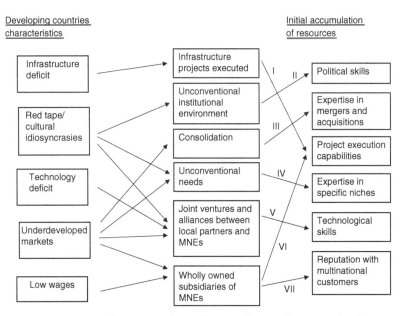

FIGURE 8.1 The process of initial accumulation of resources by the new multinationals

Bimbo, ALSA, and IESE followed this strategy for most markets, though introducing some product adaptations for the Chinese market. Gamesa and Suzlon are also global niche players, although they do need to adapt to regulatory and technical peculiarities in some countries. Discriminators, by contrast, are companies that offer a specific product-segment combination that suits the needs of each market. We came across two companies that followed this strategy: Pronovias in the bridal wear industry, and Duro Felguera in turnkey projects. In both cases, the company developed capabilities that enabled it to adapt locally so as to cater to the peculiarities of the market.

Multi-domestic generalists are firms that that offer a wide range of products or services across all market segments, but tailoring the offerings to the peculiarities of each country. Ebro Puleva and SOS in processed foodstuffs, Santander in commercial banking, Telefónica in telecommunications, Unión Fenosa in electricity and management systems, and Agbar in water and other services followed this approach. Finally, global generalists offer a full range of goods or services but without engaging in local adaptation. We identified a number of firms following this strategy, especially those in durable goods, producer goods, and publishing and information (see Table 8.1). This typology entails a simplification of the strategies that a new multinational can follow at a given moment of time. However, the strategies of the new multinationals may change over time, as Ramamurti and Singh's (2009) study of the Indian multinationals shows. The most typical pattern of evolution identified in our cases is the change from being a niche player to a generalist, a change in strategy usually based both on domestic and cross-border mergers and acquisitions, as the cases of Ebro Puleva and Bharat Forge illustrate.

CAPABILITIES AND THE EMERGENCE OF THE NEW MULTINATIONALS

The new multinationals have typically become strong international competitors on the basis of a set of capabilities that are different from the classic technological and brand assets of the established multinationals. In the preceding chapters, we emphasized the importance of organizational, managerial, project-execution, political, and network capabilities as sources of sustainable competitive advantage. In Figure 8.1 we present a dynamic framework that reflects the different patterns of capability building analyzed in the previous chapters. The process of resource accumulation by the new multinationals cannot be properly understood without analyzing the characteristics of the home countries in which they were born. A first aspect was the infrastructure gap typical of the home countries of the new multinationals, which created opportunities for certain types of firms. Firms which took advantage of them accumulated project-execution capabilities (arrow I in Figure 8.1). This demand for infrastructure projects helped firms such as Telefónica, Unión Fenosa, and Agbar develop expertise that could be exploited in other countries.

Table 8.1. *A typology of new multinationals*

Product scope:	Global integration:	
	Low	High
Generalist	**Multi-domestic generalist**	**Global generalist**
	Ebro Puleva	Inditex
	SOS	Famosa
	Telefónica	Fagor
		Electrodomésticos
	Agbar	
	Unión Fenosa	Haier
	Santander	Mabe
		Arcelik
		Ficosa
		Gestamp
		Bharat Forge
		Wanxiang
		Planeta
		Freixenet
Niche player	**Discriminator**	**Global niche player**
	Pronovias	Bimbo
	Duro Felguera	Gruma
		Arcor
		Viscofán
		Flamagas
		Zanini
		Gamesa
		Suzlon
		IESE
		ALSA

A second dimension had to do with the suffocating regulations characteristic of the home countries of the new multinationals (arrow II). Regulations and red tape not only affected firms in infrastructure sectors. For instance, the founders of Fagor Electrodomésticos acquired an existing firm in order to avoid having to work through the dense government bureaucracy to obtain a license. However, firms in infrastructure sectors subject to regulated prices and operating conditions offer the most complete illustration of this constraint, which, paradoxically, can become a source of competitive advantage if the firm learns to use it as leverage to erect entry barriers and privileged political connections (García-Canal and Guillén 2008).

A third process of capability building was related to the fact that industries in the home countries of the new multinationals tended to be fragmented, and the firms relatively small in size. Domestic mergers and acquisitions preceded the beginning of their internationalization process. Consolidation within the home country allowed the new multinationals not only to gain scale, but also to accumulate expertise in the management of mergers and acquisitions, a capability that proved valuable when expanding abroad, as illustrated by the cases we analyzed from the food-processing, producer-goods, banking, and infrastructure industries (arrow III in Figure 8.1). The companies that benefited the most from this capability were those in regulated infrastructure sectors because of the presence of many underperforming firms in foreign countries.

A fourth path to capability building was created by a combination of lags in economic development and cultural features, which produced unconventional needs in the market (arrow IV). For instance, the lack of air transportation services generated the opportunity for ALSA to innovate with services like the premium Supra bus service. In another example, IESE targeted would-be entrepreneurs and family firms among its main customers. Both companies used the expertise gained in the domestic market when expanding abroad as global niche players. Another example was the commercial strategy of América Móvil based on pre-paid mobile services.

Although strong technological skills are not typical of the new multinationals, some managed to gain access to technology in exchange for market access, which represents a fifth pattern of capability building (arrow V in Figure 8.1). Gamesa's licensing agreement with Vestas in the wind power generation industry illustrates this pattern. Collaborations between foreign firms owning technology and brands and local companies that possess resources such as know-how, project-execution, networking, and political skills is a relatively frequent pattern among the new multinationals. In general, the potential for the local partner to obtain state-of-the-art technologies is directly proportional to the size of the market and to the cultural distance with the home country of the foreign firm, as illustrated by the cases of Fagor Electrodomésticos, Haier, Mabe, and Arcelik (see Chapter 4).

A final path to resource development involves the project execution capabilities (arrow VI) and reputation (arrow VII) that can be built from serving foreign firms in the domestic market. The established multinationals, especially in the automobile industry, tend to orchestrate a process of natural selection among local suppliers with a view to selecting those that manage to develop project-execution capabilities related to the design and manufacture of components. Several of the new multinationals expanded abroad on the basis of these capabilities and reputation.

IMPLICATIONS FOR THE THEORY OF THE
MULTINATIONAL ENTERPRISE

The strategy of the new multinationals of basing their international expansion on bundles of organizational, managerial, project-execution, and network capabilities should not be regarded as second-best. As we argued in Chapter 1, one needs to adopt an evolutionary perspective and consider the dynamic aspects of capability building. The new multinationals are not giants with feet of clay, that is, companies whose technological and brand weaknesses will eventually undo them. We have documented cases of Spanish firms that have managed to catch up with their counterparts from the most advanced countries in the world, including such stellar examples as Viscofán, Inditex, Gamesa, Telefónica, Santander, and Planeta. Samsung Electronics and LG of South Korea are perhaps the best examples of new multinationals that managed to develop their own technology and/or brands. Other examples from emerging economies include Tenaris in steel tubes, Cemex in cement, Acer in personal computers, Haier in household appliances, Infosys in information services, or Embraer in aircraft, to name but a few.

These cases illustrate a common pattern that includes three key components. First, domestic and international growth helps the firm reach economies of scale, which facilitate not only investments in technology and branding, but also the development of an ample set of resources such as the ones presented in the previous section. Second, entering more sophisticated markets provides an incentive to innovate and to upgrade capabilities, as we argued in Chapter 2. And third, being a follower rather than a leader may enable the new multinational firm to leapfrog established competitors by fully utilizing its organizational, managerial, project-execution, and network capabilities at the same time that it builds new capabilities in technology and branding. Thus, the possession of technology and brands is not a prerequisite for successful foreign expansion; in the case of the new multinationals it tends to be the corollary of such expansion. Thus, it is nearly impossible to explain the existence of the new multinationals without taking into account their valuable resources and capabilities, as different as these may be when compared to those possessed by the established multinationals. In fact, a key characteristic of the new multinationals is that they have followed a pattern of international expansion by which they leveraged the resources conventional multinationals usually lack or neglect.

The rise of the new multinationals has not only turned parts of the global economy upside down, but also challenged some of the foundational ideas in the field of international business. We do not dispute the basic postulate that multinational firms must somehow surmount the liability of foreignness (Hymer 1960). Our argument has to do with the capabilities that enable firms to compete in a wide variety of markets, which need to be defined more broadly to include skills or resources other than technology and brands. As with the established multinationals from the most advanced countries, the emergence of the new multinationals required leveraging resources developed in the home country and combining them with local resources developed in the host country, via greenfield subsidiaries, acquisitions, or alliances (Hennart 1991, 2009). What the growth of the new multinationals shows is that, under some circumstances, the local resources owned by local partners in emerging countries can be a solid base to build a multinational firm. Specifically, the theoretical and empirical analysis in this book indicates that organizational, managerial, project-execution, political, and network capabilities can propel and support the internationalization process of the firm. Moreover, these capabilities can become the foundation for developing technological and branding capabilities, either internally or externally, especially if the firm exposes itself to sophisticated markets and established multinationals. That exposure can acquire different forms: buyer–supplier relationships, alliances, or competition. The rise of the new multinationals demonstrates that firm-specific capabilities are diverse, malleable, and dynamic. Their future as successful global competitors fully depends on their ability to continually transform and recombine their skill-set internally and externally.

References

Accenture. 2008. *The Rise of the Emerging-Market Multinational.* Pamphlet.

Adams/Jobson. 1996. *Adams/Jobson's Wine Handbook 1996.* New York: Adams/Jobson Publishing.

Akamatsu, Kaname. 1962. "A Historical Pattern of Economic Growth in Developing Countries." *Journal of Developing Economies* 1(1): 3–25.

Amsden, Alice H., and Takashi Hikino. 1994. "Project Execution Capability, Organizational Know-How and Conglomerate Corporate Growth in Late Industrialization." *Industrial and Corporate Change* 3(1): 111–47.

Andersen Consulting. 1994. *Worldwide Manufacturing Competitiveness Study: The Second Lean Enterprise Report.* London: Andersen Consulting.

Ariño, Africa, Esteban García Canal, Cristina López Duarte, Josep Rialp, Ana Valdés, and Llanos Gallo. 2000. "Freixenet: Strategic Alliances for Internationalization." IESE case number DG-1300-E.

Arrieta, Juan J. and José M. Ormaechea. n.d. *Caja Laboral Popular.* Textos básicos de Otalora IX. Mondragon: Mondragon Corporacion Cooperativa.

Aulakh, Preet S. 2007. "Emerging Multinationals from Developing Economies: Motivations, Paths and Performance." *Journal of International Management* 13(3): 235–40.

Baden-Fuller, Charles, and John Stopford. 1991. "Globalization Frustrated." *Strategic Management Journal* 12: 493–507.

Barney, Jay. 1986. "Strategic Factor Markets: Expectations, Luck, and Business Strategy." *Management Science* 32(10): 1231–41.

Bartlett, Christopher A., and Sumantra Ghoshal. 1989. *Managing Across Borders: The Transnational Solution.* Boston: Harvard Business School Press.

BCG. 2009. *The 2009 BCG 100 New Global Challengers.* Pamphlet.

Bell, Jim, Rod McNaughton, and Stephen Young. 2001. "Born-again Global Firms: An Extension to the Born Global Phenomenon." *Journal of International Management* 7(3): 173–90.

Biggart, Nicole W., and Mauro F. Guillén. 1999. "Developing Difference: Social Organization and the Rise of the Auto Industries of South Korea, Taiwan, Spain, and Argentina." *American Sociological Review* 64(5) (October): 722–47.

Boddewyn, Jean J., and Thomas L. Brewer. 1994. "International-Business Political Behavior: New Theoretical Directions." *Academy of Management Review* 19: 119–43.

Bonaglia, Federico, Andrea Goldstein, and John. A. Mathews. 2007. "Accelerated Internationalization by Emerging Markets Multinationals: The Case of the White Goods Sector." *Journal of World Business* 42: 369–83.

Bonardi, Jean P. 2004. "Global and Political Strategies in Deregulated Industries: The Asymmetric Behaviors of Former Monopolies." *Strategic Management Journal* 25: 101–20.

Bonet, José Luis. 1993. "La competitividad del cava: El caso Freixenet." *Papeles de Economía Española* 56: 399–401.

Buckley, Peter. J., and Mark Casson. 1976. *The Future of the Multinational Enterprise.* London: Macmillan.

Buckley, Peter J., L. Jeremy Clegg, Adam R. Cross, Xim Liu, Hinrich Voss, and Ping Zheng. 2007. "The Determinants of Chinese Outward Foreign Direct Investment." *Journal of International Business Studies* 38: 499–518.

Campa, José Manuel, and Mauro F. Guillén. 1999. "The Internalization of Exports: Firm and Location-Specific Factors in a Middle-Income Country." *Management Science* 45(11) (November): 1463–78.

Canals, Carles M. 2009. *Sabiduría práctica. 50 años del IESE.* Barcelona: Planeta.

Casanova, José. 1983. "The Opus Dei Ethic, the Technocrats, and the Modernization of Spain." *Social Science Information* 22(1): 27–50.

Casanova, Lourdes. 2002. "Lazos de familia: La inversión española en América Latina." *Foreign Affairs en Español* (web edition, summer issue).

Caves, Richard E. 1996. *Multinational Enterprise and Economic Analysis.* New York: Cambridge University Press.

Chandler, Alfred D. 1990. *Scale and Scope: The Dynamics of Industrial Capitalism.* Cambridge, MA: Harvard University Press.

Cho, Dong-Sung. 1987. *The General Trading Company: Concept and Strategy.* Lexington, MA: Lexington Books.

Clamp, Christina A. 2003. "The Evolution of Management in the Mondragon Co-operatives." Working Paper, University of Victoria.

CMT. 2009. *Informe anual 2008.* Barcelona: Comisión del Mercado de las Telecomunaciones.

Coff, Russell W. 1999. "How Buyers Cope with Uncertainty when Acquiring Firms in Knowledge-Intensive Industries: Caveat Emptor." *Organization Science* 10(2): 144–61.

Collis, David. J., and Cynthia A. Montgomery. 1995. "Competing on Resources: Strategy in the 1990s." *Harvard Business Review* (July–Aug): 118–28.

Cortright, Joseph. 2006. "Making Sense of Clusters: Regional Competitiveness and Economic Development." The Brookings Institution Metropolitan Policy Program, online, available at: www.brookings.edu/reports/2006/03cities_cortright.aspx.

Cosmen, Andrés. 2004. "Los sistemas de gestión de las empresas de transporte en China." *Economía Exterior* 30: 85–92.

Cosmen, José. 1994. "Experiencia de un empresario español en China." *Política Exterior* 38: 159–71.

Cuervo, Alvaro, and Belén Villalonga. 2000. "Explaining the Variance in the Performance Effects of Privatization." *Academy of Management Review* 25: 581–90.

Cuervo-Cazurra, Alvaro. 2008. "The Multinationalization of Developing Country MNEs: The Case of Multilatinas." *Journal of International Management* 14(2) (June): 138–54.

Cuervo-Cazurra, Alvaro, and Mehmet Genc. 2008. "Transforming Disadvantages into Advantages: Developing-country MNEs in the Least Developed Countries." *Journal of International Business Studies* 39: 957–79.

Dinica, Valentina. 2008. "Initiating a Sustained Diffusion of Wind Power: The Role of Public–Private Partnerships in Spain." *Energy Policy* 36: 3562–71.

Dunning, John H. 1979. "Explaining Changing Patterns of International Production: In Defence of the Eclectic Theory." *Oxford Bulletin of Economics and Statistics* 41: 269–96.

Dunning, John H. 2002. "Relational Assets, Networks, and International Business Activities," in *Cooperative Strategies and Alliances*, edited by Contractor, F.J., and P. Lorange. Amsterdam: Pergamon, pp. 569–93.

Dunning, John H., and Rajneesh Narula. 1996. "The Investment Development Path Revisited: Some Emerging Issues," in *Foreign Direct Investment and Governments*, edited by Dunning, J.H., and Rajneesh Narula. London: Routledge, pp. 1–41.

Economist, The. 2008. "The Challengers." *The Economist*, January 10, 2008.

ECORYS. 2008. "Study on the Competitiveness of the European Steel Sector." Retrieved April 8, 2009, from http://ec.europa.eu/enterprise/steel/docs/final_report_steel.pdf.

Eisenhardt, Kathleen M. 1989. "Building Theories from Case Study Research." *Academy of Management Review* 14: 532–50.

Elango, B., and Chinmay Pattnaik. 2007. "Building Capabilities for International Operations through Networks: A Study of Indian Firms." *Journal of International Business Studies* 38: 541–55.

Empson, Laura. 2001. "Fear of Exploitation and Fear of Contamination: Impediments to Knowledge Transfer in Mergers between Professional Service Firms." *Human Relations* 54(7): 839–62.

Erramili, Krishna M. 1990. "Entry Mode Choice in Service Industries." *International Marketing Review* 7(5): 50–62.

Fernández, Zulima, and María Jesús Nieto. 2008. "La internacionalización de ALSA," in *La internacionalización de la empresa familiar*, edited by Casillas, José C. Seville: Edición Digital @tres, pp. 199–215.

Ferrantino, Michael J. 1992. "Technology Expenditures, Factor Intensity, and Efficiency in Indian Manufacturing." *Review of Economics and Statistics* 74(4): 689–700.

Fields, Karl J. 1995. *Enterprise and the State in Korea and Taiwan*. Ithaca, NY: Cornell University Press.

Flyvbjerg, Bent. 2006. "Five Misunderstandings about Case-Study Research." *Qualitative Inquiry* 12: 219–45.

Furman, Jeffrey L., Michael E. Porter, and Scott Stern. 2002. "The Determinants of National Innovative Capacity." *Research Policy* 31(6): 899–933.

García-Canal, Esteban, and Mauro F. Guillén. 2008. "Risk and the Strategy of Foreign Location Choice." *Strategic Management Journal* 29(10): 1097–115.

García-Canal, Esteban, Cristina López Duarte, Josep Rialp Criado, and Ana Valdés Llaneza. 2002. "Accelerating International Expansion through Global Alliances: A Typology of Cooperative Strategies." *Journal of World Business* 37(2): 91–107.

García-Canal, Esteban, and Pablo Sánchez-Laorda. 2007. "One more only if it is one of us. The number of partners and the stock market reaction to domestic and international alliance formation in EU telecom firms." *International Business Review* 16: 83–108.

Gerring, John. 2007. *Case Study Research*. New York: Cambridge University Press.

Ghemawat, Pankaj. 2007. *Redefining Global Strategy*. Boston, MA: Harvard Business School Press.

Goldstein, Andrea. 2007. *Multinational Companies from Emerging Economies*. New York: Palgrave Macmillan.

Goldstein, Andrea, and Wilson Pritchard. 2009. "South African Multinationals: Building on a Unique Legacy," in *Emerging Multinationals from Emerging Markets*, edited by Ramamurti, Ravi, and Jitendra V. Singh. New York: Cambridge University Press, pp. 244–79.

Greenwood, Rystond, Stan X. Li, Rajsheree Prakash, and David L. Deephouse. 2005. "Reputation, Diversification, and Organizational Explanations of Performance in Professional Service Firms." *Organization Science* 16: 661–73.

Guillén, Mauro F. 1989. *La profesión de economista*. Barcelona: Ariel.

Guillén, Mauro F. 2000. "Business Groups in Emerging Economies: A Resource-Based View." *Academy of Management Journal* 43(3) (June): 362–80.

Guillén, Mauro F. 2001. *The Limits of Convergence: Globalization & Organizational Change in Argentina, South Korea, and Spain*. Princeton: Princeton University Press.

Guillén, Mauro F. 2002. "Structural Inertia, Imitation, and Foreign Expansion: South Korean Firms and Business Groups in China, 1987–1995." *Academy of Management Journal* 45(3) (June): 509–25.

Guillén, Mauro F. 2005. *The Rise of Spanish Multinationals: European Business in the Global Economy*. Cambridge and New York: Cambridge University Press.

Guillén, Mauro F., and Esteban García-Canal. 2009. *"La presencia de la empresa española en el exterior."* Madrid: ICEX.

Guillén, Mauro F., and Adrian E. Tschoegl. 2007. "Gamesa: Creciendo en los Estados Unidos." Case study. Centro de Experiencias of the Centro de Estudios Comerciales (CECO).

Guillén, Mauro F., and Adrian E. Tschoegl. 2008. *Building a Global Bank: The Transformation of Banco Santander.* Princeton, NY: Princeton University Press.

Gulati, Ranjay, Tarun Khanna, and Nitin Nohria. 1994. "Unilateral Commitments and the Importance of Process in Alliances." *Sloan Management Review* Spring: 61–9.

Gupta, Anuja, and Mauro F. Guillén. 2009. "Developing, Testing, and Validating Management Theory with Comparative Case Studies." Working Paper.

Haggard, Stephan. 1990. *Pathways from the Periphery: The Politics of Growth in the Newly Industrializing Countries.* Ithaca, NY: Cornell University Press.

Hall, David, and Emanuele Lobina. 2007. "Water Companies in Europe 2007." Working Paper, PSIRU, Business School, University of Greenwich.

Hamel, Gary, and C.K. Phahalad. 1993. "Strategy as Stretch and Leverage." *Harvard Business Review* (March–April): 75–84.

Hamel, Jacques. 1993. *Case Study Methods.* Newbury Park, CA: Sage.

Hawawini, Gabriel. 2005. "The Future of Business Schools." *Journal of Management Development* 24(9): 770–82.

Heenan, David A., and Warren J. Keegan. 1979. "The Rise of Third World Multinationals." *Harvard Business Review* 57 (January–February): 101–9.

Henisz, Witold J. 2000. "The Institutional Environment for Economic Growth." *Economics & Politics* 12: 1–31.

Henisz, Witold J. 2003. "The Power of the Buckley and Casson Thesis: The Ability to Manage Institutional Idiosyncrasies." *Journal of International Business Studies* 34: 173–84.

Henisz, Witold J., and Bennet A. Zelner. 2001. "The Institutional Environment for Telecommunications Investment." *Journal of Economics & Management Strategy* 10: 123–47.

Henisz, Witold J., Bennet A. Zelner, and Mauro F Guillén. 2005. "Market-Oriented Infrastructure Reforms, 1977–1999." *American Sociological Review* 70(6) (December): 871–97.

Hennart, Jean F. 1982. *A Theory of Multinational Enterprise.* Ann Arbor, MI: University of Michigan Press.

Hennart, Jean F. 1991. "The Transaction Cost Theory of the Multinational Enterprise," in The Nature of the Transnational Firm, edited by Pitelis, Christos N., and Roger Sugden. London and New York: Routledge, pp. 81–116.

Hennart, Jean F. 2009. "Down with MNE-centric Theories! Market Entry and Expansion as the Bundling of MNE and Local Assets." *Journal of International Business Studies* 40(9): 1432–54.

Hennart, Jean F., and Sabine Reddy. 1997. "The Choice between Mergers/Acquisitions and Joint Ventures: The Case of Japanese Investors in the United States." *Strategic Management Journal* 18: 1–12.

Hicks, John R. 1935. "Annual Survey of Economic Theory: The Theory of Monopoly." *Econometrica* 3: 1–20.

Hitt, Michael A., Leonard Bierman, Katsuhiko Shimizu, and Rahur Kochhar. 2001. "Direct and Moderating Effects of Human Capital on Strategy and Firm Performance in Professional Service Firms: A Resource-based Perspective." *Academy of Management Journal* 44: 13–28.

Hitt, Michael A., Leonard Bierman, Klaus Uhlenbruck, and Katsuhiko Shimizu. 2006. "The Importance of Resources in the Internationalization of Professional Service Firms: The Good, the Bad, and the Ugly." *Academy of Management Journal* 49: 1137–57.

Hymer, Stephen. [1960] 1976. *The International Operations of National Firms: A Study of Direct Foreign Investment.* Cambridge, MA: The MIT Press.

IDATE. 2008. *DigiWorld Yearbook 2008. The Digital World's Challenges.* Montpellier: IDATE.

Iñiguez de Onzoño, Santiago, and Salvador Carmona. 2007. "The Changing Business Model of B-schools." *Journal of Management Development* 26(1): 22–32.

Interbrand. 2009. "Best Global Brands: 2009 Rankings." Online, available at: www. interbrand.com/best_global_brands.aspx.

International Energy Agency. 2009. *World Energy Report.* Paris: International Energy Agency.

Jacobsson, Staffan, and Volkmar Lauber. 2006. "The Politics and Policy of Energy System Transformation: Explaining German Diffusion of Renewable Energy Technology." *Energy Policy* 34: 256–76.

Johanson, Jan, and Jan-Erik Vahlne. 1977. "The Internationalization Process of the Firm: A Model of Knowledge Development and Increasing Foreign Market Commitments." *Journal of International Business Studies* 8(1): 23–32.

Johanson, Jan, and Finn Wiedersheim-Paul. 1975. "The Internationalization of the Firm — Four Swedish Cases." *Journal of Management Studies* (October): 305–22.

Kale, Prashant, Harbir Singh, and Howard V. Perlmutter. 2000. "Learning and Protection of Proprietary Assets in Strategic Alliances: Building Relational Capital." *Strategic Management Journal* 21: 217–37.

Kenney, Martin, and Richard Florida. 1993. *Beyond Mass Production: The Japanese System and its Transfer to the U.S.* Oxford: Oxford University Press.

Khurana, Rakesh. 2007. *From Higher Aims to Hired Hands.* Princeton: Princeton University Press.

Kindleberger, Charles. 1969. *American Business Abroad.* Cambridge, MA: MIT Press.

Kipping, Matthias, Behlül Üsdiken, and Núria Puig. 2004. "Imitation, Tension, and Hybridization: Multiple 'Americanizations' of Management Education in Mediterranean Europe." *Journal of Management Inquiry* 13(2) (June): 98–108.

Knickerbocker, Frederick. 1973. *Oligopolistic Reaction and Multinational Enterprise.* Boston: Division of Research, Harvard Business School.

Kock, Carl, and Mauro F. Guillén. 2001. "Strategy and Structure in Developing Countries: Business Groups as an Evolutionary Response to Opportunities for Unrelated Diversification." *Industrial & Corporate Change* 10(1): 1–37.

Kogut, Bruce, and Nalin Kulatilaka. 1994. "Operating Flexibility, Global Manufacturing, and the Option Value of a Multinational Network." *Management Science* 40(1) (January): 123–39.

Kosacoff, Bernardo, Jorge Forteza, Maria I. Barbero, Fernando Porta, and E. Alejandro Stengel. 2007. *Globalizar desde Latinoamérica. El caso Arcor.* Argentina: McGraw-Hill Interamericana.

Kristinsson, Kari, and Rekha Rao. 2008. "Interactive Learning or Technology Transfer as a Way to Catch-Up? Analysing the Wind Energy Industry in Denmark and India." *Industry and Innovation* 15: 297–320.

Krugman, Paul R. 1979. "Increasing Returns, Monopolistic Competition, and International Trade." *Journal of International Economics* 9: 469–79.

Krugman, Paul R. 1980. "Scale Economies, Product Differentiation, and the Pattern of Trade." *The American Economic Review* 70(5) (December): 950–9.

Lall, Sanjaya. 1983. *The New Multinationals.* New York: Wiley.

Lara Bosch, José M. 2002. "Sector editorial: el caso de Planeta." *Información Comercial Española* 799: 219–24.

Lecraw, Donald. 1977. "Direct Investment by Firms from Less Developed Countries." *Oxford Economic Papers* 29 (November): 445–57.

Lecraw, Donald. 1993. "Outward Direct Investment by Indonesian Firms: Motivation and Effects." *Journal of International Business Studies* 24(3): 589–600.

Lema, Adrian, and Kristian Ruby. 2007. "Between Fragmented Authoritarianism and Policy Coordination: Creating a Chinese Market for Wind Energy." *Energy Policy* 35: 3879–90.

Li, Peter Ping. 2003. "Toward a Geocentric Theory of Multinational Evolution: The Implications from the Asian MNEs as Latecomers." *Asia Pacific Journal of Management* 22(2) (June): 217–42.

Li, Peter Ping. 2007. "Toward an Integrated Theory of Multinational Evolution: The Evidence of Chinese Multinational Enterprises as Latecomers." *Journal of International Management* 13(3): 296–318.

Lillo, Juan de. 2004. *Francisco Riberas contra su destino.* Oviedo: Ed. Nobel.

Lobina, Emanuele, and David Hall. 2007. "Water Privatisation and Restructuring in Latin America 2007." Working Paper, PSIRU, Business School, University of Greenwich.

López Milla, Julián. 2003. "1998–2002, avances y obstáculos en la expansión de la competencia en el mercado eléctrico español." *Información Comercial Española* 808 (July): 13–34.

Lovelock, Christopher H. 1999. "Developing Marketing Strategies for Transnational Service Operations." *Journal of Services Marketing* 13 (4–5): 278–89.

Margalef Llebaria, Joaquim. 2005. "El proceso de internacionalización del sector auxiliar de automoción en España. Estudio de dos casos. Maisa y Ficosa." Doctoral Dissertation, Universitat Rovira i Virgili.

Markides, Constantinos C., and Peter J. Williamson. 1996. "Corporate Diversification and Organizational Structure: A Resource-Based View." *Academy of Management Journal* 39(2) (April): 340–67.

Mathews, John A. 2002. *Dragon Multinationals: A New Model of Global Growth.* New York: Oxford University Press.

Mathews, John A. 2006. "Dragon Multinationals." *Asia Pacific Journal of Management* 23: 5–27.

McKendrick, David G., Richard F. Doner, and Stephan Haggard. 2001. *From Silicon Valley to Singapore: Location and Competitive Advantage in the Hard Disk Drive Industry.* Palo Alto, CA: Stanford University Press.

Meyer, Klaus E. 2004. "Perspectives on Multinational Enterprises in Emerging Economies." *Journal of International Business Studies* 35: 259–76.

Mínguez Sanz, Santiago. 1994. "El cava: Su producción y comercialización." *El Campo* 130 (January): 111–21.

MMAMRM. 2009. *Anuario de Estadística 2008.* Madrid: Ministerio de Medio Ambiente y Medio Rural y Marino.

Noland, Marcus. 2008. "Telecommunications in North Korea: Has Orascom Made the Connection?" Working Paper, Peterson Institute for International Economics.

Ontiveros, Emilio, Manuel Conthe, and José M. Nogueira. 2004. *"La percepción de los inversores de los riesgos regulatorios e institucionales en América Latina."* Working Paper, Washington, DC: Interamerican Development Bank.

Ormaechea, José M. 1993. *The Mondragon Cooperative Experience.* Mondragon: Mondragon Corporacion Cooperativa.

Ormaechea, José M. n.d. *El Grupo Cooperativo Mondragón.* Textos básicos de Otalora VII. Mondragon: Mondragon Corporacion Cooperativa.

Ortiz de Urbina Criado, Marta, and María Angeles Montoro Sánchez. 2007. "Las fusiones y adquisiciones de las principales empresas eléctricas europeas (2000–2006)." *Información Comercial Española* 2914: 19–30.

Ozawa, Terutomo. 1996. "Japan: the Macro-IDP, Meso-IDPs, and the Technology Development Path (TDP)," in *Foreign Direct Investment, Economic Structure and Governments: Catalysts for Economic Restructuring*, edited by Dunning, John and Rajneesh Narula. London: Routledge, pp. 142–73.

Paba, Sergio. 1986. "'Brand-naming' as an Entry Strategy in the White Goods Industry." *Cambridge Journal of Economics* 10: 305–18.

Peteraf, Margaret A. 1993. "The Cornerstones of Competitive Advantage: A Resource-Based View." *Strategic Management Journal* 14(3) (March): 179–91.

Porporato, Marcela Mª. 2004: "Configuration, Design and Uses of Management Control Systems in International Equity Joint Ventures: A Theoretical and Empirical Study." Doctoral Dissertation, IESE Business School.

Porter, Michael E. 1986. "Competition in Global Industries: A Conceptual Framework," in *Competition in Global Industries*, edited by Porter, Michael E. Cambridge, MA: Harvard Business School Press, pp.15–60.

Porter, Michael E. 1998. "Clusters and the New Economics of Competition." Online, available at: www.oregoneconomy.org/Porter%20Clusters%20New%20Economics%20 of%20Competition.pdf.

Prial, Frank J. 1996. "Getting a Kick from Champagne." *The New York Times*, September 15, Section 5, 15, 22.

Prieto Iglesias, José Manuel. 2002. "El compromiso con el conocimiento, clave para la expansion internacional de Unión Fenosa." *Información Comercial Española* 799: 189–98.

Puig, Nuria, and Paloma Fernández. 2003. "The Education of Spanish Entrepreneurs and Managers: Madrid and Barcelona Business Schools, 1950–1975." *Paedagogica Historica* 39(5): 651–72.

Pujol Artigas, José M. 1998. "Ficosa". *Cuadernos de la Federación Minerometalúrgica de Comisiones Obreras* 6: 35–7.

Quevedo, Manuel. n.d. *La Investigación e Innovación en MCC. Presente y Futuro.* Textos básicos de Otalora XI. Mondragon: Mondragon Corporacion Cooperativa.

Ramamurti, Ravi. 2009. "What Have We Learned about Emerging-Market MNEs?" in *Emerging Multinationals in Emerging Markets*, edited by Ramamurti, Ravi and Jitendra V. Singh. New York: Cambridge University Press, pp. 399–426.

Ramamurti, Ravi, and Jitendra V. Singh. 2009. *Emerging Multinationals from Emerging Markets.* Cambridge: Cambridge University Press.

Rialp, Alex, Josep Rialp, and Gary A. Knight. 2005. "The Phenomenon of Early Internationalizing Firms: What Do We Know After a Decade (1993–2003) of Scientific Inquiry?" *International Business Review* 14(2) (April): 147–66.

Roberts, Joanne. 1999. "The Internationalization of Business Service Firms: A Stage Approach." *The Service Industries Journal* 19(4): 68–88.

Rui, Huaichun, and George S. Yip. 2008. "Foreign Acquisitions by Chinese Firms: A Strategic Intent Perspective." *Journal of World Business* 43: 213–26.

Salazar, Jesús. 2009. "La estrategia de internacionalización de Grupo SOS: Vocación global." *Economistas* 119: 246–48.

Sarkar, M.B., S.T. Cavusgil, and Preet. S. Aulakh. 1999. "International Expansion of Telecommunications Carriers: The Influence of Market Structure, Network Characteristics and Entry Imperfections." *Journal of International Business Studies* 30: 361–82.

Siegel, Jordan. 2008. "Grupo Bimbo." Case 9–707–521. Harvard Business School.

Stopford, John M., and Louis T. Wells. 1972. *Managing the Multinational Enterprise*. New York: Basic Books.

Teece, David J. 1977. "Technology Transfer by Multinational Firms: The Resource Cost of Transferring Technological Know-How." *Economic Journal* 87 (346): 242–61.

Tolentino, Paz E. 1993. *Technological Innovation and Third World Multinationals*. London: Routledge.

UNCTAD (United Nations Conference on Trade and Development). 2004. *World Investment Report 2004*. New York: United Nations.

UNCTAD (United Nations Conference on Trade and Development). 2006. *World Investment Report 2006*. New York: United Nations.

UNCTAD (United Nations Conference on Trade and Development). 2008. *World Investment Report 2008*. New York: United Nations.

UNCTAD (United Nations Conference on Trade and Development). 2009. *World Investment Report 2009*. New York: United Nations.

Van Agtmael, Antoine. 2007. *The Emerging Markets Century: How a New Breed of World-Class Companies Is Overtaking the World*. New York: Free Press.

Vandermerwe, Sandra, and Michael Chadwick. 1989. "The Internationalisation of Services." *The Service Industries Journal* 9(1) (January): 79–93.

Velázquez, Cándido. 1995. "Telefónica: Una estrategia hacia la multinacionalidad." *Presupuesto y Gasto Público* 16: 187–202.

Vernon, Raymond. 1979. "The Product Cycle Hypothesis in a New International Environment." *Oxford Bulletin of Economics and Statistics* 41(4) (November): 255–67.

von Nordenflycht, Andrew. 2010. "What is a Professional Service Firm? Toward a Theory and Taxonomy of Knowledge-Intensive Firms." *Academy of Management Review* 35(1): 155–74.

Wells, Louis T., Jr. 1983. *Third World Multinationals: The Rise of Foreign Investment from Developing Countries*. Cambridge, MA: The MIT Press.

Wilkins, Mira. 1974. *The Maturing of Multinational Enterprise: American Business Abroad from 1914 to 1970*. Cambridge, MA: Harvard University Press.

Yin, Robert K. 2003. *Case Study Research: Design and Methods Revised*, 3rd edn. Thousand Oaks, CA: Sage.

Yiu, Daphne W., Chung Ming Lau, and Garry D. Bruton. 2007. "International Venturing by Emerging Economy Firms: The Effects of Firm Capabilities, Home Country Networks, and Corporate Entrepreneurship." *Journal of International Business Studies* 38: 519–40.

Zollo, Mauricio, and Harbir Singh. 2004. "Deliberate Learning in Corporate Acquisitions: Post-acquisition Strategies and Integration Capability in US Bank Mergers." *Strategic Management Journal* 25: 1233–56.

Index

Printed in the United States
By Bookmasters